The making of the GDR
1945-53

MANCHESTER
UNIVERSITY PRESS

The making of the GDR
1945-53
From antifascism to Stalinism

Gareth Pritchard

Manchester University Press
Manchester and New York

distributed exclusively in the USA by St. Martin's Press

Published by Manchester University Press
Oxford Road, Manchester M13 9NR, UK
and Room 400, 175 Fifth Avenue, New York, NY 10010, USA
http://www.man.ac.uk/mup

Distributed exclusively in the USA by
St. Martin's Press, Inc., 175 Fifth Avenue, New York,
NY 10010, USA

Distributed exclusively in Canada by
UBC Press, University of British Columbia, 2029 West Mall,
Vancouver, BC, Canada V6T 1Z2

British Library Cataloguing-in-Publication Data
A catalogue record for this book is available from the British Library

Library of Congress Cataloging-in-Publication Data applied for

ISBN 0 7190 5654 3 *hardback*

First published 2000

07 06 05 04 03 02 01 00   10 9 8 7 6 5 4 3 2 1

Typeset in Photina 10/12 pt
by Heather FitzGibbon, 11 Castle Street, Christchurch, Dorset

Printed in Great Britain
by Bookcraft (Bath) Ltd, Midsomer Norton

Contents

Acknowledgements

In the writing of this book, my thanks are above all due to the staff of the *Sächsisches Staatsarchiv Leipzig*, the *Sächsisches Staatsarchiv Chemnitz*, the *Thüringisches Hauptstaatsarchiv Weimar*, and the *Bundesarchiv* in Berlin, for their helpful and friendly assistance; to my German friends Christoph, Christine, Jens, Eveline, Nicole and Andreas, for providing me with free accommodation and a German perspective; to my colleagues Andy Croll, Ursula Masson, Chris Evans, Sharif Gemie, Peter Mercer and Neil Wynn, for doing what they could to lighten my teaching load and for putting up with my grumpiness; to Inna Margarit of Odessa State University, for her invaluable assistance; to Dr Jill Lewis of Swansea, Professor Jonathan Osmond of Cardiff and Professor Mary Fulbrook of UCL, for the opportunity to discuss and develop my ideas; and, finally, to my friend and teacher Dr Eleanor Breuning, to whom I owe more than I can ever express in words.

Glossary and list of abbreviations

Abbreviations and German words used in the text

ADGB	German General Trade Union Federation
antifa	antifascist committee
Befehl	order
Betriebsgruppe	workplace cell (of SPD, KPD or SED)
Betriebsrat	workplace council
Bezirk	district
Bezirksleitung	district leadership
Bezirksvorstand	District Area Executive
BMG	British Military Government
BPO	Workplace Party Organisation
Bürgermeister	mayor
CDU	Christian Democratic Union
CPSU	Communist Party of the Soviet Union
DSF	Society for German–Soviet Friendship
DWK	German Economic Commission
EAC	European Advisory Commission
East Germany	see GDR
FDGB	Free German Trade Union Association
FDJ	Free German Youth
GDR	German Democratic Republic (also called East Germany)
HO	trading organisation, special shops for the privileged
Junker	large landowners
Kampfgemeinschaft	'fighting community'
KPD	Communist Party of Germany
KPKK	*Kreis* Party Control Commission
KPO	Communist Party Opposition
Kreis	area
Kreisleitung	area leadership

Kreissekretariat	area secretariat
Kreisvorstand	area executive committee
Land	region
Landesleitung	regional leadership
Landesvorstand	regional executive committee
LDP	Liberal Democratic Party of Germany
LPKK	Land Party Control Commission
Mitbestimmung	co-determination
NKFD	National Committee 'Free Germany'
NKVD	Soviet People's Commissariat of Internal Affairs
NSDAP	National Socialist Workers' Party of Germany
Nurgewerkschaftlertum	'only-trade-unionism'
Oberbürgermeister	lord mayor
PDS	Party of Democratic Socialism
PKK	Party Control Commission
Reichsbanner	a paramilitary organisation for the defence of the Weimar Republic, with close links to the SPD
RFB	League of Red Front Fighters
SA	*Sturmabteilung*, the Nazi terrorist militia
SAG	Soviet joint-stock Company
SAP	Socialist Workers' Party
SED	Socialist Unity Party of Germany
SMAD	Soviet Military Administration of Germany
SOPADE	SPD leadership-in-exile
SPD	Social Democratic Party of Germany
Stimmungsbericht	report on public opinion
TAN	Technical Work Norm
Unterbezirksleitung	sub-district leadership
VEB	People's Own Enterprise
Volkspolizei	People's Police
VVN	Union of the Persecuted of the Nazi Regime
ZA	Central Committee (of SPD)
Zero Hour	*Stunde Null*, the period in 1945 immediately following the end of the Second World War
ZPKK	Central Party Control Committee

Abbreviations used in the references

BArch	*Bundesarchiv*
BAdSt Halle	*Besatzungsamt der Stadt Halle*
BdM	*Büro des Ministerpräsidenten*
BPA	*Bezirksparteiarchiv*
FO	Foreign Office

KV	*Kreisverwaltung*
MdI	*Ministerium des Innern*
PRO	Public Record Office
SAPMO	*Stiftungsarchiv der Parteien und Massen-organisationen der DDR*
SStA	*Sächsisches Staatsarchiv*
ThHStA	*Thüringisches Hauptstaatsarchiv*
VVN	*Vereinigung der Verfolgten des Naziregimes*

Notes concerning references to the East German archives

The regulations of the East German archives stipulate that personal names which occur in archival documents should not be referred to in published texts, with the exception of prominent individuals such as Walter Ulbricht or Otto Grotewohl. In order to comply with this requirement, all personal names in this book have been rendered anonymous through the use of initials (S.K., A.D., H.M., etc.). These initials have been chosen at random and are used for convenience only; they do not necessarily bear any relation to the person's real initials.

A further problem relating to the citation of archival material is that in many files the individual pages have not yet been assigned a page or *Blatt* (Bl.) number by the archivists. In such instances, the particular page of any document can only be located by finding first of all the document, and then looking up the particular page *within* that document. Other files, however, have been worked through by the archivists, who have assigned each individual piece of paper in the files a *Blatt* number. In such instances, one does not need to know the title of a document in order to track down a reference; it is sufficient to know the file number and the *Blatt* number. In the references used in this book, the titles of documents are given only where the archivists have not yet assigned a *Blatt* number.

Introduction:
the two traditions

The Red Army soldiers who marched into eastern Germany in the spring of 1945 brought with them a political tradition – Stalinism – which had evolved over the previous two decades in the Soviet Union. With the assistance of their allies and underlings in the leadership of the Communist Party of Germany (KPD), the Soviets went on, in the months and years to come, to impose this tradition upon that part of Germany which had fallen under their occupation. By the time of Joseph Stalin's death in 1953, East Germany had acquired a centrally planned economy, a grossly swollen police and security apparatus, and a ruling party which claimed to be grounded in the principles of Marxism–Leninism. To this extent, the experience of East Germany was broadly parallel to that of Poland, Romania, Hungary, Bulgaria and all the other countries which, at that time or subsequently, were absorbed into the Soviet empire.

In another sense, however, East Germany, along with the Czech part of Czechoslovakia, was unique. Marx himself had laid down that the prerequisites for Socialism were an advanced industrial economy and a numerous, class-conscious proletariat. Yet all the other countries which fell to 'Communism' were characterised by economic backwardness, small working classes and populations that were overwhelmingly agrarian. Most obviously, the Soviet Union itself had been, at the time of its creation, a backward country of peasants and farmers. The Russian working class, in the name of whom the Bolsheviks had launched their revolution, had consisted of first or second generation proletarians who retained very close ties to the countryside and who were still strongly under the influence of the superstitious, illiterate peasant culture from which they had only recently emerged. Under these circumstances, it was hardly surprising that the labour movement in Russia had only the very shallowest of roots. Towards the end of the nineteenth century, for example, the Russian Marxist movement had consisted of Georgi Plekhanov and a handful of exiled intellectuals in Switzerland. On one occasion, when they went on a boating trip,

1

Plekhanov joked to his comrades that if the boat should sink, Russian Marxism would be wiped out at a stroke. At that time, this was not too much of an exaggeration.

In East Germany and western Czechoslovakia, by contrast, the majority of the population was urban and industrial, and had been so for many decades. Moreover, particularly in the case of East Germany, there were native traditions of Socialism and Marxism stretching back well into the nineteenth century. Indeed, Germany was the homeland not just of Marx himself, but of a mass working-class movement based on Marxist principles. At the time of Plekhanov's boating trip, the Social Democratic Party of Germany (SPD) was already a huge organisation, with tens of thousands of members and hundreds of thousands of supporters and sympathisers. Its most prominent figures – August Bebel, Eduard Bernstein and Karl Kautsky – were the acknowledged high priests of the Marxist tradition and were far better known in the international labour movement than the relatively marginal figure of Lenin, let alone the Georgian non-entity Djugashvili, who would one day bear the pseudonym Stalin.

These simple facts raise a whole series of fascinating and important questions. If Stalin became powerful, it was because of his battalions, the tens of thousands of soldiers, bureaucrats and party activists in Soviet Russia and throughout the world who, whether through fear, careerism or idealism, were prepared to do his bidding. However, in East Germany, many of the activists and functionaries who laid the Stalinist foundations of the German Democratic Republic (the GDR or East Germany; 1949–90) were Social Democrats or trade unionists who were steeped in their own German traditions of Marxism. The vast majority of rank-and-file Communists, meanwhile, though loyal to the Soviet Union, had only the vaguest of conceptions of what the USSR was in fact like, and were committed to an egalitarian, millenarian vision of Socialism which had long since been abandoned by the Russian Communists. How, then, did these people react to the Stalinist occupation policies which they found themselves having to implement, but which in many ways were alien to the traditions in which they had been brought up? To what extent should the GDR be regarded, not so much as Stalin's offspring, but as the creation of this layer of East German Socialists and Communists? What impact did the Soviet and German traditions of Marxism have upon each other, and how did the relationship between the two influence the political development of the Soviet zone of occupation and the GDR which was founded in the territory of that zone?

The archival sources

Before 1989, research into questions such as those raised above was seriously impeded by the inaccessibility of the relevant archives. Since the collapse of the Berlin Wall, the East German archives have become fully available and, on the basis of the new material, it is possible for scholars to take a fresh look at many of the controversial issues of post-war German history.

The archival material that has now become available is not, however, without its problems. The functionaries and apparatchiks who created the archives did not do so for the benefit of historians and, as a consequence, the documents are often badly filed and catalogued. Despite the bravest efforts of the new authorities, the East German archives are still something of a labyrinth in which the historian must take pot luck.

Furthermore, despite the super-abundance of archival material now available, there remains a number of important themes and issues which are only poorly documented. Most obviously, very few documents are to be found which cover the first crucial weeks and months of occupation. This is hardly surprising, for the situation at the time was chaotic in the extreme, and activists and functionaries on the ground were confronted by desperate material problems. Even if they happened to have access to a supply of paper (which they often did not), they had rather more pressing issues on their minds than writing letters or compiling reports. However understandable this lacuna might be, it is still a most regrettable one.

Later on, once the machinery of state had been set in motion once again, the situation, from the point of view of the historian, improved dramatically. Indeed, by the later 1940s and early 1950s the increasingly bureaucratic East German regime was beginning to generate vast quantities of paperwork. By this stage however the party and the state were also becoming more and more authoritarian and dogmatic, as a result of which the records they kept tended to become distorted by bureaucratic and ideological jargon. Evidence of this kind obviously needs to be treated with great caution, for it often tells us far more about the mind-set of the Stalinist apparatchiks who were producing it than about the real world on which they were reporting.

On the other hand, there are also advantages to working in the archives of a defunct dictatorship. For all its authoritarianism and dogmatism, the regime was also extremely keen to find out what people were really saying and thinking. One can thus find in the archives vast numbers of internal party reports which, at least in the period before 1948, are often remarkably candid about the problems and shortcomings of the authorities. After 1948, the functionaries who compiled these reports became noticeably more reluctant to pass on bad news to their superiors. Additionally, from 1948 onwards the authorities also began to make increasing use of spies and informants, who gathered vast amounts of information, not just on the oppositional sentiments or activities of their neighbours and colleagues, but on every aspect of their working and domestic lives. In short, this extended network of spies and informants effectively conducted an exercise in 'mass observation', the results of which provide an invaluable window on the daily life of the East German population.

Focal points

Given the enormous mass of archival material which has become available over the last few years, it seemed important to keep the present study within manageable boundaries. For this reason, the book concentrates on the first eight years of Communist East Germany. The year 1953 is an obvious cut-off date, partly because it was the year of Stalin's death and partly because the workers' uprising of 17 June 1953 can in some ways be seen as the final death spasm of the East German labour movement. Thereafter, the organs of the labour movement were entirely 'Stalinised' in the sense that all power and authority inside the movement flowed in one direction only: from top to bottom.

The book also has a geographic focus, in that most (though by no means all) of the material examined pertains to the two southernmost East German *Länder* (regions) of Saxony and Thuringia. The simple reason for this is that both of these states were of unique importance in the history of the German – and, to some extent, of the world – labour movement. Saxony was one of Germany's most important industrial regions, many of whose towns and cities had a long tradition of radical working-class and Marxist politics. The great city of Leipzig, for example, was the home of such giants of the German labour movement as Wilhelm Liebknecht and Franz Mehring, and the birthplace of Karl Liebknecht. The newspaper of the Leipzig SPD, the *Leipziger Volkszeitung*, was perhaps the most important publication of the revolutionary wing of German Social Democracy, and on many occasions published articles by Rosa Luxemburg, Clara Zetkin, Maxim Gorky and Vladimir Lenin. Before and after the outbreak of war in 1914, Leipzig was a centre of the anti-war movement and, during the early months of 1918, it was once again the focal point for anti-war strikes and demonstrations. In November 1918, Leipzig was at the forefront of the wave of unrest which toppled the Kaiser and, throughout the Weimar period (1919–33), the city was a stronghold of both Communism and left-wing Social Democracy. Under the Third Reich (1933–45), the anti-Nazi underground in Leipzig was both more extensive and more successful than almost anywhere else in Germany. In short, in the words of Horst Schmollinger: 'Saxony is the motherland of the German labour movement, and Leipzig was ... one of the strongholds of its left-socialist wing in its Central German – Thuringian and Saxon – core.'[1]

Thuringia, for its part, was significant in the history of the German working class for rather different reasons. Though largely agricultural, Thuringia is studded with a number of small industrial towns which have witnessed some of the most important milestones in the development of the German labour movement. In August 1869, August Bebel and Wilhelm Liebknecht established Germany's first Marxist political party, the so-called 'Social Democratic Workers' Party', at a conference in Eisenach. Six years later, at a conference at Gotha, representatives of Bebel's and Liebknecht's party came together with representatives of Ferdinand Lassalle's 'General Union of German Workers' to found the party which was later to become known as the SPD. In 1891, at an historic conference in Erfurt, the SPD adopted a new, more radical political programme which 'adhered dogmatically to the doctrines of Marx and Engels'.[2] Thuringia was thus the birthplace of Marxism as a mass political movement. When Soviet troops marched into the region in 1945, they were, in a sense, bringing Marxism back home to the place from which it had originated.

What follows from all this is simply that, if one wants to study the relationship between working-class politics and Soviet occupation policy in eastern Germany in the period after 1945, it makes sense to concentrate one's attention on those areas or regions which possessed the largest number of workers with the strongest attachment to the traditions of the German labour movement. By so doing, one can study the interaction between the Soviet and the German traditions of Marxism at its purest and most intense. Since, with the exception of Berlin, the largest numbers of workers and the strongest traditions of working-class politics were to be found in Saxony and Thuringia, it is to these regions that we must turn our attention.

The most important focal point of this study pertains to popular working-class political attitudes and behaviour. Developments are viewed very much from the point of view of lower ranking functionaries or rank-and-file activists of the East German labour movement. High politics and the intricacies of Soviet foreign policy are only touched upon in so far as they provided the context in which popular politics developed, and were themselves influenced by the development of working-class politics. This 'bottom-up' approach to the history of the Soviet occupation is in no way intended to imply that high politics and Soviet foreign policy were unimportant. On the contrary, the course of political developments was always determined primarily by the Soviets' perception of their Great Power interests. Nonetheless, the archival evidence now available does seem to suggest that developments at the base of East German society were far more significant than has hitherto been supposed. The purpose of this study is thus not to challenge the traditional interpretations of the history of East Germany in the post-war period, but merely to cast new light on an aspect of the occupation which, due to the inaccessibility of the documentary evidence before 1989, was very much neglected.

A final limitation which should be mentioned is that this book does not attempt to examine in any depth the role of women in the East German labour movement during the post-war period. This is not in the least meant to imply that women did not play a significant role in the post-war reconstruction of East Germany. On the contrary, sheer demographic necessity impelled the participation of women in the labour movement to an extent which was without parallel in German history. It is precisely because women *cannot* be regarded as a mere footnote in the history of the labour movement that it seemed inappropriate to treat them as such by attempting to squeeze their story into a single chapter or part of a chapter. After much deliberation, it was eventually decided that it would be better to postpone dealing with the issue to later publications, where it can be explored in the depth which it deserves.

It will be clear by now that this book does not in any way attempt to provide a broad survey of East German history in the period 1945 to 1953. On the contrary, the study very much focuses on one central aspect of that history, namely, the interaction of the German and Soviet traditions of Socialism and the transformation of the labour movement from a representative organ of the East German working class to an abject tool of the Communist dictatorship. Even thus circumscribed, the topic raises a number of important and fascinating questions, which deal with the very heart of the process that led to the formation of the GDR and the division of Germany. These questions are: how did the activists of the East German labour movement respond to the policies which were being introduced from above, but which they were being expected to implement on the ground?; to what extent was the process of Stalinisation in East Germany itself tempered and modulated by the existence of a native tradition of working-class politics?; what, if anything, can the answers to the above two questions tell us about the broader issues of Stalinism and the course of German history in the twentieth century?

Notes

1 H. Schmollinger, 'Das Bezirkskomitee Freies Deutschland in Leipzig', in L. Niethammer et al. (eds.), *Arbeiterinitiative 1945*, Wuppertal, 1976, p. 219.
2 H. Grebing, *The History of the German Labour Movement* (trans. by E. Körner), London, 1969, pp. 74–75.

1

Eastern Germany at 'Zero Hour'

Most ordinary Germans had very mixed feelings about the cessation of hostilities in May 1945. On the one hand, there was relief that the guns had at last fallen silent. There would be no more terrible bombing raids. On the other hand, however, their country had been reduced to ruins, invaded and now lay prostrate before the British, French, American and Soviet occupiers. The old Germany seemed to have been utterly destroyed, but it was not at all clear what sort of system, or what sort of society, would emerge in its place. It was for this reason that people at the time began to refer to 1945 as 'Zero Hour' (*Stunde Null*): the point at which the clock of German history was turned back to zero, the point at which the past ended and an uncertain future began.

At this decisive turning point of German history, it was the interaction of three factors which shaped the course of political developments, not just in the Soviet zone, but throughout the whole of Germany. The first and ultimately most important of these was the occupation policies pursued in Germany by the victorious allied powers. Any analysis of the situation in the Soviet zone at Zero Hour must therefore commence with an examination of the occupation policies with which the Soviets arrived in East Germany, and which, over the ensuing weeks and months, they attempted to implement.

Soviet occupation policy at Zero Hour

Between December 1943 and January 1944, the allied powers reached a number of important agreements concerning the future of Germany; above all, that following the unconditional surrender of Germany, the country would be divided into zones of occupation, the borders of which were proposed by the British in January 1944 at the European Advisory Commission (EAC) in London. Shortly afterwards, on 6 February 1944, the politburo of the exiled KPD in Moscow resolved to set up a 'Working

Committee', the purpose of which was to clarify the KPD's views on a whole range of problems related to the collapse of the Nazi regime and the subsequent military occupation. Between March and August 1944, under the watchful eye of the Soviets, the Working Committee met regularly to consider a wide range of economic and political issues. The culmination of this process was the so-called *Action Programme of the Bloc of Militant Democracy* of October 1944, which was intended to serve as a platform for a broad, antifascist united front in post-war Germany. In the spring of 1945, following the Yalta conference and the great military victories of the Red Army in Poland and Eastern Germany, the policies outlined in the *Action Programme* were further refined in the *Guidelines for the Activities of German Antifascists in the Territory Occupied by the Red Army* of April 1945.

There is no need at this point to embark on a detailed examination of the particular policies and underlying political assumptions of the *Action Programme* and the *Guidelines*, for they have already been thoroughly explored by a number of western and Soviet Bloc historians.[1] However, four features of the *Action Programme* and *Guidelines* are of such enormous significance that they need at least to be mentioned.

First, both documents explicitly and repeatedly stated that there was no question of Germany being ready for a Socialist revolution, for, according to the KPD leadership, the most fundamental preconditions for this were lacking. Whereas, in Leninist orthodoxy, the existence of a powerful revolutionary party was a basic prerequisite for a proletarian revolution, Germany in the spring of 1945 did not even possess a trade union movement or a Social Democratic Party, let alone a vigorous, popular and disciplined Communist party. Whereas, according to Lenin, a successful revolution can only be launched when a significant section of the masses has attained a revolutionary consciousness, the German people in 1945 were still thoroughly imbued with Nazi ideology. In the view of the KPD leadership, any attempt to introduce socialism in Germany would have the support of an insignificant minority of the population and would hence be no more than a putschist adventure which would be doomed to failure.[2]

On the basis of this analysis, the KPD leadership arrived at the conclusion that, rather than indulging in puerile, ultra-left fantasies about socialist revolution, anti-Nazis in Germany should concentrate instead on completing the tasks left unfinished by the abortive German revolution of 1848. Instead of attempting to seize power for itself, the German working class, in alliance with the peasantry and the progressive bourgeoisie, should establish in Germany a parliamentary democracy in which civil and property rights were guaranteed, and in which the basic motor of economic reconstruction would be private free enterprise.[3]

The second salient feature of both the *Action Programme* and the *Guidelines* was the assertion that, although Germany was nowhere near ready for Socialism, there would nonetheless have to be a period of sweeping reforms to get rid not just of the Nazis and of Nazism, but of the material roots from which Nazism had sprung. The Communists, for example, had always regarded the Nazi regime as the political representative of the so-called 'monopoly capitalists', who, it was alleged, had financed Hitler's rise to power and who had used the Nazis to crush the German labour movement. Once the Nazi regime had been defeated, it would therefore be necessary to smash the economic power of the barons of German industry by expropriating them and by breaking up their cartels.[4]

Similarly, the Communists had also long regarded the large landowners (*Junker*) as the backbone of German militarism. Accordingly, the *Action Programme* of October 1944 called for sweeping land reform to destroy forever this perennial source of reaction. Significantly, however, the *Action Programme* did not call for collectivisation, but, in accordance with the moderate temper of KPD policy at this time, it was argued that the estates of the *Junker* should be split up amongst the small peasants and landless agricultural labourers. This, it was asserted, would create an unbreakable alliance between the peasantry and the working class, which, in turn, would allow the new democratic republic of Germany to be established on a firm political foundation.[5]

A third significant feature of the policies drawn up by the Working Committee of the exiled KPD leadership in the period February 1944 to April 1945 was the great stress which was placed on the obligation of the Germans both to pay reparations and to accept the redrawing of the Eastern border of Germany. The majority of the German people, it was argued, had supported the Nazis to the very end and therefore could not escape a share of the responsibility for the crimes which the Nazis had perpetrated in their name. Once the Nazi regime had finally been destroyed, the countries which had suffered so cruelly at the hands of the Nazi aggressors, above all the Soviet Union, had a right to demand restitution. Only by acknowledging the justness of these demands, and only by meeting them in full, could the German people begin to win back their place amongst the community of civilised nations.[6]

Finally, the fourth important area covered by the *Action Programme* and the *Guidelines* concerned the means by which the other three main goals were to be achieved. In order to create a bourgeois democratic republic, to implement the necessary anti-Nazi reforms and to ensure the acceptance by the German people of the post-war territorial changes and reparations, it would be necessary to create the broadest possible united front. This organisation, which would be called the 'Bloc of Militant Democracy', would encompass the working class, the peasantry, the progressive bourgeoisie, petty bourgeoisie and intelligentsia. By working under the guidance and direction of the 'Bloc', the broad mass of the German people, it was argued, could re-learn the habits and practices of democracy, and prepare themselves for the day when Germany was allowed to resume its position as a sovereign and independent nation. Though it would be a genuine, cross-class alliance, the leading role in the Bloc would be played by the working class, which – as the section of the population which historically had proved most resistant to reactionary ideology – would be the best guarantor of the new, democratic order.[7]

With regard to the internal structures and organisation of the 'Bloc of Militant Democracy', two possibilities were envisaged by the *Action Programme*; either the Bloc would consist of a formal alliance of political parties, or it would be an over-arching body in which all anti-Nazi political tendencies would be subsumed.[8] By the spring of 1945, however, the views of the Soviets on this matter seem to have been influenced by their increasingly pessimistic assessment of the political situation within Germany. Despite the fact that the war was manifestly lost, and despite the increasing barbarism and madness of Hitler's policies, the loyalty of the German people to the Nazi regime did not appear to have been broken. Accordingly, the Soviets concluded that the Germans were a thoroughly bad lot who had given themselves up entirely to Nazism. At the Yalta conference of January 1945, Stalin asserted that 'the Germans are savages and seem to hate with a sadistic hatred the creative work of human beings'.[9]

On the basis of this very negative assessment of the political character of the German people, the Soviets decided that it would take many years of reform and re-education before Germany would be ready for a resumption of normal party politics. In the meantime, all political activity would take place under the direction of the Bloc, which in turn would be covertly controlled by reliable Communists. According to Wolfgang Leonhard, Communist exiles in Moscow in the spring of 1945 were told, shortly before being returned to their homeland, that political developments in Germany would lag behind those in the other countries of Eastern and Central Europe. It might, Leonhard and his fellow Communists were informed, be years before political parties were allowed, and even the creation of the 'Bloc of Militant Democracy' was not imminent.[10]

Taken together, these four salient features of KPD planning in the period February 1944 to April 1945 give us a good picture of the immediate tasks which the Soviets had set themselves, and their Communist henchmen, in the part of Germany which had been allotted to them by the EAC proposals of January 1944. One can, of course, argue about how genuine these policies were. Wilfried Loth maintains that Stalin's commitment to the gradual creation of a non-socialist democracy in Germany was vague but nonetheless sincere.[11] Manfred Wilke, by contrast, sees the Soviet and KPD conversion to the idea of a democratic and capitalist Germany as little more than a 'tactical interim goal'.[12] However, whatever Stalin's long-term purpose in promoting this cautious, moderate approach to the German question, in the short term at least both the Soviet military government and the KPD leadership remained true to it.

Material conditions in East Germany

Although East German politics in the immediate post-war period were dominated by the presence of the Soviets, it would be a grave error to interpret political developments purely in terms of Soviet policy. The Soviets were not operating in a vacuum. Nor did the formation and implementation of Soviet policy remain uninfluenced by native German conditions. Policies drawn up on paper under wartime conditions in Moscow often took on a rather different shape when exposed to the harsh realities of post-war East Germany. The second of the three critical factors in East Germany at Zero Hour was thus the appalling material problems with which the Soviets were confronted and to which they, no less than the other occupying powers, had to attempt to find solutions.

In purely physical terms, the bombing campaigns of the British and American airforces, coupled with the passage of allied armies, had reduced the major towns and cities of the region to rubble. The great city of Leipzig, for instance, had been bombed on thirteen separate occasions, on five occasions heavily.[13] As a result, some 25 per cent of all dwellings in the city had been destroyed. Chemnitz had been even more badly hit, losing 38 per cent of its available accommodation through bomb damage. The capital of Saxony – Dresden – had suffered a particularly destructive raid in February 1945, as a result of which 65 per cent of dwellings in the city had been rendered uninhabitable. In Plauen, where the devastation was even worse, some 75 per cent of dwellings had been destroyed by bombs.[14]

The physical destruction of buildings was the most visible but by no means the only legacy of the allied bombing campaigns. The war had also had a devastating impact on the provision of essential public services. In almost all of the region's towns and cities, the trams had ceased to run, the gas and electricity had been cut off, the taps had run dry and the post had long since ceased to be delivered. In Dresden, the sewage system had been penetrated by bombs and there was grave danger of disease. The streets of the city were pitted by 1,700 bomb craters, many of which had penetrated to the gas and water mains.[15]

The transport and communications network had also been devastated, not just by British and American bombs, but also as a result of the 'scorched earth' policy which the Nazis had pursued during the last desperate months of the war. No fewer than three quarters of locomotives and 60 per cent of carriages in the Soviet zone were no longer usable, whilst 970 railway bridges had been partially or completely destroyed.[16] As a result, even the major towns and cities were isolated from the outside world, whilst smaller towns and villages were almost completely cut off. It would be many months before communications with outlying localities would be restored to anything like normality. According to one report from the small Saxon town of Leubnitz:

No trains ran, no post was delivered, no newspaper came. In Dresden a provisional state administration had been set up, although at first we didn't notice it much, for there were still no post or rail connections. The telephone system, too, came only slowly and haltingly back into service. All messages went by courier, as in the middle ages and with the same difficulties.[17]

Alongside this material destruction, the wheels of East German industry had almost entirely ceased to turn. In Leipzig, for example, 14,393 of 16,154 concerns (89 per cent) had entirely stopped functioning.[18] This was partly a result of the direct material destruction of plant and equipment. According to one East German source, some 45 per cent of the productive capacity of the Soviet zone of occupation had been physically destroyed during the war.[19] More importantly, even where factories were still intact, the breakdown of the transport network meant that it was almost impossible to acquire either raw materials or components. Elsewhere, owners and managers had simply fled from the approaching Red Army, often absconding with vital pieces of equipment and machinery.[20]

The most serious material problem of the Soviet zone at Zero Hour was the chronic shortage of food. In the countryside, years of neglect and over-exploitation had reduced the productivity of the soil. Moreover, the hundreds of thousands of slave workers who had hitherto toiled to feed the German people had been released from their bondage by the allied victory. Most importantly, the paralysis of the transport network meant that the flow of agricultural produce from rural to urban areas had almost entirely dried up. As a result of these factors, most Germans were compelled to go hungry, not just at Zero Hour, but for many months and years to come. For most people, food remained an overwhelming, all-absorbing concern. In order to find food, ordinary Germans were compelled repeatedly to travel into the countryside where they bought or bartered or stole food from local farmers. For the individuals concerned this was often an exhausting, humiliating, not to mention impoverishing process. According to one contemporary report from Sonneberg in Thuringia: 'The worker is compelled by the general hunger to part with his last items of clothing to the farmer in order to obtain a little something extra [to eat].'[21] For the economy, the need of workers repeatedly to absent themselves from work in order to travel into the countryside was a major obstacle to recovery. As late as 1947, a typical factory in Thuringia reported that the average worker took fifty-five hours off every month in order to go scavenging in the countryside.[22]

These desperate shortages of commodities and especially of food, coupled with the rampant inflation which beset post-war Germany, created the ideal conditions in which the black market could flourish. For ordinary civilians – and especially for those who, on account of old age or sickness, were unable to make trips into the countryside – the black market meant the misery of being dependent on ruthless speculators, the Harry Lime characters who proliferated amidst the squalor and the rubble. In economic terms, the all-pervasiveness of the black market was a further serious obstacle to recovery. Contemporary Soviet and German reports are full of accounts of desperately needed supplies disappearing from warehouses, only to re-emerge on the street corners at many times the official price. According to Dietmar Keller, even as late as 1948 no less than 25 per cent of all consumer goods in Saxony found their way, by one route or other, on to the black market.[23] Clearly, in a situation where one quarter of industrial production disappears into the black economy, rational economic planning becomes a virtual impossibility.

The chaos left by the war affected not only Germany's economy, but also her civil administration, which, during the final cataclysmic weeks of the war, had almost entirely disintegrated. As the Nazi regime collapsed, the whole machinery of government came crashing down as well. By 1945 Germany had become a nation without a state; a country with no civil service, no education system, no executive and no judiciary. Throughout most of East Germany, this created a vacuum of power which was filled only partially by the armies of occupation. Most seriously, the disintegration of the German army and police force, coupled with the desperate material circumstances, led to a severe breakdown of law and order. In the cities and towns there was widespread looting by civilians and even, on occasion, by feral German policemen.[24] In the countryside, hungry and often armed bands of former slave labourers and POWs rampaged at will, looting and killing as they went.[25] In areas overrun by the Red Army, groups of drunken and violent Russian soldiers constituted a massive threat to civilian life and property. The cumulative impact of these perils was to impose a reign of terror on the population, particularly in the smaller and more isolated towns and villages. According to one eye-witness account, again from the Saxon town of Leubnitz:

> all kinds of shady riffraff made the area unsafe. Scattered Nazis and war criminals were roaming around. Robbery and murder were the order of the day ... Nobody left the locality without a pressing reason or without a sturdy companion. From seven o'clock in the evening to five o'clock in the morning it was absolutely forbidden to leave the house. Only to the foreign workers did this ban not apply. Naturally, many of these ruled the streets at night, exploiting their advantage to the full for their acts of thievery and violence.[26]

Finally, a circumstance which exacerbated all these problems was the huge influx of refugees from East Prussia, Pomerania, Silesia and the Sudetenland. Hundreds of thousands of Germans had, in the spring of 1945, fled from the advancing Red Army. Throughout the mid- and late 1940s, millions more were expelled from territories annexed by the Soviets and the Poles, and from regions elsewhere in Eastern Europe which had traditionally been the home of German-speaking communities. Despite the losses of war, the Soviet zone in 1946 contained nearly two million more inhabitants than the same area had possessed in 1939.[27] To make matters worse, not only did the Soviet zone have to cope with refugees settling permanently in the area, it also had to provide for the millions who were passing through on their way to destinations in the western zones of occupation. For example, no fewer than four million people travelled across the province of Saxony in the post-war period.[28] The Saxon city of Chemnitz, having lost 38 per cent of its dwellings during the war, nonetheless had to find temporary accommodation for the 250,000 refugees who passed through on their way to the West.[29]

The cumulative impact of all these desperate economic and administrative problems brought about a situation without parallel in the history of the twentieth century. Never before had a modern, industrialised society been brought so close to total economic and social collapse. This, of course, presented the German people with enormous difficulties, but the circumstances were also problematic for the various armies of occupation. Having defeated Germany in battle, the victors would now, at the very least, have to ensure that millions of Germans did not starve to death or succumb to disease. Some minimal level of law and order would have to be restored. Somehow or other, the administrative vacuum left by the collapse of the Nazi state would have to be filled. These would have been gargantuan tasks even for armies of trained administrators fluent in the German language and familiar with German conditions. But the new masters of Germany were fighting men, not bureaucrats or civil servants, and possessed little in the way of relevant experience or expertise. In any case, the Soviets, like the other occupying powers, simply lacked the personnel to be able effectively to cope with the appalling material problems of Germany at Zero Hour. Nor was the Red Army immune from the prevailing difficulties of transport and communication. During the chaotic early days and weeks of occupation, local Soviet commanders – just like their American, British and French counterparts – often had very little contact with their superior officers, and were hence compelled to rely on their own initiative to find solutions to desperate local problems.[30]

In addressing the immediate material and organisational difficulties which confronted them, the Soviets did, however, possess one important instrument which was not available to the western armies of occupation. Several hundred Communist émigrés, who had been thoroughly schooled in the Soviet Union, returned to Germany in the wake of the advancing Red Army. In particular, three 'initiative groups' of high-ranking Communists, under the leadership of Walter Ulbricht, Gustav Sobottka and Anton Ackermann, were dispatched to Berlin, Mecklenburg and Saxony respectively. Each of these three groups, under close Soviet supervision, immediately began to reconstruct the apparatus of public administration. Anti-Nazi politicians of Weimar vintage were sought out and installed as mayors

(*Bürgermeister*) or as officials of local government. Anti-Nazi policemen, who had been thrown out of the police force after 1933, were re-appointed by the initiative groups to their former offices. All kinds of anti-Nazi activists were contacted by the initiative groups and set to work. In short, the Soviets were able to employ these 'Moscow Communists' as a catalyst, one of the prime functions of which was to foster and accelerate the process of reconstruction. Even if Red Army commanders had little knowledge of local conditions, they did have at their disposal a body of disciplined and reliable functionaries who were both fluent in German and conversant with local circumstances. The 'Moscow Communists' gave the Soviets an initial head start in the tasks of post-war reconstruction, though it remained to be seen whether the German population would follow the lead they provided.[31]

The political mood of the German people

If the first critical factor in East Germany at Zero Hour was Soviet occupation policy, and if the second was the desperate material situation, the third was the political mood of the German people. When they were drawing up their plans for post-war occupation, the Soviets and the leadership of the KPD could only guess what sort of political situation would confront them on their entry into Germany. The fact that the majority of the population remained loyal to the Nazi regime did not bode well. The poor record of the anti-Nazi resistance movement seemed to be another depressing sign that it would take a long time before the Germans could emerge from the political shadow of Hitler. It was partly as a result of such pessimistic assumptions about German politics that the Soviets and the KPD leadership were so cautious in their planning.

In the event, the political conditions which the Soviets and KPD leadership encountered in Germany did not altogether correspond to their expectations. Like the other occupying powers, the Soviets discovered that the political situation in the territories they had conquered was highly chaotic and contradictory. Indeed, the political mood of the German people at Zero Hour was so contradictory that, ever since, historians' accounts of the time have been extremely inconsistent. A number of historians speak of the overwhelming passivity and fatalism of the population, and the lack of support for left-wing or radical ideas. F. Roy Willis, for example, has asserted that the average German in 1945 was stunned by the 'overwhelming shock of total defeat and ruin', which 'made him a pliant, passive object under the direction of military government'.[32] According to Mary Fulbrook, meanwhile:

> On the whole, the political attitude of most Germans may be characterised in terms of apathy, a weariness in relation to 'politics' ... and an overriding concern with sheer physical survival from day to day. Only a minority at either end of the spectrum were ideologically committed and active.[33]

Beating hard on the same drum, Leonard Krieger has argued that

> politics for the average German was associated with Nazism, which was bad, or
> with Weimar, which was worse. Hence when, immediately after the Nazi
> collapse, the crushed remnants of the local Social Democrat and Communist
> party machines began unofficially to reconstitute their organisations, they
> attracted little mass support.[34]

Other historians have asserted that the left-wing and radical temper
which prevailed throughout Europe at this time was also apparent in
Germany. William Carr, for example, has argued that Germany, like the rest
of Europe, displayed an 'anti-capitalist' mood in which radical and left-wing
politics were expected to thrive.[35] According to Volker Berghahn:

> capitalism had become discredited in the eyes of many [Germans] who
> associated it with the disaster of the great slump, the rise of Hitler, and the
> subsequent catastrophes of German history. The mood in all four zones of
> occupation was distinctly 'socialist' in the early years after the war.[36]

In fact, despite their seeming incompatibility, Krieger's view that Germany
in 1945 was passive and conservative, and Berghahn's depiction of
Germany as radical and 'distinctly Socialist', both contain elements of truth,
for a fundamental characteristic of Germany at Zero Hour was the polarising
effect which twelve years of Nazism and war had had upon political opinion.
On the one hand, the majority of the population which had actively
supported or passively accepted the Nazi regime emerged from the ruins in
1945 in a state of profound exhaustion. This passive section of the population was generally suspicious of politics in general and of left-wing politics in
particular, and was overwhelmingly concerned with the difficult task of day-
to-day survival. On the other hand, the minority of the population which
had never accepted Nazi rule or ideology wanted, in 1945, to see a root-and-
branch transformation of German society, and was prepared to engage in
radical political activity in pursuit of that goal. This polarisation of political
opinion had occurred in all the zones of occupation, and was apparent to
many contemporary observers. A political report from the Saxon town of
Waldheim, for example, noted that:

> If we are to give [an accurate] report ... [on public opinion] we must make one
> thing clear right at the outset, namely, that divided opinions continue to be found
> here, that is to say the opinions of the antifascist-thinking population and of those,
> who although they cannot be described as fascists or reactionaries, cannot quite
> rid themselves of the past.[37]

The fault line which ran through German society – dividing the 'passive
majority' on the one hand from the 'active minority' on the other – was of

enormous significance, not just at Zero Hour, but in the months and years to come. In 1947, for example, a British visitor to the Soviet zone noted that: 'The contrast between the passive hostility [to the project of radical, anti-Nazi reconstruction] adopted by a fairly large section of the German population and the enthusiasm shown by those who are pressing forward with the tasks of rebuilding, overshadows everything.'[38] In the same year, another British visitor in the western zones noted that: 'Though the bulk of the population may be tired and apathetic, there is an active, enthusiastic minority busy trying to restart life again.'[39] The roots of this division lay in the very different ways in which the twelve years of the Third Reich had impacted on different sections of the German population.

The 'passive majority'

The political passivity of the majority of the German population is not difficult to explain. After the trauma of the battlefield and the long years of terror bombing, it was hardly surprising that most Germans wanted simply to be left alone to pick up the pieces of their shattered personal lives. A further massive disincentive to participation in political activity was of course furnished by the appalling material conditions, which compelled most people to devote a huge amount of time and energy to the desperate struggle to find food, shelter and warmth. A significant part of the population suffered from chronic malnutrition, and displayed the lethargy and listlessness which so often accompany that condition. Nor did the apparent bleakness of the future help to promote a willingness to engage in political activity. As one contemporary report from Plauen observed: 'The attitude of the population ... was in general one of severe depression, hopelessness, despair, not seeing any way out or what else the future might bring.'[40]

There were also political reasons underlying the passivity of the majority. It had been impossible, under the conditions of Nazism, for individuals to engage in open political discussion, and the faculty to develop one's ideas in free debate with other people did not spontaneously re-emerge in 1945. Moreover, twelve years of Nazi rule had accustomed most Germans to the *Führerprinzip*,[41] thereby eroding their ability to act independently, rather than blindly obeying orders handed down from above. In all the zones of occupation, the new masters of Germany continually noted the passivity and sometimes cringing servility of most of their German subjects.[42]

If most Germans were, however, reluctant to engage in political activity, this did not mean that they were entirely devoid of political ideas and opinions, confused and inchoate though these often were. There still existed in Germany, for example, significant numbers of die-hard Nazis, many of whom had flourished under the Third Reich, but who, since the defeat of their 'Führer', had fallen on hard times. After the Soviet invasion, thousands of Nazis lost their homes, their jobs and their privileges. Thousands more were carted off to internment camps where they were compelled to live (and, not infrequently, die) in the most squalid circumstances.[43] Though quiescent for the moment, unrepentant Nazis would return to the political stage in the months and years to come, particularly in West Germany (i.e. the Federal Republic of Germany). Even in East Germany, where there were fewer possibilities for overt Nazi activity, the authorities continued to note sporadic signs of pro-Nazi sentiment, mainly taking the form of graffiti, hate mail addressed to local officials and home-made leaflets. Above all, as one contemporary report from Plauen noted, pro-Nazi Germans would in private express the hope 'that everything would once again change and that a return to National Socialism lay within the bounds of possibility'.[44]

More numerous by far than the die-hard Nazis were those who, whilst recognising that the policies of the Nazis had led to disaster, were still very much under the influence of Nazi ideology. Many millions of ordinary Germans, it should be remembered, had voted for the Nazis before 1933, hoping that Hitler would deliver them from economic distress and the threat of Communist revolution. In the years after the Nazi seizure of power, millions more were so gratified by Hitler's perceived economic and foreign policy successes that they were content to come to terms with the new dispensation. In return, the Nazis went to considerable lengths to ensure the material well-being of the bulk of the population. Rather than forcing the Germans to pay for Hitler's re-armament programme out of their own pockets, the government pursued a 'guns and butter' policy which destabilised the whole economy, and this in turn provided Hitler with a pressing material incentive for his war of aggrandisement.

During the war itself, this sizeable section of the German population had of course suffered terribly as a result of Hitler's expansionist fantasies. It should be remembered, however, that these sufferings were inflicted, not directly by the regime itself, but as a result of the activities of the allied armies and air forces. Indeed, during the war years many Germans had directly profited from the xenophobic and imperialistic policies of the Nazi government. Thousands of Germans were able to take over the businesses or property of Jews, Poles or Czechs who had been murdered or expelled. Thousands more were the recipients of looted goods which had been sent back to Germany by husbands, sons and brothers serving abroad. The entire German economy benefited enormously from the ruthless plundering of the economies of occupied countries, and from the brutal exploitation of the labour of slave workers and concentration camp inmates.

As a result of their experiences, this 'passive majority' of the population emerged from the rubble in 1945 disillusioned and demoralised. The traumas of war had disabused these millions of Germans of their erstwhile faith in Nazism, but instead of turning to anti-Nazism, they tended to lapse into apathy and cynicism towards all political ideologies. According to a report from Plauen in December 1945:

The major part of the population still remains politically reserved. In particular the middle classes, which lived through the period of the Wilhelmine system and the period of the Weimar Republic to their great disappointment, but which took fresh hope from National Socialism and which are now witness to the downfall of the National Socialist regime, have lost faith in everything. Trust in any new political movement does not yet exist amongst them.[45]

Despite this overt apoliticism, these passive millions of Germans were still very much under the influence of Nazi propaganda. Bark and Gress have asserted that the German people were effectively denazified by their traumatic experiences during the cataclysmic final years of the Second World War.[46] In fact, twelve years of intense Nazi propaganda had left a deep imprint on people's attitudes and political behaviour. The Nazis had succeeded in deepening the anti-Communism which had already been present in the Weimar period, and, from the very outset of the post-Second World War period, political reports submitted by local KPD groups were full of complaints that their efforts to win the trust of the population were being blocked by an impenetrable wall of suspicion and hatred, above all in localities which had been Nazi strongholds.[47] Ideas about Lebensraum and the superiority of the German race were still prevalent, particularly with regard to the Czechs, Poles, Russians and other 'inferior' Slavonic races. There were still abundant traces of the 'Führer myth': the idea that, whilst the regime as a whole might have led to Germany's downfall, Hitler himself had been a man of destiny and a true patriot and leader. Most importantly, the majority of Germans displayed a profound inability to grasp the true criminal character of the Nazi regime. Their own complicity in the crimes of the regime made them unwilling to think too much about the past.[48]

Thus the Second World War was generally seen, not as a criminal enterprise, but simply as a catastrophic mistake. The Nazis' greatest single felony was that they had lost the war. The atrocities committed by the Nazis were condemned, but were nonetheless regarded as just another regrettable episode, different neither in quantitative nor qualitative terms from atrocities perpetrated by other nations during the war.[49] This utter failure of many Germans to acknowledge the enormity of the barbarism which the Nazis had unleashed upon the world is succinctly encapsulated in a letter addressed by an irate citizen of Leipzig to the city council in October 1945, complaining bitterly that a concert he had recently attended had been preceded by a political speech. 'I believe', wrote the anonymous Leipziger, 'that old Goethe would be turning in his grave if he knew that his name had been mentioned in the same breath as that of Karl Marx. Is that free democracy? That is an even worse dictatorship than that of the Nazis.'[50] Clearly, anyone who can say that a political speech given before a concert is worse than the systematic butchery of millions of people has no comprehension whatsoever of the true bestiality of Nazism.

Not only was there little understanding of the magnitude and uniqueness of the crimes committed by the Nazis, but there was an equal reluctance to acknowledge that the millions of Germans who had supported Hitler were hence partly responsible for the disaster which Hitler had visited upon the country. As Norman Naimark has pointed out: 'The Germans tended to blame everyone but themselves for the catastrophe that had engulfed them.'[51] In particular, most Germans ascribed their problems in the immediate post-war period, not to the failure of a criminal war of aggression, but to the various occupying armies and the German political authorities which had been installed by the allies. In a typical report from Plauen from October 1945, the local Communists complained resentfully that the majority of Germans

> do not always regard the present circumstances as the cause [sic: clearly 'result' is meant] of the past twelve years, but are convinced that the blame for these circumstances belongs to the men who are in charge today. We have not yet been able to counter this false point of view, nor to demonstrate the guilt of the German people sufficiently effectively to convince at least the majority.[52]

The final important point which must be made about the political orientation of the 'passive majority' of the German population is that it was deeply and bitterly anti-Soviet, as a result partly of Nazi propaganda, and partly of the brutalising experience of warfare on the Eastern Front.[53] The anti-Soviet inclinations which the majority of Germans entertained before 1945 were then massively increased by the behaviour of Red Army troops on the invasion of Germany in 1945. The true extent of the looting, murdering and raping which occurred during the Soviet invasion will probably never be known. Norman Naimark suggests that as many as two million German women may have been raped by Soviet soldiers. What is beyond question, however, is that the experience of being conquered by the Soviets was, for the majority of Germans, profoundly traumatic, and stamped them with indelible hatred, or at the very least fear, of all things Russian.[54]

The 'active minority'

If the experience of Nazism and war had demoralised and depoliticised the bulk of the German people, for a radical, anti-Nazi minority of the population, the preceding twelve years had had precisely the opposite effect. In the weeks immediately following the end of the war, thousands of anti-Nazi Christians and liberals, and tens of thousands of Communists, Social Democrats and trade unionists, emerged from the rubble of Germany's towns and cities and began, spontaneously, to organise at a grass-roots level. Though relatively few in number, such anti-Nazi radicals dominated the German political stage for the simple reason that they were the only people left standing upon it. The National Socialist Workers' Party of Germany (NSDAP), and with it the entire machinery of the state, had completely disintegrated. The old political parties of the centre and right were dispersed, demoralised, and discredited by the feeble resistance they had offered to the Nazis. For the time being, the radical, anti-Nazi section of the population constituted the sole active force in German domestic politics. It is for this reason that most contemporaries and many historians arrived at the conclusion that the 'mood in all four zones of occupation was distinctly "socialist" in the immediate postwar period'.

Among the most obvious manifestations of the activism and radicalism of this section of the population were the so-called 'antifascist committees' (*antifas*) which sprang up in great profusion in the spring and summer of 1945. The *antifas* were essentially citizens' committees based on the idea of direct, participatory involvement in the immediate and pressing tasks of reconstruction. With great energy and enthusiasm, the *antifas* set about restoring some degree of order out of the chaos. Throughout the length and breadth of the country, the *antifas* 'brought the supply of electricity and water back into order, began to take charge of and distribute the scarce supplies of food, organised transport and set about – in most cases without having been asked to by the local commandant – denazifying the administration, courts and factories'.[55]

Of equal importance were the workplace councils (*Betriebsräte*) which also emerged spontaneously amidst the ruins of German industry. Germany's long tradition of workplace councils had been suppressed by the Nazis on their accession to power. With the demise of the regime, however, the tradition was resurrected. In the chaotic conditions of 1945, many of these councils were able to attain a position of real power and influence in industry. Where the old owners and managers had either fled or been killed, many of these factory councils took over effective day-to-day control of their workplaces. Where the old owners and managers remained, the councils often forced on them some degree of 'co-determination' (*Mitbestimmung*). In the Soviet zone of occupation, the workplace councils, in the weeks and months following the end of the war, would go on to make 'an important contribution to the revival of Soviet zone industry'.[56]

A third manifestation of the activism of this anti-Nazi section of the population, alongside the *antifas* and factory councils, was the rapid re-emergence of party political life. In the last days and weeks of the war, small groups of Social Democrats and Communists began to meet in order to make their preparations for the return to legality. Once the war had finally ended, vast numbers of these small but very active local party cells sprang into existence. During the first days and weeks after their liberation, these rank-and-file activists played a central part in setting up local factory councils, trade union cells, and *antifas*. Most importantly, Communists and Social

Democrats often descended on the local town hall, deposed the Nazi Bürgermeister, and divided the various posts of local government between themselves. In the longer term, these local party cells went on to become the nuclei of the re-emerging zonal parties.[57]

As a result of their experiences, the anti-Nazi activists in the *antifas*, factory councils and rank-and-file party cells were motivated at least in part by a passionate loathing of Nazism and the Nazis. Through the twelve long years of Nazi oppression, thousands of Socialists, Communists and trade unionists had perished at the hands of the Gestapo, whilst tens of thousands had spent shorter or longer amounts of time in prisons and concentration camps. Not surprisingly, anti-Nazis who survived the camps displayed thereafter a hatred of Nazism of an intensity which is simply beyond the comprehension of those who have not themselves suffered such brutal oppression. Typical is the comment of the former Buchenwald inmate Hermann Brill, speaking at a meeting of Social Democrats in Thuringia in July 1945: 'Perhaps it sounds terrible but nonetheless I'll say it – a Nazi is not a human being, he just looks like one.' According to the minutes of the meeting, Brill's comment was met with stormy applause from the anti-Nazi audience.[58]

Hatred of Nazism, however, was by no means confined to the ranks of former concentration camp inmates. Many thousands of anti-Nazi workers who had escaped torture and imprisonment had nonetheless spent twelve years living in fear and isolation. Many workers, especially during the latter stages of the war, had been subject to ruthless labour discipline and exploitation.[59] Now, at last, the time had come for revenge. In the wake of the collapse of the Hitler regime, there was thus a wave of fiery and vengeful anti-Nazism, the intensity of which can be easily demonstrated. In Annaberg, the former Gauleiter of Saxony, Martin Mutschmann, had been captured by local anti-Nazi activists and was being held prisoner at the local town hall. According to a report written by one of the activists responsible for guarding Mutschmann:

> During the course of the morning the population of Annaberg stormed up to the Rathaus and demanded: 'show us the criminal, we want to see the man who must answer for our misery.' We were responsible for him and this was a real problem for us, for the mass of the people would have liked to tear him to pieces.[60]

In Waldheim, also in Saxony, a meeting was held in September 1945 which dealt in depth with the crimes perpetrated by the Nazis in Auschwitz and elsewhere. As one report of this event puts it: 'The mood of the population was such that, if the antifascist population had been given free rein, there would have been violence. People kept saying that these criminals should be dragged out here. Their punishment could never be severe enough and so on and so forth.'[61]

However, the anti-Nazi minority of the population wanted far more than simply a settling of scores with their erstwhile tormentors. Amongst this section of the German people, it was generally accepted that it was not enough simply to obliterate Nazism; the material roots from which Nazism had grown had also to be destroyed. As far as most of these anti-Nazi activists were concerned, these material roots could be located in the capitalist system. The disaster of Nazism, they reasoned, demonstrated once and for all that the capitalist system was morally and politically bankrupt, and needed to be replaced by a more humane and rational form of social organisation. In particular, the finger of blame was pointed at the traditional power elites, such as the 'monopoly capitalists', the *Junker*, and the German officer corps, who had constituted the backbone of German reaction in the days of imperial Germany (1871–1918) and the Weimar Republic, and who had also, in the view of the anti-Nazis, been the driving force behind Nazism. In order to break the perceived stranglehold of these reactionary groups on German society, the radical anti-Nazis advocated far-reaching political and economic reforms, such as land reform, sweeping nationalisation and thorough demilitarisation.[62] In 1945, the majority of such anti-Nazi activists believed that the prospects for a radical overhaul of German society were good. The Hitler state had been cast down and destroyed. The forces of the Right were dispersed and demoralised. The old state machine, which in imperial Germany and the Weimar Republic had proved to be a massive obstacle to social progress, had disintegrated utterly. There seemed to be no remaining barriers to the accomplishment of the dream for which they had struggled so long and suffered so much. Beneath this optimism, however, the years of Nazi rule had left deep and lasting wounds. The health of many had been ruined by years of malnutrition and maltreatment at the hands of the Nazis, and they were compelled thereafter to spend much of their time in sanatoria and convalescent homes. Others were left emotionally scarred by their experiences in the concentration camps and torture chambers of the Third Reich. Often they would be plagued for years afterwards by nightmares, in which they would hear once again 'the dreadful screaming' of their friends and comrades under torture.[63]

The experiences of the past had left many anti-Nazi activists, not just with physical and psychological wounds, but also with political ones. In the words of Detlev Peukert: 'The history of the resistance is the history of defeat.'[64] Accordingly, many anti-Nazis felt burdened by the sense of past failure. They believed that they had failed in 1914 to resist the nationalistic and chauvinistic tide which had swept Germany at the outbreak of the First World War. They had, they believed, failed once again in the period 1918 to 1919, when they had squandered the opportunity to crush their class enemies. They had failed yet again in 1933 to prevent the rise to power of the Nazis. In the period 1933 to 1945, they had failed to undermine the Nazi regime. They were painfully aware that the Nazi regime had met its nemesis, not through the efforts of the German resistance, but at the hands of the victorious allies. After such a dismal record of failure and defeat, it was hardly surprising that so many German anti-Nazis after 1945 were plagued by a deep lack of self-confidence. In the words of one Social Democrat, speaking at a meeting in Schwarzenberg in January 1946:

> We have lifted up our Socialist banner once again. We have done so timidly, as if we did not really have the right to grasp it again. It was, after all, wrested from us, and for twelve years we, in our impotence, had to conceal it. It is only the victors and liberators who have enabled us to unfurl our red flag.[65]

The anti-Nazi minority was also disorientated after twelve years of isolation. Between 1933 and 1945 the world had been transformed, but most anti-Nazi activists had had little or no opportunity to discuss these changes or to stay in touch with the ideas of their exiled political leaders. There was consequently a great deal of confusion and, linked to this, an enormous diversity of political opinion. Anti-Nazis in one locality, who had been effectively cut off for twelve years, had often developed in a very different direction to anti-Nazis in a neighbouring locality. This diversity of opinion at grass-roots level was a salient and important feature of the political scene throughout the first year or so of occupation.

Another very important point which should be made about the anti-Nazi minority of the population is that, at least to begin with, it was favourably disposed towards the Soviet Union. For most Communists, the USSR was of course the country of Lenin and the October Revolution; it was the fatherland of the international proletariat. Their faith in the Soviet Union had been, for many, one of the main sources of the strength and hope which had sustained them through the Nazi period. In the 1920s, for example, the Communist workers at the Presto-Werk in Chemnitz had been presented with a Soviet trade union banner. After 1933 the flag was hidden by the workers, firstly sewn into a pillow, then buried in a back garden. At great personal risk, the Presto-Werk Communists had thereby protected the banner from the local Gestapo until the time came, in 1945, to dig it up once again.[66] For Communists such as these, their faith in the Soviet Union had served, quite literally, as a banner of hope and defiance during the long nightmare of Nazism.

However, if the continued loyalty of Communists to the USSR was hardly surprising, it was also the case that the majority of Social Democrats were also deeply aware of the debt they owed to the Red Army. At political meetings during the first weeks and months of occupation, Social Democrats continually expressed their sense of gratitude to the Soviets for their liberation.[67] This, coupled with the radicalising impact of twelve years of Nazism, led many Social Democrats to display what Henry Krisch has called 'an open-minded willingness to reconsider their traditional views of the Soviet Union'.[68] Even Social Democrats who had problematic relations with the Soviet Military Administration of Germany (SMAD),[69] such as Hermann Brill in Thuringia, were prepared to admit that, although a Bolshevik-style government would not be the answer to Germany's problems, it was and remained the only progressive possibility in Russia. This view seems to have been shared by a majority of SPD functionaries.[70]

It is worth mentioning that the attitude of many anti-Nazi activists towards the Soviet Union was often deeply influenced by their personal experiences of being liberated from prisons and concentration camps by the Red Army. One female anti-Nazi from Chemnitz, for example, gives the following emotional account of her release:

> I was woken suddenly in the night by the singing and shouting of the French women prisoners in the dormitory above my cell ... Soon I too could hear the approaching rumble [of Soviet vehicles] along the nearby road. I clambered up to the window and saw lights appear in the courtyard of the prison. Suddenly I heard Russian speech, which filled me with delight.
>
> I shall never in my whole life forget what happened next. In our wildest dreams we had never imagined that our liberation would be like this. At the unceasing cries of the prisoners, Russian soldiers appeared and in a flash they opened the cell doors. We embraced each other, and, amidst tears and laughter, we sang the Internationale together.[71]

A similar account of liberation by the Red Army is given by another anti-Nazi who was also a prisoner in Chemnitz in May 1945:

> Towards midnight, suddenly, came the rumble of tank tracks. From cell window to cell window the cry went up 'The Russians are coming'. What happened next can scarcely be described. From a hundred throats the Internationale resounded into the night... Shortly thereafter Soviet soldiers opened the cell door with the words 'Comrade, you are free' ... People hardened in the struggle against fascism, in prison, in the torture chambers of the Gestapo and in the concentration camp, fell into the arms of the Soviet comrades, and nobody felt ashamed of the tears rolling down their cheeks.[72]

Unfortunately, not all East German anti-Nazis had such positive memories of liberation. Many female anti-Nazis fell victim to the wave of indiscriminate rape. Many male anti-Nazis had wives and daughters who were assaulted by Soviet soldiers. Not surprisingly, such harrowing experiences often destroyed any positive feelings which the individuals concerned might have harboured towards the Soviet Union.[73] Nonetheless, the point remains that whereas for the bulk of the population the Soviet invasion was an occasion of trauma and of fear, for the anti-Nazi minority it represented a blessed release from twelve years of oppression. In not a few cases the Red Army rescued anti-Nazis, at the very last moment, from SS or Gestapo firing squads.[74] Just as the Russian invasion confirmed the 'passive majority' in its fear and hatred of the Soviet Union, so did the liberation of the anti-Nazi minority from Nazi tyranny confirm them in their pro-Soviet sentiments.

Thus, twelve years of Nazism and six years of war had clearly had a divisive effect on the German population. What was of profound significance for the future, however, was not just that the Germans were divided, but that this division was in many ways extremely bitter. The Nazi regime which had pampered and cosseted the conformist majority had at the same time tortured and imprisoned the minority of the population which had refused to collaborate. Whilst millions of Germans participated in Nazi parades, the regime to which they were showing their hysterical devotion was at the very same time murdering Communists, Socialists and trade unionists in the concentration camps.

Similarly, many anti-Nazis had been repelled by the rapacious cruelty which they were forced to witness in their compatriots. One anti-Nazi member of a Wehrmacht punishment battalion, for example, records the revulsion he felt on encountering German soldiers, laden with plundered money and jewellery, who openly boasted of their participation in mass executions during the Warsaw uprising. In the aftermath of the uprising, the soldiers had been told by their officers that 'anyone who goes with Polish women is a race defiler [*Rassenschänder*]. But we have nothing against it, provided you shoot them after use.' With disgust the anti-Nazi notes that this was precisely what 'the majority indeed did'.[75]

It is hardly surprising, then, that many anti-Nazi activists in 1945 displayed a deep distrust and animosity towards the majority of a population which had actively supported or passively accepted the regime which had so tormented them. This resentment was exacerbated by the failure of most Germans to acknowledge the criminal character of the Nazi regime, and by the tendency of the majority of Germans to blame their post-war troubles not on Hitler and his cohorts but on the anti-Nazis who were attempting to rebuild what the Nazis had destroyed.[76] These feelings of animosity and resentment, moreover, were entirely reciprocated. Former resisters were often viewed with suspicion because of their close relations with the Russian invaders. Former inmates of concentration camps were also given better rations and access to superior accommodation, a fact which provoked considerable anger and envy amongst ordinary Germans.[77] An anti-Nazi worker in a Chemnitz engineering factory records how former concentration camp inmates were derided as being 'a real rabble'.[78] Elsewhere, former victims of Nazi persecution were mocked and accused of having brought their sufferings on their own heads, an accusation which naturally infuriated people who had endured years of abuse and incarceration.[79]

Clearly, the twelve years of Nazism had left a bitter and divisive legacy. Even without the allied partition of the country into zones of occupation, Germany in 1945 would in any case have been a deeply divided nation.

Notes

1 See, e.g.: A. Fischer, 'Antifaschismus und Demokratie', in E. Deuerlein, *Potsdam und die deutsche Frage*, Cologne, 1970, pp.16–17; E. Fischer, 'Die Entwicklung der Staatsauffassungen der KPD in der Zeit der faschistischen Diktatur in Deutschland', in K. Schöneberg (ed.), *KPD und Staatsfrage*, Staatsverlag der DDR, [East] Berlin, 1986, pp. 141–51.

2 Ibid., pp. 104–09.

3 Institut für Marxismus–Leninismus beim Zentralkomitee der SED, *Geschichte der deutschen Arbeiterbewegung*, Kapitel XI, [East] Berlin, 1968, pp. 190–93.

4 H. Laschitza, *Kämpferische Demokratie gegen Faschismus*, [East] Berlin, 1969, pp. 109–10.

5 Ibid., pp. 112–13.

6 Ibid., pp. 93–94.

7 Ibid., pp. 111–12.

8 G. Sandford, *From Hitler to Ulbricht*, Princeton, NJ, 1983, pp. 12–18.

9 US Department of State, *Foreign Relations of the United States, Diplomatic Papers: The Conferences at Malta and Yalta*, Westport, CN, 1955, p. 571.

10 W. Leonhard, *Die Revolution entläßt ihre Kinder*, Frankfurt/M, 1961, pp. 266–69.

11 W. Loth, *Stalins ungeliebtes Kind*, Berlin, 1994, pp. 33–34.

12 M. Wilke, 'Die Staatskonzeption der KPD-Führung im Moskauer Exil 1944' (paper given at the International Conference of the Institute of Contemporary History, Academy of Sciences of the Czech Republic, 9–11 September 1993), p. 5.

13 H. Arndt, 'Leipzig in den Jahren der Weimarer Republik under der faschistischen Diktatur', in K. Czok & H. Thieme (eds.), *Leipzig: Geschichte der Stadt in Wort und Bild*, [East] Berlin, 1966, p. 15.

14 J. Heise & J. Hofman, *Fragen an die Geschichte der DDR*, [East] Berlin, 1988, p. 2.

15 G. Schaffer, *Russian Zone*, London, 1947, p. 33.

16 Institut für Marxismus–Leninismus beim Zentralkomitee der SED, *Geschichte der deutschen Arbeiterbewegung*, Band 6, [East] Berlin, 1966, p. 15.

17 SStA Chemnitz, BPA Karl-Marx-Stadt, V/5/198, Bl. 31–32.

18 Arndt (n. 13 above), p. 87.

19 Heise & Hofman (n. 14 above), p. 22.

20 S. Suckut, *Die Betriebsrätebewegung in der sowjetisch besetzten Zone Deutschlands* (doctoral thesis, University of Hanover, 1978), pp. 104–05.

21 ThHStA Weimar, MdI, 142, Bl. 64.

22 Ibid., Bl. 45.

23 Quoted in D. Staritz, *Sozialismus in einem halben Land*, [West] Berlin, 1976, p. 104.

24 See, e.g.: SStA Leipzig, BPA Leipzig, letter from the KPD Ortsgruppe Zwenkau to the KPD Unterbezirksleitung Leipzig, 21.7.45.

25 N. Naimark, *The Russians in Germany*, Cambridge, MA, 1995, pp. 104–05.

26 SStA Chemnitz, BPA Karl-Marx-Stadt, V/5/198, Bl. 31–32.

27 Suckut (n. 20 above), p. 25.

28 A. Schellbach, 'Die antifaschistisch-demokratische Umwälzung in Halle', in E.

Könnemann et al. (eds.), *Halle: Geschichte der Stadt in Wort und Bild*, [East] Berlin, 1983, p. 103.

29 SStA Chemnitz, BPA Karl-Marx-Stadt, V/5/165, Bl. 4.

30 Naimark (n. 25 above), Chapter 1.

31 See, e.g.: Leonhard (n. 10 above), Chapter 7; H. Vosske, 'Über die Initiativgruppe des Zentralkomitees der KPD in Mecklenburg-Vorpommern', in *Beiträge zur Geschichte der deutschen Arbeiterbewegung*, Nr. 3, 1964.

32 F.R. Willis, *The French in Germany*, Stanford, CA, 1962, pp. 182–83.

33 M. Fulbrook, *The Divided Nation*, London, 1991, pp. 134–35.

34 L. Krieger, 'The Inter-Regnum in Germany: March–August 1945', in *Political Science Quarterly*, vol. 64, no. 4, 1949, p. 512.

35 W. Carr, *A History of Germany*, 1815–1985, 3rd edition, London, 1987, p. 270.

36 V. Berghahn, *Modern Germany*, 2nd edition, Cambridge, 1987, p. 185.

37 SStA Chemnitz, BPA Karl-Marx-Stadt, 1/3/29, 'Bericht Waldheim', 15.11.45.

38 Schaffer (n. 15 above), p. 26.

39 M. Lambert, 'Back from Germany', in *Points of Contact*, Book III (1947?), p. xx.

40 SStA Chemnitz, BPA Karl-Marx-Stadt, I-4/26, 'Politischer Bericht für Monat August 1945 von der Kreisleitung Plauen', Bl. 121.

41 This is the notion that all authority in society flowed down from the Führer and that subordinates should therefore obey the orders of their superiors as if they came from Hitler himself.

42 See, e.g., Schaffer (n. 15 above), p. 104.

43 See G. Adge, *Sachsenhausen bei Berlin*, Berlin, 1994, and M. Klonovsky and J. von Flocken, *Stalins Lager in Deutschland*, Munich, 1993.

44 SStA Chemnitz, BPA Karl-Marx-Stadt, I/4/26, Bl. 121.

45 SStA Chemnitz, BPA Karl-Marx-Stadt, I/4/27, Bl. 173.

46 D. Bark & D. Gress, *From Shadow to Substance*, Oxford, 1989, pp. 80–86.

47 See, e.g., KPD reports from the Saxon towns of Plauen and Pausa for the summer and autumn of 1945, SStA Chemnitz, BPA Karl-Marx-Stadt, I/4/25 and I/4/26.

48 A.J. Merritt & R.L. Merritt, *Public Opinion in Occupied Germany*, Urbana, IL., 1970.

49 See, e.g., Schaffer (n. 15 above), pp. 27–28.

50 Quoted in U. Oehme, *Alltag in Ruinen*, Dresden, 1995, p. 54.

51 Naimark (n. 25 above), p. 18.

52 SStA Chemnitz, BPA Karl-Marx-Stadt, I-4/25, Bl. 169.

53 See, e.g., O. Bartov, *The Eastern Front*, 1941–45, Basingstoke, 1985.

54 Naimark (n. 25 above), Chapter 2.

55 D. Staritz, *Die Gründung der DDR*, 2nd edition, Munich, 1987, p. 97.

56 Sandford (n. 8 above), pp. 32–37.

57 See Chapter 3.

58 ThHStA Weimar, BPA Erfurt, II/1-001, 'Rede des Genossen Brill am 8. Juli 1945', Bl. 3.

59 Laschitza (n. 4 above), pp. 33–35.

60 SStA Chemnitz, BPA Karl-Marx-Stadt, V/5/112, Bl. 6.

61 SStA Leipzig, BPA Leipzig, I/3/29, 'Bericht über die Stimmung und Gespräche unter der Bevölkerung, Waldheim', 1.10.45.

62 See Chapter 4.

63 See, e.g., SStA Chemnitz, BPA Karl-Marx-Stadt, V/5/218.

64 D. Peukert, 'Volksfront und Volksbewegungskonzept im kommunistischen Widerstand', in J. Schmädeke & P. Steinbach (eds.), *Der Widerstand gegen den Nationalsozialismus*, Munich and Zurich, 1986, p. 867.

65 SStA Chemnitz, BPA Karl-Marx-Stadt, II-2/17, Bl. 124.

66 SStA Chemnitz, BPA Karl-Marx-Stadt, V/5/059.

67 See, e.g.: SStA Leipzig, BPA Leipzig, I/3/01, Bl. 6; ThHStA Weimar, BPA Erfurt, II/1-001, 'Protokoll von der ersten Landeskonferenz der SPD Thüringen', 8.7.45, Bl. 2; SStA Chemnitz, BPA Karl-Marx-Stadt, III, 4/03, Bl. 9.

68 H. Krisch, *German Politics under Soviet Occupation*, New York, 1974, p. 33.

69 SMAD was the Soviet military government of Germany, which exercised sovereignty in the Soviet zone until the creation of the GDR in October 1949.

70 ThHStA Weimar, BPA Erfurt, II/1-001, 'Wie kommen wir zur sozialistischen Einheit der deutschen Arbeiterklasse?', Bl. 18–19.

71 SStA Chemnitz, BPA Karl-Marx-Stadt, V/5/081.

72 SStA Chemnitz, BPA Karl-Marx-Stadt, V/5/170.

73 Naimark (n. 25 above), p. 117.

74 See, e.g., SStA Chemnitz, BPA Karl-Marx-Stadt, I-4/26, 'Bericht, Plauen', 22.10.45, Bl. 203–05.

75 SStA Chemnitz, BPA Karl-Marx-Stadt, V/5/331.

76 For examples of such resentments, see G. Pritchard, *German Workers under Soviet Occupation* (doctoral thesis, University of Wales, 1997), p. 47, notes 105–07.

77 E. Reuter & D. Hansel, *Das kurze Leben der VVN von 1947 bis 1953*, Berlin, 1997, Chapter 2.

78 SStA Chemnitz, BPA Karl-Marx-Stadt, V/5/077, Bl. 4.

79 SStA Chemnitz, BPA Karl-Marx-Stadt, V/5/149, Bl. 1.

2

Antifascist committees and workplace councils

The German labour movement had been crushed by the Nazis in the early and mid-1930s, and thereafter did not pose a serious threat to the regime. Though many thousands of Communists, Socialists and trade unionists did continue to engage in resistance activities in the late 1930s and the early 1940s, they were isolated from and had little influence over the vast bulk of the population, and were primarily concerned with surviving the attentions of the Gestapo. Nonetheless, despite this record of failure, the German labour movement sprang back to life in 1945 with a vigour which, under the circumstances, was quite remarkable. Though only a minority of the German proletariat participated in this revival, many tens of thousands of workers did become involved in the antifascist committees and workplace councils which proliferated in every major German city, and in many of Germany's towns and villages. At Zero Hour, these grass-roots organs of working-class politics were the only organised force on the domestic political stage and were hence, for the time being at least, far more significant than their size would otherwise have warranted.

The existence of these organisations presented the Soviets with both problems and opportunities. On the one hand, such manifestations of grass-roots, working-class activism were anathema to the bureaucratic traditions of Stalinism. Moreover, their activities threatened to alienate the broad masses which the Soviets and the KPD leadership wanted to bring under their political control. Yet, if the rank-and-file activists were simply suppressed, this might result in their energies finding outlets which were harmful to Soviet interests. Furthermore, the rank-and-file activists were, by and large, the people who were most favourably disposed towards the Soviets, and most prepared to co-operate in the implementation of Soviet occupation policy. This was important, for the Soviets simply lacked the experience and the personnel to be able to achieve their goals entirely through their own efforts. As Norman Naimark has pointed out: 'The Soviets' lack of preparation for the occupation dictated that they use Germans' help in rebuilding an orderly and peaceful Germany wherever they could.'[1] For the time being at least, the Soviets needed the activists.

The solution the Soviets found to their dilemma was to adopt a two-pronged strategy towards the 'active minority'. On the one hand, they moved quickly either to suppress or to tame these rank-and-file initiatives. On the other hand, they tried to provide alternative avenues for the energies of the rank-and-file activists which were more in accordance with Soviet interests. In short, the Soviet response to the grass-roots activism of the 'active minority' was to try and divert its political energy into channels which could be controlled from above. To this end, however, the Soviets would have to modify many aspects of the occupation policies which had been developed in Moscow in the period 1944 to 1945, but which now needed to be fine-tuned to cope with the unexpected circumstances which they had encountered on the ground in East Germany.

The antifascist committees

During the war, the Soviets and the exiled leadership of the KPD had repeatedly called upon German anti-Nazis to form 'People's Committees' (*Volks-ausschüsse*), which, it was hoped, would not only help to destroy the Nazi regime, but would also serve as the building blocks for a new, anti-Nazi democracy in post-war Germany. In the *Action Programme* of October 1944, it was envisaged that such committees would be the primary organs through which the masses would participate in the construction of a 'militant democracy', first of all at a local, then at a district, regional and, ultimately, national level. According to Anton Ackermann, a leading figure in the drawing up of the KPD programme, the 'planned incorporation of the hitherto illegal People's Committees in the state administration' would lead to the emergence in post-war Germany of a new kind of participatory democracy.[2]

The hope, however, that a mass anti-Nazi movement, centred on People's Committees, would emerge to topple the Nazi regime, proved illusory. When, by the spring of 1945, no such anti-Nazi movement had materialised, the Soviets and their underlings in the KPD abandoned their concept of the People's Committees. In the *Guidelines* of April 1945, it was envisaged that the primary motive force for the construction of a new democratic order would come, not from People's Committees set up by Germans on their own initiative, but from a revived apparatus of local government established under the close supervision of the Soviets. Rather than trying to construct People's Committees, it would be the duty of German anti-Nazis to place themselves at the disposal of the new, Soviet-sponsored public administration.[3]

At Zero Hour, the Soviets and the KPD leadership were thus basing their policies on the assumption that German anti-Nazis would not form themselves into People's Committees and would not, on their own initiative, try to destroy the vestiges of the Nazi regime or address themselves to the pressing tasks of post-war reconstruction. This assumption, however, proved to be false. In the last weeks and days of the war and in the first days and weeks of occupation, vast numbers of antifascist committees sprang into existence. Though they were be to found almost everywhere in Germany, these '*antifas*' were particularly thick on the ground in industrial regions such as Saxony and the other traditional strongholds of the German labour movement. In the area around Gotha, for example, there were some fifty-four separate antifascist committees.[4] In the Mansfeld region there were fifty local *antifas*, whilst in the Dresden area, no fewer than sixty-eight *antifas* have been recorded.[5]

Despite the fact that almost all major towns and cities witnessed the emergence of these organisations, the *antifas* themselves were of extremely diverse origins. Some – such as the 'National Committee "Free Germany"' (NKFD) in Leipzig or the 'Antifascist Working Group of Central Germany' in the Mansfeld region – had begun life as wartime resistance circles.[6] More commonly, as in the Saxon town of Flöha, *antifas* were only established during the final weeks or days of the war.[7] In other cases, particularly in smaller towns and villages, *antifas* were created only after the allied armies had arrived. In Chemnitz, on the very day on which it fell to the Red Army, a crowd of anti-Nazis, after having held a demonstration to welcome the Russian tanks, retired to a local hostelry to establish an *antifa*.[8] In Limbach, a local *antifa* was set up two days after the town had been taken by the Americans.[9] In the small Saxon town of Niederwiesa, an *antifa* was not set up until the end of May 1945, some three weeks after the arrival of the Red Army.[10]

The *antifas* were equally diverse in terms of their size. In the smaller towns and villages, the *antifas* might contain no more than a handful of members. In the small Saxon town of Olbernhau, for example, the local *antifa* consisted of just six members: three former Communists and three Social Democrats.[11] In Eilenburg, in the vicinity of Leipzig, the local *antifa* had nine members, six of whom were Communists or Social Democrats, and three of whom were liberals or progressive Christians.[12] In the larger towns and cities, by contrast, the *antifas* sometimes recruited thousands of members and became genuine mass movements. At the end of April, the NKFD in Leipzig consisted of no fewer than thirty-eight local committees with 4,500 members and 150,000 supporters.[13] According to Wolfgang Leonhard, the 'Antifascist People's Committee' in Dresden had between 20,000 and 30,000 members.[14]

These striking differences in terms of origin and size were reflected in the diverse political orientations of the antifascist committees. In some places, antifascist committees were self-consciously revolutionary organisations which predicated their activities on the assumption that the collapse of the Third Reich constituted the end of the road for German capitalism, and that the presence of the Soviet invaders created the conditions for the establishment of a proletarian dictatorship. In the Saxon town of Meissen, the local antifascist committee demonstrated its commitment to Socialist revolution by calling itself the 'Council of People's Commissars'. In accordance with its revolutionary perspective, the Meissen *antifa* then set about creating a miniature Soviet republic. Factories were expropriated and proclaimed to be 'socialist property'. The homes and apartments of the wealthy were seized from their owners and handed over to working-class families. Throughout the town, buildings were bedecked in red flags and five-pointed Soviet stars.[15] All this was very far removed from the cautious and moderate politics at that time being espoused by the Soviets and the KPD leadership.

Elsewhere, however, local antifascist committees agreed with the basic proposition of the KPD leadership that Germany was not yet ripe for socialism, and hence that the *antifas* could not serve as the basis of a proletarian dictatorship. But in many cases, even these more moderate *antifas* envisaged that the *antifa* movement would play a central role in the reconstruction of Germany. The NKFD in Leipzig, for example, argued that the *antifa* movement should serve as 'the point of political crystallisation, around which all the antifascist forces in Germany must gather'. Although it accepted the necessity of establishing a 'Popular Front Government' (*Volksfrontregierung*) based on bourgeois, parliamentary principles, it also insisted that, within this democracy, the driving force would be the working class organised in People's Committees.[16] In short, though the programme of the Leipzig NKFD had much in common with the *Action Programme* of October 1944, it was well to the left of the more moderate *Guidelines* of April 1945, in which the Soviets and the KPD leadership had abandoned the whole concept of 'People's Committees'.

But for all these differences in terms of origin, size and political orientation, *antifas* everywhere engaged in similar practical activities. Whatever their origin or size, the nature of the material situation ensured that the practical tasks confronting the antifascist committees were the same. For those antifascist committees founded in areas still under the control of the Nazis, an immediately pressing task was the undermining of the fighting morale of the German armed forces and the securing of a peaceful and bloodless surrender. In Leipzig, NKFD activists attempted, sometimes successfully, to persuade local Wehrmacht and *Volkssturm* (the German equivalent to the British Home Guard) units to give up without a fight. Leaflets were distributed on the streets calling upon the citizens of Leipzig to avoid senseless bloodshed and to display either red or white flags from their windows.[17] Similarly, *antifa* members in Halle launched a campaign to persuade the population to display white flags from their houses and apartments. On the night of 14 April, the Halle anti-Nazis distributed 2,000 leaflets, calling upon the defenders of Halle to offer 'no resistance to the advancing Americans, otherwise thousands of bombers will reduce your city to rubble and ashes and destroy you, your wives and children'.[18] Elsewhere, *antifas* attempted to ensure that the Gestapo and the SS did not murder their prisoners as a final act of revenge. The local *antifa* in Zwickau, for instance, successfully negotiated the release of political prisoners from the nearby Schloss Osterstein.[19]

In a number of cases, antifascist committees went beyond simply calling for a bloodless surrender and seized control of their towns and villages. In Flöha, a band of anti-Nazis deposed the Nazi *Bürgermeister* at gun-point and disarmed the local police, seizing their weapons. An armed, anti-Nazi police force, sporting red armbands, took effective control of the town and began to prepare for the entry of the approaching Red Army. Barricades and mines were cleared from the streets, explosives were removed from nearby bridges, and the town was draped in red and white flags. A depot of Wehrmacht weapons and supplies at the local railway station was seized and placed under armed guard. By the time Soviet units eventually arrived in Flöha, they found the town firmly under the control of the local antifascist committee.[20]

Once the Nazis had finally been defeated, most antifascist committees devoted themselves to trying to solve the most pressing material problems which were afflicting the population. The scope and significance of the activities of many *antifas* at this time were recollected by one of the leading members of the main *antifa* in Chemnitz:

> The city's administrative organs – such as the Rathaus, local health insurance office, labour exchange, police headquarters [had] to be occupied by reliable antifascists. The fascist apparatus of house wardens had collapsed, and had to be reconstructed as quickly as possible, for the supply of provisions to the Chemnitz population was largely dependent on it. In all enterprises, and above all in municipal enterprises, good comrades had to take over management and guarantee the supply of gas, water and electricity to the population. It was a similar story on the trams and the railway... In particular it should be mentioned that, through the initiative of the *antifa*, the very first weeks saw the deployment of voluntary labour [in order to clear the streets of rubble] in which tens of thousands of people participated. The highest level of participation in a single week was 46,000 people.[21]

A similar story is told by a prominent member of the *antifa* in Leubnitz, a small town situated a few miles west of Zwickau. In Leubnitz, an 'Action Committee' composed of former Social Democrats and Communists constituted the only organised body in the district, and it was therefore compelled to take 'into its hands the fate of the five thousand inhabitants of Leubnitz'. In the weeks that followed, the members of the Action Committee were ceaselessly active in their efforts to restore the town to some degree of normality. Every member of the Action Committee took over a particular department such as food supplies, accommodation, agriculture, industry, transport, welfare and health... This of course does not mean that each individual would only work in his [or her] own field, for everything was still wildly confused. However, every individual endeavoured to do his [or her] bit and the population soon became accustomed to this system.[22]

Perhaps one of the most important tasks of the antifascist committees, at least in the short term, was the preservation of public order. In the small town of Olbernhau, which is situated in the Erzgebirge mountains on the border between Saxony and (the then) Czechoslovakia, the local *antifa* played an important role in restoring public order and preventing looting. The Olbernhau *antifa* seized control of remaining stocks of basic commodities, such as groceries, soap, electric light bulbs and toilet paper. Weapons were rounded up and secured, as were cars, trucks and other means of transport.[23] In Leipzig, meanwhile, the NKFD moved energetically to bring to a halt the wave of looting which was threatening to destroy the remaining stockpiles of vital foodstuffs and commodities. An English journalist, who visited Leipzig in 1947, was told of the following incident:

> On one occasion a crowd of several thousand was bent on plundering the food stores. Six members of the committee faced them, in danger at any moment of being trampled underfoot. There were moments of tension and then someone from the crowd shouted 'these are the right people'. The mood of the crowd changed and they eventually dispersed...
>
> I was given copies of the posters which the Leipzig Free German Committee somehow succeeded in printing in the first days of liberation and with which they plastered the town. These called on the people to stop looting and explained that by denuding the stores the looters would threaten the town with starvation, and called on all sections of the people to begin the reconstruction of their country.[24]

However, throughout most of East Germany, the greatest single threat to public safety was posed not by German looters but by the bands of Red Army soldiers and former slave workers who roamed at large across the countryside, looting, raping and killing as they went. Here, again, local *antifas* often played a key role in defending the population from physical attack. In Olbernhau, the *antifa* established contact with local Red Army units, as a result of which 'dealings with the occupation troops were regularised'. The Olbernhau *antifa* also established a workers' militia, which defended the civilian population 'day and night... even under the mortal threat of being attacked by the occupation troops'. The anti-Nazi militia also fought off the gangs of hungry and violent Czechs which had swarmed across the border in pursuit of food, booty and revenge.[25]

The Soviets and the *antifas*

The unexpected vitality displayed by the *antifa* movement confronted the Soviets with two options. They could revert to their original policy with regard to the People's Committees, outlined in the *Action Programme* of October 1944, and use the *antifas* as the basic building blocks of the new state apparatus. Alternatively, the Soviets could stick to the new line, set forth in the *Guidelines* of April 1945, according to which the People's Committees would play no part in the processes of political and economic reconstruction.

In the event, the Soviets and the KPD leadership, during the first month or so of occupation, do not appear to have followed a consistent policy towards the antifascist committees. In many places, those KPD leaders who had returned to Germany with the Red Army suppressed *antifas* wherever they were found, and encouraged anti-Nazis to place themselves at the disposal of the new organs of public administration being set up under the close supervision of the Soviets.[26] Elsewhere, however, *antifas* were tolerated or even encouraged by Soviet officers. In Chemnitz, local anti-Nazis were able 'to create from the very first discussion a favourable relationship with the commanding officers of the Red Army, and to obtain for ourselves a free hand for our work in the *antifa*'.[27] In Pockau, a local Communist, with the explicit support of the Red Army, was able to form a workers' militia (sporting red armbands on which was printed the five-pointed Soviet star) and, one week later, an antifascist committee.[28] Even in Meissen, the revolutionary activities of the 'Council of People's Commissars' enjoyed, at least to begin with, the 'complete support' of the local Soviet commandant.[29]

There are several possible ways in which we might explain these inconsistencies in Soviet policy towards the *antifas*. It is possible that at this stage the Soviets simply did not possess a coherent strategy with regard to the *antifas*, and that variations in policy between regions were no more than a reflection of confusion at the highest level. Alternatively, local Red Army commanders, as a result of the prevailing chaos and the difficulties of transport and communication, may simply have been unaware of what was going on elsewhere in the zone. Accordingly, local officers may have had to decide, on their own initiative, how to respond to antifascist committees in areas under their control. Possibly, as Gregory Sandford argues, *antifas* were tolerated in more provincial and outlying areas because, unlike in Berlin and the other major cities, there was at that time no possibility of replacing them with more orthodox organs of local government.[30]

A full understanding of the evolution of Soviet policy towards the *antifas* must await further research in the Soviet archives. What is beyond question, however, is that from the beginning of June 1945, a clearer and more consistent policy towards the *antifas* began to emerge. On 26 May, in a sudden reversal of previous policy, a Soviet directive announced that four political parties were to be established immediately in the Soviet zone: a Communist party (the KPD), a Social Democratic party (the SPD), a Christian Democratic party (Christian Democratic Union or CDU), and a liberal party (the LDP). Shortly thereafter, at the beginning of June 1945, KPD leaders were summoned to Moscow for discussions with the Soviet leadership about how this new policy was to be implemented. At the same time, at a meeting with Stalin, Molotov and Zhdanov on 4 June, the KPD leaders were informed that the antifascist committees were to be disbanded as quickly as possible. According to notes made at the meeting by Wilhelm Pieck, 'the formation of antifascist committees ... is not useful, because the danger exists that they will have independent power next to that of the city and local government'.[31]

The reasons for this sudden and dramatic change of policy are not clear, but it seems likely that the decision to suppress the *antifas*, and the decision to allow political parties, were closely linked. The reluctance which the Soviets had hitherto displayed about the refounding of political parties was predicated upon a pessimistic assessment of the degree to which Nazism had infected the German people in general and the German working class in particular. It is conceivable that the vigour of the *antifa* movement furnished the Soviets with living proof that sections of the working class were rather less infected by Nazism than they had originally supposed. Conceivably, the Soviets concluded that it would perhaps be possible to increase the tempo of political reconstruction – hence the early refounding of political parties. Alternatively, perhaps the Soviets felt they needed to provide a safe and controllable outlet for the energies of activists of the *antifa* movement. The *antifa* movement was an amorphous, heterogeneous phenomenon and was therefore not particularly amenable to Soviet and Communist manipulation. Orthodox political parties, by contrast, had the advantage of possessing established bureaucratic structures and procedures which could quite easily be subordinated to Soviet influence or control.

Whatever the reason for the decision to re-legalise political parties in the Soviet zone, the impact of the decision on the evolution of the *antifa* movement was considerable. From June 1945 onwards, in all areas under Soviet control, *antifas* were dissolved and their members encouraged to join one or other of the new political parties.[32] By and large, there seems to have been little resistance to the suppression of the *antifas*. Wolfgang Leonhard asserts that many *antifa* members retired, disillusioned, into private life, and played no further part in politics.[33] Whether or not this claim is true, it was certainly the case that many thousands of *antifa* members did go on to join and play an active role in the SPD, KPD or even in the LDP and CDU. What resistance there was seems, ironically, to have come from rank-and-file Communists, for reasons which will be outlined in the following chapter.

The workplace councils

In the towns and cities of Germany, the *antifas* had been the primary means through which the 'active minority' of the German population had addressed itself to the pressing material and political tasks with which it was confronted. In the factories and workplaces of Germany this role was fulfilled by the workplace councils (*Betriebsräte*). Like the *antifas*, the workplace councils sprang up in great profusion in the weeks immediately preceding and following the end of the war. They were also, again like the *antifas*, particularly in evidence in industrial regions such as Saxony, where there was a long tradition of labour activism.

In some cases, these councils had their origins in wartime resistance circles. In the Venuswerke in Chemnitz, for example, the workplace council began life as an illegal committee of anti-Nazis, the main purpose of which had been to alleviate the sufferings of the slave workers employed at the plant.[34] More commonly, workplace councils emerged spontaneously upon liberation, usually at the instigation of a small number of activists. At the Firma Schumann, in the Leipzig suburb of Engelsdorf, the initiative to found a workplace council came from a single former Communist, who, to this end, organised a mass meeting of 100 of his colleagues.[35] Similarly at the Elt-Werk in Chemnitz, a small group of Communists, just two days after the capture of the city by the Russians, called a mass meeting of the workforce at which a workplace council was appointed under the chairmanship of a former Social Democrat.[36] At the Firma Eberhard Schreiber in Leipzig, the initiative came from a Social Democrat, a Communist and a non-party activist, who constituted themselves as a 'Three-Person Committee' (*Dreierausschuß*), and who thereafter exercised the functions of a workplace council.[37] In Leipzig alone, there were no fewer than eighty-six such Three-Person Committees by May 1945, twelve in large, twenty in medium-sized, and fifty-four in smaller workplaces.[38]

There were a number of reasons for this spectacular revival of the workplace council movement at Zero Hour. First, the workplace councils in the 1920s and early 1930s had enjoyed great popularity on the shop-floor, and, although the Nazis had been able to suppress the workplace councils as organisations, they had never been able entirely to eradicate the councils either from memory or from tradition. Throughout the Nazi period, despite the best efforts of the Gestapo, the workplace councils had often continued to lead a shadowy existence as loose networks of personal relationships. Of particular importance in this regard were those workers who had escaped conscription into the Wehrmacht, either on account of their age, or because they possessed irreplaceable skills and who, as a result, had remained in their factories throughout the war. These older, skilled workers, who were often the most politically conscious section of the workforce, had been the backbone of the workplace council movement before 1933. Once the Nazi regime had collapsed it was precisely this section of the workforce which went on to play a leading role in the revival of the workplace council movement. In many instances members of the pre-Nazi workplace council, upon the arrival of the occupying armies, simply resumed their old positions and functions.[39]

A second important reason for the rapid revival of the workplace councils was that the destruction of the Nazi regime, and the concomitant disintegration of the German state, had profoundly undermined both the confidence and the authority of employers. Many owners and managers had been enthusiastic members of the NSDAP, or had exploited the labour of foreign slave workers, or had in some other way blotted their copy books. Now that their Nazi paymasters and protectors had been overthrown, they had good reason to fear that their past misdeeds would catch up with them. Many employers were further undermined by the fact that, with the collapse of the Nazi state, they could no longer rely on outside agencies to bolster their authority in the workplace. In the absence of any external authority, employers nervously eyed their workers across what was left of German industry, knowing that the only remaining check on the workers' behaviour was the rather threadbare tradition of deference and respect.

In thousands of workplaces throughout the Soviet zone, employees took advantage of these relatively favourable circumstances to alter significantly the balance of power on the shop-floor. In many factories, the newly constituted workplace council simply seized control of the firm's finances or imposed a wages ceiling to ensure that managers and foremen did not cream off remaining funds at the expense of the ordinary workers.[40] Elsewhere, workplace councils summarily abolished clocking-in machines and piece-work, or equalised wages.[41] At the Firma Eberhard Schreiber in Leipzig, the workplace council informed the management that henceforth 'no decision of the management will be accepted unless it has first been fully discussed with us'.[42] In the Saxon town of Böhlen, one particularly active and militant workplace council dismissed four out of the five directors and set up a political department, under reliable anti-Nazis, to vet all new appointments.[43] At the sugar refinery in Halle, a large company employing 800 workers, the chairman of the workplace council took over as the plant's technical director. In Erfurt, the director of the Olympia-Büromaschinen-Werke, a personal friend of Gauleiter Fritz Sauckel, was replaced by two ordinary workmen. At the giant Leuna works, south of Halle, the managing director was compelled, once a week, to give a detailed account of his activities to the workplace council, and to allow the workplace council unrestricted access to all the company's papers.[44] No doubt many employers in East Germany at this time would have sympathised with one Leipzig entrepreneur who lamented in the pages of his diary: 'I can hardly believe it. The workers simply will not accept my authority.'[45]

A third important reason for the vigour of the workplace council movement at Zero Hour was the desire of many antifascist workers to revenge themselves on former Nazis, many of whom had flourished before 1945 at the expense of their non-Nazi or anti-Nazi colleagues. In particular, many Nazi foremen and managers were hated because of the draconian labour discipline they had imposed upon their workers. In many factories, such as the Leipziger Wollkämmerei, the workplace councils simply turned out all former Nazis onto the street.[46] At one large factory in Böhlen, nobody who had joined the Nazi party before 1933 was allowed to work for the firm, whilst nominal Nazis were allowed to stay on, albeit under close supervision.[47] Elsewhere it was thought more expedient not to kick former Nazis out of the workplace, but to punish them by reducing their wages, taking away their company homes and forcing them to do menial or physical labour.[48] According to one contemporary account of the activities of the workplace council at the giant Espenhain plant near Leipzig: 'All Nazis were weeded out of key positions; they were not made unemployed, but put to work in the scrap yard and on the coal heaps.'[49] In Radebeul, a number of workplace councils did not confine their attentions to former Nazis, but insisted on the dismissal of all unpopular foremen and managers.[50]

The fourth, and by far the most important, reason for the remarkable revival of the workplace council movement at Zero Hour was sheer economic necessity. Unlike the farmers, the workers could not satisfy their own food requirements. Unlike most country dwellers, the urban proletariat could not easily go hunting for rabbits or foraging for fruits or edible wild plants. Unlike the wealthier urban classes, most workers had little or nothing which they could exchange for food on the black market. For most workers, the only way to survive was by producing commodities which could be sold or bartered. For the working class as a whole, the rapid revival of production was absolutely necessary for sheer physical survival.

In a great number of workplaces, however, the former employers had either been killed during the war or had fled from the approaching Red Army. In Saxony alone there were no fewer than 3,000 of such 'masterless' (*herrenlos*) workplaces.[51] Under such circumstances, workers had little alternative but to take matters into their own hands, and to attempt, on their own initiative, to bring their workplaces back into operation. However, even where the former owners and managers were still at their posts, they often had little interest in reviving production. The collapse of the currency and the prevailing economic chaos dictated that, whilst production for need was still possible and necessary, production for profit was no longer feasible. In any case, many employers, disbelieving Soviet and Communist assurances that private enterprise would not be interfered with, did not see a bright future for themselves in East Germany. Given their lack of commitment to the economic future of the Soviet zone, many owners and managers saw little reason why they should throw themselves into the immediate tasks of reconstruction.[52]

Above all else, the workplace councils were a pragmatic and logical means by which workers could fill the gap between their own pressing need to revive production and the inability or unwillingness of owners and managers to foster such a revival. In hundreds of workplaces throughout the Soviet zone, workplace councils began to play an important or even decisive role in the organisation of economic production. At the Firma Eberhard Schreiber, the company's fifty employees returned to the factory immediately after Leipzig had fallen to the Americans and, under the guidance of the newly constituted workplace council, held a mass meeting to discuss how the factory might be switched from wartime to peacetime production. Since, for the time being, there would not be enough work for all the firm's employees, the workforce decided that twenty men, selected according to their anti-Nazi credentials and family circumstances, should be set to clear up the site and ready the plant for peacetime production. The rest of the workers were sent on unpaid leave, but still attended the weekly meetings at which the progress of the company was discussed by the entire workforce.[53]

On many occasions, the desire of the workplace councils to foster a rapid economic recovery led to a clash of interests with incumbent owners and managers. At the Firma Erich Brangsch in the Leipzig suburb of Engelsdorf, the workplace council complained that it was being continually hampered by the 'inhibiting lack of decisiveness' of the factory owner.[54] At the Döhlitzer-Kohlenwerke, the managing director was suspected of deliberately failing to run the plant at full capacity. In response, the angry workers held a mass meeting at which, led by their workplace council, they decided to take matters into their own hands.[55] At the Elite-Diamantwerke in Chemnitz, so impatient did the workplace council become with the irresolute leadership of the manager that it entirely took over the running of the enterprise.[56]

The enormously difficult task of reconstruction could not be carried out without sacrifice. Under the leadership and guidance of their workplace councils, many workers proved willing to supply their own tools, work extra shifts, go without wages and even, on occasion, to donate money to their enterprises.[57] At the Espenhain plant near Leipzig, the workplace council persuaded the employees that they had to work longer hours if the plant were to be restored to full production. At the Firma Erich Brangsch, which had been hit by no fewer than fifty-two bombs, special Sunday shifts were worked in order to fill in the bomb craters, and 'everybody voluntarily took on extra work without asking about immediate recompense'. At the Radio-Graetz plant in Rochlitz, which had been given over entirely to war production, the workers, under very difficult circumstances, began to produce cigarette lighters, portable immersion heaters and, eventually, radios. At first they had to fashion these items out of whatever scrap metal they could scavenge or reclaim. Once all available supplies of scrap had been exhausted, the workers at Radio-Graetz went out on their bicycles to beg or borrow materials from neighbouring factories. In order to overcome the firm's cash-

flow problems, the workers not only agreed to go temporarily without payment, they even donated some of their own money to the enterprise.[58]

Soviet policy and the workplace councils

The KPD in Weimar Germany had always championed the rights of
workplace councils vis-à-vis the employers, and of the autonomy of the
workplace councils from the SPD-dominated trade union movement. In
1944, however, when the KPD leadership-in-exile turned its attention to the
position of workplace councils in post-war Germany, the radical rhetoric of
the Weimar period was quietly forgotten. Where workplace councils were
mentioned at all, which was rarely, they were spoken of only in the vaguest
of terms. Though the *Action Programme* of October 1944 did call for the
'democratic guidance and supervision' of the economy through the trade
unions and workplace councils, no specific details were spelt out. When,
shortly afterwards, Anton Ackermann mentioned the necessity of passing a
new workplace council law, he did not envisage that it would go much
beyond the old, moderate Weimar law of 1920. In the KPD 'Appeal' (*Aufruf*)
of 11 June 1945, in which the KPD leadership outlined its basic platform and
most fundamental principles, the workplace councils were not even
mentioned.[59]

Given the enthusiasm with which the Communists had espoused the
workplace council movement in the 1920s, the new-found moderation of
the KPD leadership on the issue is striking, but hardly surprising. Though
sharply at odds with old KPD policies of the pre-Nazi period, the new,
reserved approach to the workplace councils was very much in keeping with
the scrupulously moderate politics at that time being peddled both by the
Kremlin and by the various European Communist parties. If, as the Soviets
and the KPD leadership asserted, Germany was not yet ripe for socialism,
then it followed that the major role in post-war reconstruction would be
played, not by the organisations of the working class, but by private enterprise. If, as the KPD leadership argued, the prime task of all anti-Nazis was to
establish a cross-class 'popular front' stretching from the Communist Party
to progressive capitalists, then the slogans of workers' control and
Mitbestimmung could only have the effect of disrupting the popular front and
alienating those sections of the bourgeoisie and petty bourgeoisie which the
Soviets and the KPD leadership were so keen to win over.

Accordingly, the wartime literature of the KPD-in-exile, whilst rarely
mentioning the workplace councils, stressed repeatedly and explicitly that
the KPD had no intention of abolishing private property or interfering with
small-scale private production.[60] Moreover, in its eagerness to win over the
middle class, the KPD not only pledged to refrain from intruding on traditional property rights, but also promised actively to foster small businesses
and manufacturers. The *Action Programme*, for example, advocated generous

state credits to restore small artisanal and commercial enterprises.[61]

The Soviets and the KPD leadership at Zero Hour were thus basing their industrial strategy on the assumption that workplace councils would play, at most, a marginal role on the post-war economic scene. Once again, however, the East German labour movement was to take the Soviets and the KPD leadership by surprise. Moreover, as in the case of the *antifas*, the process of adjusting their policies to cope with unexpected circumstances proved highly problematic.

On the one hand, the Soviets were almost as eager as the East German workers to see a rapid economic recovery, partly for propaganda reasons, partly because they did not want an economic disaster on their hands and partly because they wanted to extract reparations from current production. The workplace councils, potentially at least, were a very useful ally in this task. They too were committed to raising production as rapidly as possible. They were in general far more favourably disposed towards the Soviets and the Communists than the owners and managers. They might, if handled properly, become an instrument through which the Soviets and the KPD leadership could increase their grip on the economy.

On the other hand, the rank-and-file democracy of the workplace councils was alien to the authoritarian and bureaucratic spirit of Soviet Communism. As early as 1918, the Bolsheviks had suppressed the vigorous workplace council movement in Russia which had emerged out of the Revolution. Perhaps more importantly, the radical activities of the hot-headed militants in the workplace councils might scare off the German middle class, hence rupturing the broad, cross-class alliance which the Soviets and the KPD leadership were intent on constructing. Both at the time and subsequently, leading Communists (and also Social Democrats) expressed their reservations about the 'anarcho-syndicalist' views on workers' control which were flourishing in many workplaces.[62] A particular problem, from the point of view of the Soviets, was that many workplace councils were taking revenge, not just on reactionary owners and managers, but also on humble, rank-and-file members of the NSDAP, many of whom possessed skills which were needed in the tasks of reconstruction. Not only was the dismissal or demotion of such people counter-productive in economic terms, it also – in the view of the Soviets – divided the working class and made it more difficult to persuade the masses of small-time Nazis to come to terms with the new political order.[63]

In the event, during the first chaotic months of occupation the Soviets and the KPD leadership adopted no clear policy towards the workplace councils. Torn by their ambiguous attitudes towards the councils, and impeded by their inability to intervene consistently on the shop-floor, the Soviets veered erratically between ignoring the workplace councils, tolerating them and attempting to suppress them. Between May and the first half of June 1945, the Soviets made no attempt either to foster or to stifle the workplace councils, and the matter was not even mentioned in official Soviet or KPD publications.[64] From the middle of June onwards, calls were made for the dissolution of the workplace councils and their replacement by official trade union committees, but no attempt seems to have been made to enforce this policy. On the contrary, local Red Army officers and Communist functionaries often developed good relations with workplace councils, and in some cases even instigated their formation where they did not already exist.[65] There also seems to have been some confusion at the very highest ranks of the KPD with regard to the future of the workplace councils. Walter Ulbricht, the most powerful figure within the KPD, consistently denied the value and importance of the workplace councils. Yet Hans Jendretzky, the party's expert on trade union matters, publicly called for the passing of a new law which would re-establish workplace councils on a firm legal footing.[66]

The confusion in the Soviet and KPD response to the workplace councils lasted until the late summer of 1945, when the authorities suddenly began to adopt a more consistent and positive approach. According to Siegfried Suckut, it had by this time become clear that private enterprise was not going to generate a rapid economic revival in East Germany. If an economic catastrophe were to be averted, the authorities therefore had little choice but to work with the councils, for they constituted the one active and constructive force in East German industry. The first intimations of the new policy appeared at a trade union delegate conference in Thuringia towards the end of August, at which a motion was passed demanding the creation of workplace councils in all workplaces. On 26 August, at a trade union conference in Brandenburg, a resolution was carried which explicitly demanded the election of workplace councils in all East German enterprises, and the restoration of their rights and privileges as guaranteed under the old workplace council law of the Weimar period. Three days later, Walter Ulbricht, who hitherto had been one of the foremost critics of the workplace council movement, gave a speech at a trade union conference in Halle in which he bemoaned the lack of initiative shown by managers and entrepreneurs, and affirmed that the workplace councils had a central role to play in reconstruction. By the end of September 1945, all traces of the former, negative approach to the workplace councils had disappeared, although this remarkable shift in policy was acknowledged neither by Communist leaders at the time nor in subsequent GDR historiography.[67]

The main thrust of the new Soviet policy was to exert greater control over the workplace council movement by bringing it under Communist influence. From August 1945 onwards, Communist workers were hence instructed to play an active and, if possible, a leading role in the workplace councils. As a consequence, workplace KPD cells began to devote an increasing amount of energy and attention to winning workplace council elections. KPD members were urged to attempt either to recruit existing delegates to the KPD or, at the very least, to bring them under Communist influence.[68] At the same time, Communist speakers began to use a language and rhetoric which were calculated to appeal to the rather syndicalist leanings of the workplace council activists. At a conference of workplace council delegates held at Waldheim on 17 October, for example, the principal Communist speaker explicitly stated that the workplace councils should henceforth keep the employers and managers on a very tight rein:

> No entrepreneur may do as he pleases, but must abide by certain guidelines. This is where the workers' councils must once again take a leading role. They must make the entrepreneur feel their commitment to reconstruction, for many entrepreneurs do not yet have any interest in throwing themselves into the new [regime of] production. Such individuals should if necessary be replaced by the workers' councils... The workers' councils should in every case be consulted about all decisions and all questions which arise.[69]

However, at the same time as the Communists were trying to place themselves at the head of the workplace council movement by appealing to the syndicalist proclivities of the activists, they were also attempting to nudge the movement away from its ultra-left radicalism and on to a more disciplined path. At meetings and conferences of workplace council delegates, Communist speakers continually reminded their audiences that if the councils had more powers than ever before, they also now had more responsibilities. In particular, workplace councils in 'masterless' workplaces now had 'an enormous responsibility'. According to the new KPD policy, it was now the responsibility of the workplace councils to oversee appointments and dismissals and to monitor prices in order to prevent profiteering.[70] The workplace councils would be expected to guard against sabotage and implement controlled and responsible denazification. Above all, it would be the duty of the workplace councils to do everything in their power to raise output and to fulfil the production plans which were assigned to enterprises by the authorities. In the words of one Communist speaker, it would be the primary task of the workplace councils to be 'the bearers and the backbone of the implementation of the production plan'.[71] As part of this duty, workplace councils would also have to persuade the workers to work longer hours, to forego unreasonable pay increases, and to abstain from carrying through measures, such as the abolition of piece-work, which might impede production.[72]

These, then, were the arguments with which the Communists sought to place themselves at the head of the workplace council movement in order to tame it, discipline it and transform it into a vehicle for KPD policy.[73] The degree to which this strategy enabled the KPD successfully to harness the energy of the workplace councils is dealt with in Chapters 6 and 8. For the time being, however, one further point needs to be made about the new Soviet approach to the workplace councils. Whilst the Soviets and KPD leadership did indeed, in August 1945, resign themselves to the fact that they were not yet in a position to suppress the workplace councils, they never abandoned their attempt to build up viable alternatives.

Thus, at the same time as KPD speakers throughout the Soviet zone were trumpeting the virtues of the workplace councils, the KPD was also busily constructing an official trade union (the Free German Trade Union Association or FDGB) as an adjunct to, and perhaps one day a replacement of, the workplace councils. Under the close supervision of Walter Ulbricht, the FDGB gradually emerged as a highly bureaucratic and centralised organisation, which was far more amenable to being manipulated from above than the workplace councils could ever be.[74]

In addition, the Soviets and the KPD leadership also installed 'trustees' (*Treuhänder*) to manage factories where the original owners had died, fled or been expropriated. For the time being these trustees usually worked closely with the workplace councils, and only in exceptional cases were they imposed against the will of the workers. Indeed, in many cases the authorities selected trustees from the ranks of the workplace council movement. In Saxony, some 47 per cent of trustees had originally been workers in the factories which were entrusted to them.[75] Nonetheless, for all their rank-and-file credentials, the trustees were, in the final analysis, accountable not to the workers but to the authorities who had installed them. Over time, the authorities would be able – through subtle bribery, gentle or not-so-gentle threats, and indoctrination – to sever the links that still bound the trustees to the workers from whose ranks they had come. Though, for the time being, the East German working class enjoyed far more power on the shop-floor than ever before in its history, the Soviets and the KPD leadership were quietly constructing the instruments through which this new-found autonomy would eventually be obliterated.

The historical significance of the *antifas* and workplace councils

Since the 1940s there has been a considerable amount of debate concerning the overall historical significance of the *antifas* and the workplace councils. Broadly speaking, one can identify three currents of thought in this controversy.

First, a significant number of left-inclined but anti-Stalinist historians have pointed to the *antifas* and workplace councils as concrete examples of participatory, democratic Socialism in action. Historians of this school of thought are keen to emphasise the importance, universality and popularity of the *antifas* and workplace councils, whilst playing down the role played in these rank-and-file workers' initiatives by the Communists. Lutz Niethammer, for example, argues that the *antifas* were not mere tools of the KPD, but were expressions of a genuine working-class unity which spanned the old sectarian divisions.[76] In his study of the largest and most successful *antifa* of them all – the NKFD in Leipzig – Horst Schmollinger concludes that the organisation was a genuine alliance of a broad spectrum of anti-Nazis, who put aside their differences to work shoulder to shoulder in the pressing tasks of reconstruction.[77] For Gabriel Kolko, meanwhile, the activists involved in the *antifas* and workplace councils were the bearers of a tradition of libertarian Socialism which had little in common with either the bureaucratic reformism of the old SPD or the authoritarian Stalinism of the KPD:

> The German radicals... were neither organised nor disciplined, but they were deeply committed to a far more libertarian view of the Left than was compatible with Bolshevism. They descended, for the most part, not from Lenin and Stalin nor Kautsky and Bernstein, but from the tradition and mood of Luxemburg and the early Spartacists.[78]

At their most extreme, historians of radical but anti-Stalinist proclivities argue that the *antifas* and workplace councils were potentially revolutionary organisations which bore within themselves the seeds of a new kind of Socialist society based on direct, participatory democracy. Germany in 1945, it is claimed, had the chance to go down a 'third way': neither capitalism nor Stalinism but genuine, democratic Socialism. According to writers such as Wolfgang Leonhard, however, all four of the occupying powers, including the Soviets, were determined to prevent the emergence of real Socialism in Germany, and they therefore intervened systematically to neutralise the potential of these independent stirrings of the German working class.[79]

The second school of thought in the debate about the historical importance of the *antifas* and workplace councils consists of mainstream western historians who downplay the vitality and significance of such working-class initiatives, and who reject any suggestion that it might have been possible for Germany to tread a revolutionary path at Zero Hour. Rolf Steininger and Theodor Eschenburg, for instance, have asserted that the anti-Nazi movement was weak, lacking in popular support and of purely local significance. The German people, they maintain, were apathetic, politically indifferent and only interested in personal survival. The type of direct participatory democracy practised by the *antifas* and workplace councils therefore appealed only to a tiny minority.[80] Only very rarely did large numbers of ordinary people become involved in such initiatives, and, for the most part, they were little more than front organisations of the KPD. In any case, the ease with which such initiatives were suppressed can hardly be seen as being indicative of a vigorous and powerful movement. In short, as Eschenburg concludes: 'In this post-war situation, the antifascist committees did not represent a serious political alternative.'[81]

The third and final tendency in the debate about Zero Hour was represented by the historians and scholars working in the GDR. Ironically, many of the arguments put forward by these East German historians were rather similar to those of their mainstream western counterparts. Like Steininger and Eschenburg, East German scholars emphatically denied that the situation in Germany in 1945 was in any way revolutionary. Like the majority of western historians, they stressed that the *antifas* and workplace councils enjoyed the support of only a minority of the population. East German historians also accused the likes of Niethammer and Schmollinger of greatly exaggerating the independence of the *antifas* and workplace councils and of seriously underestimating the role played in these organisations by the KPD.[82]

However, if revolution was not on the agenda, it followed that the only progressive possibility under the circumstances was a broad anti-Nazi coalition, the purpose of which would be to fulfil the 'bourgeois democratic revolution' which had been left unfinished in 1848. According to East German scholars, the most appropriate vehicles for the achievement of this task were the four antifascist political parties, the democratised state apparatus and the FDGB. The *antifas* and workplace councils were hence no more than a temporary expedient, which served as a focus for working-class politics during the first chaotic weeks and months of occupation, but which were no longer necessary once the four political parties and the 'democratic self-administration' had been established, and once the official trade unions had been fully developed. Far from being hostile to the *antifas* and workplace councils, the Soviets and the KPD leadership had welcomed the anti-Nazi enthusiasm of the activists, but had simply 'explained' to them how much more effectively their energies could be utilised in the newly founded parties and in the re-emerging apparatus of local government.[83]

In short, the East German historians concluded, there was no 'third way' which Germany might have taken at Zero Hour. Germany, they asserted, was confronted by only two alternatives; either, as in the Soviet zone, the forces of anti-Nazism would unite on a moderate but progressive platform in order to destroy the roots of Nazism once and for all or, as in the western zones, the evil of German reaction would be allowed to re-constitute and re-assert itself.[84]

Since the collapse of the GDR in 1989 and the opening up of the East German archives, historians can now take a fresh look at the whole debate about Zero Hour, the *antifas* and the workplace councils. In general, the documentary evidence which is now available seems to support the arguments of the mainstream western historians and even, to an extent, of the East German historians, whilst undermining the rather exaggerated claims of the anti-Stalinist radicals.

Thus, historians such as Kolko, Niethammer and Schmollinger are at pains to distance their beloved *antifas* from the KPD, for only by doing so can they claim that the *antifa* movement belonged to their tradition of libertarian Socialism, rather than the Stalinist traditions of the Communist Party. In fact, however, the evidence strongly suggests that the Communists played a much more important role in the *antifas* than the radical historians would care to admit. For example, according to one of its foremost activists, the *antifa* in Chemnitz was initially composed 'almost exclusively' of KPD members. Although a number of non-Communists were eventually persuaded to join, the organisation remained under effective Communist control.[85] The *antifa* in nearby Flöha, meanwhile, was 80 per cent KPD in composition,[86] whilst in Limbach, the decision to found an *antifa* was made by a small number of Communists at a private meeting.[87] In Düben, not only had the local *antifa* been set up by Communists, but they regarded it primarily as a means of recruiting promising individuals into the party.[88] In the vicinity of Weimar, *antifas* were set up in April 1945 by a small column of Communists from the concentration camp at Buchenwald, who travelled around local towns and villages, staging anti-Nazi rallies as a preliminary step to the formation of antifascist committees.[89] Even in Leipzig – where, in the view of Schmollinger and others, the anti-Nazi movement was based on a genuine alliance of anti-Nazi forces – the archival evidence now available suggests that the Communists were always the primary driving force. According to Stanislaw Trabalski, the leading figure in the Leipzig SPD, the NKFD was 'unfortunately no more than a Communist organisation' and the presence of Social Democrats in the NKFD committees was 'not always desired'.[90] The successor organisation to the NKFD, the so-called 'Antifascist Bloc', was – as the Communists frankly admitted in private – 'an instrument of the party'.[91]

If the radical historians of the Niethammer stable have underestimated the degree to which the *antifas* were dominated by the Communists, they have also tended to exaggerate the strength and vitality of the workplace council movement. Whilst it was true that the balance of power on the shop-floor shifted in favour of the workers, and whilst it was certainly the case that a significant number of workplace councils became extremely powerful, one must be careful not to make too much of these tendencies. In many factories, the class consciousness of the workforce had been diluted during the war by the conscription of many workers into the Wehrmacht and by the influx of relatively apolitical women or people of middle-class origins.[92] Once the war had ended, the fresh influx of dispirited and bitter 'resettlers' from the lost eastern provinces tended further to water down the militancy of many workplaces.[93] Even amongst the anti-Nazi workers, the twelve years of dictatorship had often left political scars which healed only gradually. In a report of December 1945, the KPD in Plauen stated that the mood amongst many workers was still cautious because they had not yet re-learned openly to speak their minds and because, after twelve years of turmoil, they lacked confidence in the stability of the current situation.[94] In August 1945, it was noted by the KPD in Leipzig that, particularly in the smaller workplaces, the workers were still under the influence of the *Führerprinzip*, and were reluctant to speak their minds in the presence of their employers.[95] At a conference of workplace council delegates in October 1945, the Communist speaker reported that, in a recent visit to a number of Leipzig factories, he had found that the majority of workplace council delegates were still far too passive and submissive: 'A proportion of the workplace council delegates have ... a considerable influence on the employers, but the majority do not. The consequence of this is that the majority of entrepreneurs are already asserting themselves quite actively against the workforce ... Therefore the workplace councils must display more activity.'[96]

On balance, the archival evidence would thus seem to suggest that, contrary to the claims of the most extreme of the radical historians, neither the antifascist committees nor the workplace councils were powerful enough to serve as the revolutionary beginnings of a new Germany. To understand why this was the case, however, one must bear in mind the political polarisation of the German people which was discussed in Chapter 1. As a result of the gulf dividing the 'passive majority' from the 'active minority' of the population, any progress towards a 'third way' in Germany at Zero Hour was confronted by a simple but insuperable obstacle, namely the fact that the majority of the population were indifferent or hostile to such a project. The *antifas* could and did appeal to the large numbers of anti-Nazis, most commonly of working-class origin, who wanted to see a root-and-branch transformation of Germany. However, given the domination of the *antifas* by the Communists, and given the deep-seated anti-Communism of most Germans, it is quite simply inconceivable that the *antifas* could ever have become a genuine mass movement except in places such as Leipzig or Chemnitz where there was a long history of labour radicalism. The workplace councils, meanwhile, were far too weak a force to have stood any realistic chance of becoming the nuclei of Socialist economic relations in German industry.

In this sense, the scholars of the GDR were absolutely right when they argued that Germany could either follow the East German pattern of development or the West German, but that there was no alternative path. Far-reaching political and economic reforms could only be pushed through against the wishes of the majority, which would be undemocratic. This, of course, is precisely what was to happen in the Soviet zone of occupation. Alternatively, as the West German example clearly demonstrates, if the German people were given the chance to determine their own future in free and democratic elections, they would vote in overwhelming numbers for parties of the Centre and Right. Germany in 1945 was thus confronted with the choice of either democracy or Socialism, but it could not have both.

Yet, even if historians such as Eschenburg and Steininger are correct in asserting that the *antifas* and workplace councils did not constitute 'a serious political alternative', they are wrong to belittle their historical significance and overall impact. In at least two different respects, the *antifas* and the workplace councils between them had a considerable influence on the course of later events. First, many activists in the *antifas* and workplace councils during the heady days of 1945 were both exhilarated and inspired by what they had experienced.[97] As Norman Naimark has argued: 'East German memoir literature by "activists of the first hour" underlines the fact that the first months of liberation and occupation ... were the most exciting and fruitful periods in these veterans' political lives.'[98] These positive experiences seem, in turn, to have coloured their views and political behaviour for years to come. In East Germany, for example, the recollections of the idealism and spontaneity of 1945 served only to increase the dissatisfaction of many veterans with the stifling bureaucratisation of political life in the Soviet zone during the later 1940s and early 1950s. On the other hand, their pride in the achievements of 1945 made it all the more difficult for them to reject the state, the foundations of which they themselves had laid during the first hectic months of occupation. As is argued in Chapter 7, the existence of these ambiguous sentiments amongst a whole stratum of activists – many of whom went on to become important figures in the GDR – was a fact of no little significance.

Second, and much more importantly, the different approaches of the Soviets and the western powers to the *antifas* and workplace councils set East and West Germany on very different trajectories of political development. In the western zones of occupation, the British, French and Americans did everything they could to ensure that the 'active minority' did not retain the dominant position which it had claimed for itself at Zero Hour. The *antifas* were suppressed but, unlike in the Soviet zone, no alternative was provided for the energies of the rank-and-file activists.[99] The workplace councils in the western zones were reined in to a far greater extent than was at first the case in the Soviet zone of occupation.[100] Above all, a blanket ban was imposed on all forms of political activity, which, during the first weeks and months of occupation, considerably hampered the endeavours of the 'active minority'. At the same time as frustrating the Left, the western powers also set about reconstructing the old German state machine from the ground up, whilst covertly fostering the political organisations of the Centre and Right, such as the CDU and the churches.[101] By 1949, the political balance in West Germany had been restored, and the western allies felt confident enough to permit the resumption of normal democratic politics. The result was a decisive electoral defeat for the parties of the Left, and the beginning of a seventeen-year period of conservative government.[102]

The Soviets, by contrast, may have felt suspicious towards the radical anti-Nazis, but they did not initially attempt to block their activities altogether. Instead, they sought to channel their energies into the official trade unions, the state apparatus and the newly founded political parties. As a result, the Soviets effectively confirmed the dominance of the 'active minority' in East German politics, albeit in a different form and within strict limits. In the course of time, the political ascendancy of the 'active minority' in the eastern zone of occupation was mutated by Soviet policy into the dictatorship of the Communist apparatus. The first step towards the division of Germany thus came about not as a result of any preconceived Russian plan to impose an alien and unwanted system upon the Soviet zone of occupation, but as a consequence of the response of the Soviets to a dilemma – the unexpected activism of the German Left – which they had neither created nor foreseen.

Notes

1   N. Naimark, *The Russians in Germany*, Cambridge, MA, 1995, p. 41.
2   H. Laschitza, *Kämpferische Demokratie gegen Faschismus*, [East] Berlin, 1969, pp. 111–15.
3   Ibid., pp. 131–44.
4   R. Büchner & H. Freundlich, 'Zur Situation in den zeitweilig englisch oder amerikanisch besetzten Gebieten der sowjetischen Besatzungszone', in *Beiträge zur Geschichte der deutschen Arbeiterbewegung*, 1972, p. 995.
5   G. Benser, 'Antifa-Ausschüsse–Staatsorgane–Parteiorganisation', in *Zeitschrift für Geschichtswissenschaft*, Nr. 14, 1978, pp. 785–87.
6   H. Arndt, 'Leipzig in den Jahren der Weimarer Republik und der faschistischen Diktatur', in K. Czok and H. Thieme (eds.), *Leipzig: Geschichte der Stadt in Wort und Bild*, [East] Berlin, 1978, pp. 87–89; Naimark (n. 1 above), pp. 263–65.
7   SStA Chemnitz, BPA Karl-Marx-Stadt, V/5/245, Bl. 5–7.
8   SStA Chemnitz, BPA Karl-Marx-Stadt, V/5/126, Bl. 106.
9   SStA Chemnitz, BPA Karl-Marx-Stadt, V/5/219, Bl. 3–4. N.B. The western part of the Soviet zone was initially liberated by British and American troops, and remained under British and American occupation for several weeks. At the beginning of July 1945, the British and Americans withdrew from this area, to be replaced by the Red Army.
10 SStA Chemnitz, BPA Karl-Marx-Stadt, V/5/120, Bl. 123 and 128.
11 SStA Chemnitz, BPA Karl-Marx-Stadt, I-4/23, Bl. 30.
12 SStA Leipzig, BPA Leipzig, I/3/27, 'Entwicklungs- und Tätigkeitsbericht der Ortsgruppe Eilenburg', 28.8.45.
13 H. Schmollinger, 'Das Bezirkskomitee Freies Deutschland in Leipzig', in L. Niethammer et al. (eds), *Arbeiterinitiative 1945*, Wuppertal, 1976, p. 640.
14 W. Leonhard, *Die Revolution entläßt ihre Kinder*, Frankfurt/M, 1961, p. 325.
15 See: Naimark (n. 1 above), pp. 265–67; D. Staritz, *Die Gründung der DDR*, Munich, 1987, p. 98.
16 SStA Leipzig, BPA Leipzig, I/3/17, 'KPD Sekretariat, Information Nr. 14', 28.4.45.
17 Schmollinger (n. 13 above), pp. 231–33.
18 W. Piechoki, 'Das geschah vor 30 Jahre', in *Freiheit*, Nr. 81, 5.4.75.
19 SStA Chemnitz, BPA Karl-Marx-Stadt, V/5/054, Bl. 1.
20 SStA Chemnitz, BPA Karl-Marx-Stadt, V/5/198, Bl. 5–10.
21 SStA Chemnitz, BPA Karl-Marx-Stadt, V/5/126.
22 SStA Chemnitz, BPA Karl-Marx-Stadt, V/5/198, Bl. 31–32.
23 SStA Chemnitz, BPA Karl-Marx-Stadt, I-4/23, 'Zustände vom 8.–12. Mai'.
24 G. Schaffer, *Russian Zone*, London, 1947, p. 16.

25 SStA Chemnitz, BPA Karl-Marx-Stadt, I-4/23, 'Zustände vom 8.–12. Mai'.
26 Leonhard (n. 14 above), pp. 313–20.
27 SStA Chemnitz, BPA Karl-Marx-Stadt, V/5/126, Bl. 53.
28 SStA Chemnitz, BPA Karl-Marx-Stadt, V/5/220, Bl. 206–11.
29 N. Naimark (n.1 above), p. 266.
30 G. Sandford, *From Hitler to Ulbricht*, Princeton, NJ, 1983, pp. 26–27.
31 H. Bodensieck, 'Wilhelm Piecks Moskauer Aufzeichnungen vom 4.6.45' in A. Fischer (ed.), *Studien zur Geschichte der DDR*, Berlin, 1993.
32 For examples, see SStA Chemnitz, BPA Karl-Marx-Stadt: V/5/012, Bl. 9; V/5/126, Bl. 108; I-4/23, Bl. 4. See also Naimark (n. 1 above), p. 259.
33 Leonhard (n. 14 above), p. 325.
34 SStA Chemnitz, BPA Karl-Marx-Stadt, V/5/011.
35 SStA Leipzig, BPA Leipzig, III/21, 'Bericht über die Betriebsausschußwahl bei der Firma Schuman Engelsdorf'.
36 SStA Chemnitz, BPA Karl-Marx-Stadt, V/5/232, Bl. 4.
37 SStA Leipzig, BPA Leipzig, III/21, 'Betriebsbericht der Fa. Eberhard Schreiber', 30.4.45.
38 S. Suckut, *Die Betriebsrätebewegung in der sowjetisch besetzten Zone Deutschlands* (doctoral thesis, University of Hanover, 1978), p. 145.
39 Ibid., pp. 43, 74, 120, 127, 135–36.
40 See: SStA Leipzig, BPA Leipzig, I/3/01, 'Protokoll der Unterbezirks-Partei-Delegiertenkonferenz', 18-19.8.45, Bl. 61–62 & 70–71; *Leipziger Volkszeitung*, 25.6.45, p. 5.
41 Suckut (n. 38 above), p. 196.
42 SStA Leipzig, BPA Leipzig, III/21, 'Betriebsbericht der Fa. Eberhard Schreiber', 30.4.45.
43 SStA Leipzig, BPA Leipzig, I/3/01, Bl. 170.
44 H. Jendretzky, *Neue deutsche Gewerkschaftspolitik*, [East] Berlin, 1948, pp. 133–34.
45 *Leipziger Volkszeitung*, 18.6.45, p.2.
46 SStA Leipzig, BPA Leipzig, III/21, 'Besprechung des gewerkschaftlichen Ausschusses Nord bei der Firma Gebrüder Joachim Patz'.
47 SStA Leipzig, BPA Leipzig, I/3/01, Bl. 170.
48 Suckut (n. 38 above), p. 189.
49 SStA Leipzig, BPA Leipzig, I/3/01, Bl. 61–62.
50 SStA Leipzig, BPA Leipzig, III/21, 'Bericht über die bisherige Betriebsarbeit (Radebeul)'.
51 SStA Leipzig, BPA Leipzig, I/3/28, Bl. 3.
52 Suckut (n. 38 above), pp. 108–25.
53 SStA Leipzig, BPA Leipzig, III/21, 'Betriebsbericht der Fa. Eberhard Schreiber', 30.4.45
54 *Leipziger Volkszeitung*, 21.6.46, p. 2.
55 SStA Leipzig, BPA Leipzig, III/21, 'Bericht des Betriebsrates der Gewerkschaft Leipzig-Döhlitzer-Kohlenwerke', 18.5.45.
56 SStA Chemnitz, BPA Karl-Marx-Stadt, V/5/199, 'Denkschrift über die Tätigkeit des Betriebs-Gewerkschaftsausschusses der Elite-Diamantwerke A-G, Siegmar-Schönau'.
57 Suckut (n. 38 above), p. 197.

58 *Leipziger Volkszeitung*, 15.6.46, p. 1.
59 Suckut (n. 38 above), pp. 167–73.
60 Ibid., pp. 164–66.
61 Sandford (n. 30 above), pp. 32–34.
62 See: F. Selbmann, 'Die sowjetischen Genossen waren Freunde und Hilfer', in F. Rosner et al. (eds.), *Vereint sind wir alle*, [East] Berlin, 1966, pp. 365–66; D. Staritz, *Sozialismus in einem halben Land*, [West] Berlin, 1976, p. 96.
63 Sandford (n. 30 above), pp. 32–34.
64 Suckut (n. 38 above), p. 160.
65 SStA Chemnitz, BPA Karl-Marx-Stadt, V/5/232, Bl. 4.
66 Suckut (n. 38 above), pp. 76–77 & 162–63.
67 Ibid., pp. 221–29.
68 See, e.g.: SStA Chemnitz, BPA Karl-Marx-Stadt, I/3/10, 'Protokoll der Gebietskonferenz der KPD Leipzig', 18.12.45, Bl. 74; SStA Leipzig, BPA Leipzig, I/3/28, 'Bericht über die am 11.9.45 stattgefundene Mitgliederversammlung', Bl. 2.
69 SStA Leipzig, BPA Leipzig, I/3/28, 'Bericht über die Arbeiterräte-Vollsitzung am 17.10.45'.
70 Ibid., Bl. 3.
71 SStA Leipzig, BPA Leipzig, I/3/10, Bl. 72.
72 SStA Leipzig, BPA Leipzig, I/3/28, 'Bericht über die Arbeiterräte-Vollsitzung am 17.10.45'.
73 For further examples, see G. Pritchard, *German Workers under Soviet Occupation* (doctoral thesis, University of Wales, 1997), p.87, n. 106.
74 Sandford (n. 30 above), pp. 59 & 70.
75 Staritz (n. 62 above), p. 96.
76 L. Niethammer, 'Aufbau von unten: die Antifa-Ausschüsse als Bewegung', in L. Niethammer et al. (n. 13 above), pp. 705–06.
77 Schmollinger (n. 13 above), p. 421.
78 G. Kolko, *The Politics of War*, New York, 1968, p. 507.
79 Leonhard (n. 14 above), pp. 319–20.
80 T. Eschenburg, *Geschichte der Bundesrepublik Deutschland: Jahre der Besatzung, 1945-49*, Stuttgart, 1983, pp. 136–37.
81 Ibid., p. 107.
82 See, e.g., Benser (n. 5 above), pp. 792–93.
83 See, e.g.: ibid., pp. 799–802; R. Badstübner et al., *DDR: Werden und Wachsen*, [East] Berlin, 1975, pp. 15–18.
84 W. Ulbricht, *Zur Geschichte der neuesten Zeit*, [East] Berlin, 1955, pp. 175–208.
85 SStA Chemnitz, BPA Karl-Marx-Stadt, V/5/126, Bl. 53.
86 SStA Chemnitz, BPA Karl-Marx-Stadt, V/5/245, Bl. 16.
87 SStA Chemnitz, BPA Karl-Marx-Stadt, V/5/219, Bl. 3–4.
88 SStA Leipzig, BPA Leipzig, I/3/27, '1. Versammlung der Kommunistischen Partei in Gräfenhainichen', 15.7.45, Bl. 2–3.
89 ThHStA Weimar, BPA Erfurt, I/1-002, Bl. 113.
90 SStA Leipzig, BPA Leipzig, II/1/01, Bl. 35.
91 SStA Leipzig, BPA Leipzig, I/3/05, 'Sekretariatssitzung', 24.8.45, Bl. 4.
92 Suckut (n. 38 above), pp. 31–33 & 74.

93 Naimark (n. 1 above), pp. 148–50.
94 SStA Chemnitz, BPA Karl-Marx-Stadt, I-4/29, Bl. 1.
95 SStA Leipzig, BPA Leipzig, I/3/01, Bl. 94–95.
96 SStA Leipzig, BPA Leipzig, I/3/28, 'Bericht über die Arbeiterräte-Vollsitzung', 17.10.45.
97 See, e.g., SStA Chemnitz, BPA Karl-Marx-Stadt: V/5/02, Bl. 3–5; V/5/012, Bl. 9; V/5/198, Bl. 31–40.
98 Naimark (n. 1 above), p. 272.
99 See, e.g., B. Marshall, *The Origins of Post-War German Politics*, London, 1988, Chapter 5.
100 See, e.g., ibid., pp. 70–80.
101 See: D. Bark & D. Gress, *From Shadow to Substance*, Oxford, 1989, pp. 136–40; J. Gimbel, *The American Occupation of Germany*, Stanford, CA, 1968, pp. 233–37; *The Economist*, vol. CL, 1946, pp. 99–100; B. Marshall, 'The Democratisation of Local Politics in the British Zone of Germany: Hanover, 1945-47', in *Journal of Contemporary History*, vol. 21, no. 3, 1986, pp. 418–20; V.F. Eliasberg, 'Political Party Developments', in G.A. Almond (ed.), *The Struggle for Democracy in Germany*, Chapel Hill, NC, 1949, pp. 227–30.
102 G. Pritchard, 'National Identity in a United and Divided Germany', in R. Bideleux & R. Taylor (eds.), *European Integration and Disintegration*, London & New York, 1996, pp. 155–57.

3

The rebirth of
the KPD and SPD

The re-establishment of the KPD and SPD in June 1945 was an attempt by
the Soviets and the KPD leadership to harness the energy of the reviving
labour movement by offering it channels through which it could express
itself. As such, the new line represented a shift to the left from the political
perspective outlined in the *Guidelines* of April 1945, in which no early
re-foundation of political parties had been foreseen. However, the Soviets
were still chary of allowing the political compass to swing too far to the left,
probably for fear of disrupting the broad, cross-class alliance which they were
so eagerly attempting to construct. The new political course was thus an
attempt to balance the radicalism of the 'active minority' with the
cautious passivity of the majority of the German population. The intention of
the Soviets seems to have been to create a political programme which was
radical enough to mobilise all those who wanted to see fundamental political
changes, without being so radical that it would alienate the broad masses.

Thus, on the one hand, the 'active minority' was offered the right to
engage in open political activity, and was given the promise that leading
Nazis, war criminals and *Junker* would be made to pay for their past misdeeds. However, at the same time, the pronouncements of the KPD leadership carefully avoided making revolutionary demands or using revolutionary
language. On 12 June 1945, Walter Ulbricht proclaimed that the central
political task confronting Germany was not to create a workers' dictatorship,
but, on the contrary, to fulfil the 'bourgeois-democratic' revolution
which had been left unfinished in 1848. According to Ulbricht: 'The democratisation of Germany must therefore be carried out. We are against the
establishment of a Soviet state in Germany. We must say this openly to the
people.'[1]

The main declaration of the aims and principles of the KPD leadership was
the so-called 'Appeal' of 11 June 1945, which was signed by sixteen
Communist leaders, and which provided the theoretical justification for
almost everything the Communists were to do in the following twelve
months or so. Whilst acknowledging that the German people as a whole

could not escape their share of the blame for what the Nazis had done, the 'Appeal' directed its main venom at the Nazi leaders, their 'hangers on and accomplices', as well as the 'active supporters of German militarism' such as the large banks and industrial cartels. In order, once and for all, to remove the allegedly reactionary influence of these groups, the 'Appeal' demanded the expropriation of the entire property of the 'Nazi big shots and war criminals', and the bringing of all essential public services, such as water, gas and electricity, into public ownership.[2]

All these demands were calculated to appeal to that section of the population which was most bitterly anti-Nazi and, above all, to the anti-Nazi working class. These concessions to the radicals were, however, balanced by an even more forthright promise that the Communists would make no attempt to Sovietise East Germany or introduce Socialist economic relations. Accordingly, the 'Appeal' explicitly endorsed the 'completely unimpeded development of free trade and of private entrepreneurial initiative on the basis of private property'. Similarly, the 'Appeal' promised that the expropriated estates of the *Junker* would not be taken over by the state, but would be distributed amongst the small and medium farmers and landless agricultural labourers. Above all, the 'Appeal' assured the German population that no attempt would be made to interfere with their civic freedoms or democratic rights. The goal of the KPD's policies was, it was claimed, not the creation of a workers' dictatorship, but the establishment of an 'antifascist, democratic regime, a parliamentary-democratic republic with all democratic rights and freedoms for the people'.[3]

In accordance with its moderate orientation, the newly re-founded KPD in Berlin also redefined its own sphere of political activity. Rather than returning to the revolutionary and subversive role it had played under the Weimar Republic, the KPD would henceforth, according to the leadership, become a model of conscientious responsibility. It would work shoulder to shoulder with the other antifascist parties and would respect the verdict of the ballot box. It would strive to participate constructively in the political and economic tasks now confronting the German people. In particular, the KPD would abandon its status as a cadre party of the German proletariat and would become instead a 'people's party' (*Volkspartei*), in which farmers, housewives, artisans, Christians and even small business people, would be made equally welcome. In internal party circulars, KPD members were told that one of the most fundamental tasks of the KPD was 'to gain the trust of the masses' and, to this end, that Communists should no longer feel themselves to be 'a special caste'.[4]

Thus, despite the Soviet decision to permit a more rapid reconstruction of political parties than had originally been envisaged, the policies outlined in the 'Appeal' were still scrupulously moderate. On the basis of these moderate policies, the KPD leadership in Berlin, under close Soviet tutelage, began to reconstruct the party organisation from the top down. Shortly thereafter, the newly created leaderships of the SPD, CDU and LDP issued their own political platforms and, like the KPD, set about constructing their respective party organisations. On 14 July, the final piece of the new political system of the Soviet zone was slotted into place with the creation of the so-called 'Antifascist Bloc', a coalition of the four antifascist parties, all of which pledged themselves to struggle side by side in the tasks of denazification, democratisation and reconstruction.[5] From the point of view of the Soviets, the machinery had now been created through which, at least in theory, they could direct and control the political development of East Germany. From its headquarters in the Berlin suburb of Karlshorst, SMAD could pull the strings of the KPD leadership, which in turn could guide and manipulate the activities of the other members of the 'Antifascist Bloc'. Each of the four party organisations would, in their turn, act as further 'transmission belts', through which Soviet policy could be carried to almost every section of the population.

This, at least, was the theory. In reality, the success or otherwise of the Soviets' strategy rested upon two rather shaky assumptions. First, the Soviets were assuming that both the 'active minority' and the 'passive majority' of the population could be embraced by the united front politics which had been outlined by the KPD leadership in the 'Appeal'. However, as will be seen, the chasm dividing the anti-Nazis from the bulk of the population was so enormous that any attempt to bridge it was bound to be fraught with difficulties. The political orientation of the Soviets and the KPD leadership was always in danger of falling between two stools: neither radical enough for the activists nor conservative enough for the Nazi-influenced masses. As a result, the whole united front strategy was inherently unstable, for it presupposed a degree of political cohesion in the population that simply did not exist.

The second assumption of the Soviets was that the newly established party leaderships in Berlin would be able to impose their authority on rank-and-file members in the provinces. Only thus would the system of political cogs and transmission belts be able to convey policies originating in Karlshorst to the whole of the zone's population. It was relatively easy for the Soviets to control political developments at the very apex of the new party system in Berlin, but this would be of little value if the party leaderships could not transmit these policies via their own party apparatuses.

For a whole number of reasons, however, it proved extremely difficult for the new party leaderships, and in particular the leaderships of the KPD and SPD, to impose effective discipline on functionaries and members at lower levels of the party hierarchies. After twelve years of Nazism, the rank-and-file members of both parties were confused and uncertain, lacking in political discipline and ideological cohesion. This was highly significant, for if the Soviets' attempt to construct a political mechanism through which to control the development of the zone should fail, then the only instrument remaining through which they could accomplish their goals would be force.

Communists and Social Democrats at Zero Hour

Long before the newly refounded KPD and SPD leaderships in Berlin began to reconstruct their respective party apparatuses from above, rank-and-file Communists and Social Democrats in the provinces had begun to re-establish their party organisations from below. In the small Saxon town of Niederwiesa, for example, four veteran Communists began to have discussions about the future in February 1945, the purpose of which was to ensure that the local KPD would be able 'to seize the initiative as soon as the existing [state] power collapses and to place our comrades in the most important positions in local government'.[6] In Pockau, close to the border between Saxony and Czechoslovakia, the Nazi *Bürgermeister* approached a veteran KPD functionary several weeks before the end of the war and promised him that, in the time remaining before the arrival of the Red Army, he would allow the local KPD complete freedom of manoeuvre. The Pockau Communists were only too pleased to take the *Bürgermeister* at his word, and in the following weeks they 'often came together in order to discuss the political situation and to establish what measures to take when Pockau was liberated by the Soviet army'.[7] In Chemnitz, the loose network of former Communists began to take on a more organised character as early as the spring of 1944. Discussion circles were organised, and Communist cells re-established in the city's factories and workplaces.[8] Though these organisational preparations were greatly disrupted by the wave of arrests which followed the failed coup d'état of 20 July 1944, they were taken up again with renewed vigour in the spring of 1945. By the time the Red Army arrived in May, Chemnitz possessed an illegal KPD cadre organisation encompassing the whole of the city.[9]

Though they were generally less active than their Communist counterparts, the Social Democrats, at least in certain towns and cities, began to reconstruct their party apparatus and to make plans for their post-war activities. According to Stanislaw Trabalski, who later became the leader of the SPD in Leipzig:

> Ten days before the entry of the Americans we were already able to disband camps in our district. In the meantime I had also made contact with the major general of the *Volkssturm*, who had promised me to disband it. Already by 6 April we were demanding that the police lay down their responsibilities... When, in 1945, the Americans marched in, we were already organised.[10]

These preparations for the collapse of the Third Reich paid dividends upon the entry of the Americans or Soviets into a particular district. In localities where Communists and Social Democrats had already laid their plans and reconstituted their organisations, they were able to spring immediately into action. In Niederwiesa, which was taken by the Red Army on 8 May, a group of local Social Democrats and Communists met in the town hall on the following day in order to establish an anti-Nazi public administration. A Communist was chosen as the new *Bürgermeister*, and other posts were divided according to pre-existing plans. In particular, two members of the new administration were delegated to form a group of 'auxiliary police' from reliable anti-Nazi workers.[11] In Limbach, where the local Communists had long been preparing themselves for their post-war tasks, 'the comrades of the KPD set about their work... immediately after the entry of the Americans on Sunday 15 April 1945'. Having met in one of the members' homes in order to form a party working group, a band of Communists descended on the offices of the local NSDAP, only to find that the Nazis had burnt all incriminating documents, and that the Nazi *Bürgermeister* had shot his wife and his five children before himself committing suicide.[12] The leader of the local Communists in Pockau, meanwhile, presented himself to the Soviets upon their entry into the town on 9 May 1945. Having received from them a slip of paper which confirmed his right to issue instructions, the KPD veteran 'went to the town hall, dismissed the Nazi *Bürgermeister*, and took over the running of the local administration'.[13] In Friedersdorf, a small village situated about ten miles south-east of Freiberg, a single Social Democrat took the fate of the village into his own hands, appointed himself to the post of *Bürgermeister*, and set about constructing an anti-Nazi administration.[14]

Not surprisingly, these Communists and Social Democrats, emerging in such numbers from the woodwork in the spring of 1945, proved to have been deeply influenced by their experiences of the previous twelve years. In some ways, one can see common patterns in the ways they responded to what had happened to them. All Communists and Social Democrats were eager to avenge themselves on the Nazis. All wanted to ensure that Nazism could never recur. To this end, almost all Communists and Social Democrats wished to see fundamental economic and political changes such as land reform and nationalisation.

On the other hand, and in contrast to these common themes, one of the most important legacies of the Nazi dictatorship was political confusion and diversity. For twelve long years, the majority of Communists and Social Democrats had been almost completely isolated from their respective party leaderships and party apparatuses. This simple fact was to have an enormous impact on the political development of rank-and-file Communists and Social Democrats, not just during the years of Nazism, but also in the immediate post-war period.

For the majority of Social Democrats, all contact with the SPD leadership had been severed when the party was banned in July 1933. In some parts of Saxony, it was possible for a time to maintain a tenuous link with the SPD leadership-in-exile (SOPADE) which between 1933 and 1939 was located in

Prague. However, even for Social Democrats living in a city such as Chemnitz, which is situated just forty miles north of the Czech border, the journey across the mountains into Czechoslovakia was difficult and dangerous, and contact with the exiled leadership remained, at best, sporadic. After the German invasion of Czechoslovakia in March 1939, any direct contact with SOPADE (now relocated in London) was, of course, out of the question.[15]

The Communists, meanwhile, had, during the first months and years of the Nazi dictatorship, been able to maintain a coherent underground organisation which was in touch with the exiled party leadership. By 1936, however, the ferocity of Nazi persecution had largely smashed the illegal party organisation, thereby severing the chain of command which linked rank-and-file Communists in Germany to the exiled party leadership and, ultimately, to Stalin. It was still possible for some Communists to keep in touch with the fluctuations of Communist and Comintern policy by listening to radio broadcasts from outside Germany. Occasionally, as in the Saxon town of Limbach, Communists were able to receive KPD literature which had been smuggled into Germany.[16] Most Communists, however, knew very little about the great about-turns of Soviet and Communist policy of the period 1935 to 1943, such as the abandonment of the thesis of 'Social Fascism', the adoption of the politics of the 'Popular Front' and, later on, the dissolution of Comintern. When, in June 1937, a KPD instructor held a meeting with a group of Communists in Munich, he found that they were 'seriously out of touch and knew little or nothing of the Party's new methods of work'. Similarly, a KPD instructor based in Amsterdam commented that a German underground functionary with whom he was in contact until 1939 'knows nothing of our present policy, absolutely nothing. He is still living in the year 1933.'[17] In a report drawn up by the Leipzig KPD in the summer of 1945, it was concluded that the 'almost hermetic' isolation of party members had made it extremely difficult for them to keep up with events and to interpret correctly the national and international situation.[18]

The Nazi dictatorship isolated rank-and-file party activists, not just from their respective party leaderships, but also from each other. In most towns and cities, all that remained of the Social Democratic or Communist resistance by 1936 were isolated groups of individuals, which, for security reasons, usually contained no more than four or five people.[19] Under the circumstances, such resistance cells had little option but to act autonomously, and they were often ignorant of the existence of other resistance cells in the same town or city.[20] Even where cells were aware of the presence of other groups nearby, there was generally very little attempt to co-ordinate activities, partly for security reasons and partly because the arrest of so many functionaries had removed the natural organisers of such activities. As one Social Democrat from Chemnitz put it: 'our leaders were arrested one after the other, so that each comrade had to become his own leader'.[21] Only in a few instances were resisters able to maintain a significant illegal organisation. According to one account, the SPD in Leipzig succeeded in building up an extensive system of 'five-person groups' (*Fünfergruppen*) which embraced at various times between 5,000 and 11,000 people and which, though often damaged by arrests, was never broken altogether.[22] In this respect, however, Leipzig was quite exceptional, and for most Social Democrats and Communists in East Germany, the Nazi years were spent in political solitary confinement.

Given the isolation of most resisters and their lack of knowledge about events in the wider world, it was almost inevitable that personal and local circumstances came to play a dominant role in the shaping of their political development. Since these circumstances naturally differed considerably from one individual to another, and from one locality to another, the end result of this process was enormous diversity. The SPD, even before 1933, had been a 'broad church', embracing a wide variety of political tendencies. Now, after twelve years of Nazism, these tendencies had developed along such divergent paths that they could no longer be easily contained within the same party. However, even in the ranks of the KPD, which before 1933 had placed a premium on political discipline and ideological conformity, twelve years of Nazism had led to a great deal of confusion and heterogeneity. Norman Naimark believes that the views of Communists 'at the end of the war were remarkably consistent, given the lack of any central underground Communist organisation'.[23] In fact, as the evidence clearly shows, the Communists in 1945 were in almost as great a state of ideological disarray as the Social Democrats. One Communist functionary, speaking at a meeting in Böhlen in March 1946, declared:

> We have amongst our comrades in the party the most varied ideas and opinions, which can partly be explained by the fact that we spent twelve years under Nazism, that we had no contacts, that we had no antifascist literature. Moreover, we know in our hearts – and anyone who is honest has seen it in himself – that fascism struck a chord with us. It is quite clear that from all this various opinions and differences have arisen.[24]

This ideological diversity and confusion amongst rank-and-file Communists and Social Democrats manifested itself in differences of opinion on a whole range of issues, such as women's emancipation, the role of the peasantry and attitudes to the western powers and the USSR. The two most important issues upon which the Left was divided were, however, the question of Socialism and the question of working-class unity, and these two central issues will therefore be explored separately.

The question of Socialism

One important issue dividing the Left was the question of how, and how quickly, Germany should proceed along the road to Socialism. Inside both of the left-wing parties there were at Zero Hour extremely divergent views on this central matter.

In the SPD, for example, the majority of Social Democrats had no desire to return to the moderate, reformist politics which their party had pursued during the Weimar period, for, in their eyes, the rise to power of Hitler had conclusively demonstrated the bankruptcy of this approach. Instead, they longed to see a profound and rapid transformation of German society which would destroy for ever the roots of Nazism at the same time as ushering in a new era of Socialism. In the concentration camp at Buchenwald, for instance, a group of Social Democrats around Hermann Brill produced a manifesto which called for the immediate creation of a Socialist economy and the establishment of a 'People's Republic', in which the basic units of political organisation would be 'People's Committees'.[25] In the ensuing weeks, Brill repeatedly argued at public and party meetings, before enthusiastic audiences, that the creation of a Socialist society in Germany was 'not a question of the distant future, but an immediate task of the present'. In Brill's opinion: 'The era of Social Democracy is over... The facts which revealed themselves to us in 1933 show us that we have entered a new epoch of – if I may put it like this – permanent social revolution.'[26]

A significant number of Social Democrats, however, had not abandoned the Weimar model and wanted to pick up the pieces where they had left them in 1933. Unlike their more radical colleagues, such SPD members and functionaries did not accept that the Weimar Republic had been fatally flawed, or that the SPD had made any fundamental errors in the period 1914 to 1933. In Chemnitz, a group of leading but moderate SPD functionaries publicly argued that, with the demise of the Nazi regime, Germany should return to democracy, which, as far as they were concerned, meant returning to the Weimar political system.[27] In Leipzig, the KPD noted a strong tendency amongst a number of SPD functionaries to defend the reformist politics of Weimar Social Democracy on the grounds that the lack of an SPD majority in the Reichstag had made any other course impossible.[28] Often, such moderate Social Democrats looked for inspiration, not to the Soviet Union, but to Britain, where the new Labour government furnished an example of a different road to Socialism, based entirely on parliamentary politics and eschewing any alliance with the Communists.[29]

Despite its more authoritarian and centralist traditions, there was almost as much diversity inside the KPD on these issues as inside the SPD. Very large numbers of Communists still passionately believed in Socialist revolution and the creation of a workers' dictatorship. After having been denied their proletarian revolution in 1933, and after having endured twelve years of unrelenting persecution, many Communists felt that, with the collapse of the old state machinery and the entry into Germany of the Red Army, the era of Socialism had dawned. Internal KPD documents from this period complained repeatedly that: 'Many [Communists] believe that with the destruction of the Nazi army in Germany, Socialism is at hand.'[30] At the first conference of KPD functionaries in Thuringia, held shortly after the entry of the Red Army into the area, the main speaker acknowledged: 'In our ranks, too, there are very many comrades who thought that with the Red Army would come the dictatorship [of the proletariat] at the head of which we Communists would place ourselves. That was the wish of many comrades.'[31]

Worse still, from the point of view of the KPD leadership and the Soviets, many of these radical Communists were able, under the prevailing conditions of chaos, to indulge their ultra-left fantasies, thereby threatening to wreck the cross-class united front which was so central to Soviet policy. Communists in Leubnitz, for example, seized the dwellings of the rich at gun-point.[32] In the Thuringian town of Suhl, local Communist functionaries were reported to be engaging in arbitrary and 'infantile' activities, such as the arbitrary requisitioning of the dwellings of middle-class citizens.[33] In the Saxon town of Pirna, the local Communists even went so far as to change the day of rest from Sunday to Friday and to insist that citizens greet each other with the old KPD slogan 'Red Front', rather than with 'Good day'.[34] In some places, Communists also took the opportunity to revenge themselves on the 'passive majority' of the population which so consistently in the past had shunned the KPD and embraced or tolerated the NSDAP. In Leubnitz, for example, the leader of the local Communists reported that: 'Even our own comrades tended to adopt authoritarian methods [*Führermethoden*], partly out of feelings of hatred and revenge, partly out of convenience.'[35]

In view of this widespread desire for a rapid transition to Socialism, it is hardly surprising that when the moderate character of the 'Appeal' of the KPD leadership became known, many rank-and-file Communists, who knew nothing of the rightwards drift of KPD politics in the period 1935 to 1943, responded with both incredulity and disappointment. According to an internal party report on the activities of the KPD in Plauen, the greatest threat to the party's policies came from radical Communists who were extremely hostile to the current party line. Even many functionaries, the report asserted, were following the party line 'more out of discipline than conviction'.[36] KPD functionaries in Leipzig noted that their members were continually complaining 'that the KPD had given up its goals',[37] and asking 'whether the Communist Party was still the party of the revolutionary class struggle'.[38] Throughout East Germany, internal party reports complained that it was above all the veteran comrades who clung to the radical politics of the Weimar period, and that new members often had a better under-standing of the party line than people who had been in the KPD since the 1920s.[39]

One aspect of the new political line which particularly troubled many rank-and-file Communists was the proposal that the KPD abandon its status as a cadre party and become instead a 'People's Party', which would be open, not just to the working class, but to farmers, peasants, Christians, intellectuals and business people. Many Communists were deeply attached to viewing themselves as a political élite to which the forces of historical progress had assigned a special and uniquely important role. Furthermore, the tendency of many Communists to regard themselves as a caste apart had been greatly accentuated by the persecution they had suffered under the Nazi dictatorship. Whilst the Communists had been languishing in the torture chambers and dungeons of the Third Reich, the very people whom the leadership were now proposing to recruit to the KPD had been out on the streets, clapping and cheering the 'Führer'. For many Communists, the idea of letting such elements directly into their beloved KPD, without, at the very least, an extensive period of political fumigation, was too much to stomach. Indeed, the corruption and rottenness which most German Communists saw in their compatriots provided yet another reason for wanting to keep the KPD ideologically pure. In the words of one rank-and-file Communist: 'Germany looks like an apple which is three-quarters rotten. Just as the knife must be stainless and sharp in order to clean the apple, so must our party members be.'[40]

Rather than encouraging the masses to enter the KPD, a very large number of Communists at Zero Hour wanted to rely upon the antifascist committees as the primary means through which the masses could be both mobilised and re-educated. Inside the *antifas*, an ideologically pure KPD would then be able to act as a covert leadership. Thus, in April 1945, the provisional district leadership (*Bezirksleitung*) established by the liberated Communists at Buchenwald regarded the creation of antifascist committees as one of its primary tasks.[41] Similarly, on 28 April the KPD in Leipzig instructed its members that only through 'the widest mass mobilisation' would it be possible for the German people to overcome the enormous political and material tasks which confronted them. However, since the party could not, under the prevailing circumstances, become a mass party, but would have to remain 'a cadre made up of the best comrades', the 'crystalli- sation point' for the mobilisation of the masses would have to be the antifascist committees.[42] In Gräfenhainichen, a small town some twenty miles north of Leipzig, the local Communists openly denounced the policies of Walter Ulbricht and the party leadership as being contrary to the teachings of Lenin. Rather than attempting to recruit the masses directly into the party, the KPD should build up the *antifas*, within which the party would play a leading role. In order to do this, however, the KPD should remain a cadre party containing only 'reliable and upright Communist fighters'.[43]

The ultra-left orientation of the bulk of the Communist rank-and-file was a major preoccupation of the Soviets and KPD leadership, and, in the summer and autumn of 1945, a great effort was therefore made to re-impose discipline and ideological conformity on the party. For a variety of reasons, however, this was not going to be an easy task. The situation inside Germany was still very chaotic, communications were poor and rank-and-file Communists either did not know, or did not believe, what Ulbricht was saying in Berlin. Confronting dire material problems which needed immediate resolution, Communists often had to act on their own initiative, without waiting for instructions from above. Many local Soviet commandants made the situation worse by tolerating or encouraging the activities of the extremists.[44]

Perhaps most importantly, the experiences of the previous twelve years had undermined old Communist habits of conformity and obedience to the party line. Given the conditions obtaining under the Nazi dictatorship, many Communists had had little alternative but to learn to think and act for themselves. Moreover, the twists and turns of KPD and Soviet policy in the period 1933 to 1945 had shaken the faith which many Communists had formerly had in the party leadership and in the USSR. Above all, the Nazi-Soviet pact of 1939 had come as a terrible shock to many rank-and-file Communists inside Germany. According to one Communist from Limbach: 'Many comrades did not understand the non-aggression pact, and many regarded it as a betrayal.'[45] In the words of a Communist from Chemnitz: 'Given the brutal terror against all progressive elements and the fact that thousands of our best comrades had been murdered, Stalin's action remained incomprehensible to them.'[46]

When, in 1945, the KPD leaders returned to Germany and began to re-impose their authority on the rank-and-file, they discovered that many Communists were reluctant to subordinate themselves once again to the party apparatus. In Naundorf, for example, a veteran Communist and anti-Nazi resister was expelled from the KPD for alleged breaches of party discipline. In response, his comrades in the local group sent a resolution to the area leadership (*Kreisleitung*) denouncing the undemocratic manner in which the veteran had been dismissed and demanding his immediate reinstatement.[47] In the northern districts of Leipzig, a group of KPD functionaries complained about being continually hampered in their work by the local party leadership, 'since we are always having to wait for guidelines from above'. In a resolution sent to the Leipzig sub-district leadership (*Unterbezirksleitung*), Communist functionaries accused the party leadership of being too high-handed and dictatorial, and of failing to listen either to the rank-and-file of the KPD or to the working masses. According to the disgruntled functionaries:

Since the present membership of the party... comprises the cadre of the coming mass party, it is surely necessary to get them to develop an inner trust in the party. This can only be done by showing our comrades that they do not simply have to carry out orders, but that as Communists they may also make use of their democratic rights within the party. Only thus can it be guaranteed that the supporters of the party become convinced that we do not just speak of democracy, but put it into practice.[48]

Eventually, after a considerable amount of time and effort had been expended, the Soviets and the KPD leadership did manage to bring the party membership more securely under their control. The establishment of SMAD in June 1945 and the creation of more orderly chains of command inside both the KPD and the military government helped matters. The intensive schooling of party members began to bear fruit. In Plauen, for example, the local KPD could report by November 1945 that its strenuous efforts 'to create clarity amongst our comrades' were having an impact, and that 'the comrades who take up today the same position as in 1933 are becoming fewer, which is a sign of our work'.[49]

Most importantly, it was a deliberate policy of the KPD leadership to dilute the influence of the 'sectarian' KPD veterans by changing the composition of the party through mass recruitment.[50] As part and parcel of this process of undermining the KPD veterans, younger, more pliable members, many of whom had only very recently been converted to Communism, were rapidly promoted up the party and state apparatus, whilst older members were continually criticised and held back. In Leipzig, for instance, the KPD leadership sent out the instruction that older KPD members 'who are no longer so flexible ... may not insist on being given posts which are beyond their capabilities'.[51] This created tensions between what became known as the 'New Communists' and the 'Old Communists', and significant numbers of the latter group fell by the wayside.[52] In his autobiography, Oskar Hippe asserts that 'many older comrades turned their backs on the party because they were not prepared to tolerate the policies of Walter Ulbricht... At demonstrations, they watched from the sides of the streets as bystanders.'[53] However, the strategy of isolating and undermining the ultra-left KPD veterans achieved its primary purpose, and by the late autumn of 1945 the KPD had regained something of the discipline and cohesion which it had possessed during the Weimar years.

The question of working-class unity

The question of the degree to which the struggle against the Nazis led to a rapprochement between rank-and-file Communists and Social Democrats has greatly exercised historians. East German writers always argued that the common battle against the Nazi dictatorship led to a 'Fighting Community' (*Kampfgemeinschaft*) between Communists and 'honest' Social Democrats, which in turn paved the way for the eventual merger of the KPD and SPD in April 1946 to form the Socialist Unity Party of Germany (SED). According to Joachim Heise and Jürgen Hofman: 'The will to unity grew in the antifascist defence front, in illegality, in the dungeons of the Gestapo, in the fascist prisons and concentration camps, in exile, in the trenches and in air-raid shelters. Unity was forged in common suffering, in the common struggle against the fascist enemy.'[54]

Many western historians, by contrast, have tended to downplay the degree to which Communists and Social Democrats co-operated in the resistance and have argued that old animosities did not fade away. The implication of this line of argument is that, if the eventual unification of the SPD and KPD in the Soviet zone did not come about as a result of anti-Nazi unity, then it must have been accomplished at the point of Red Army bayonets. Henry Krisch, for example, maintains that:

> Any study of the post-war relationship of the KPD and SPD must take into account the legacy of mutual hostility of the SPD and KPD. The actual measure of co-operation between the KPD and SPD attained in the 1935–1945 period was very small – much less, in fact, than in such countries as France or Spain... Thus, in the post-war period, the notion of collaboration, or even unification, rested more on hopes, slogans and programmes than on any record of accomplishment.[55]

Other historians from the West have claimed that, although it is true that the exiled leaderships of the SPD and KPD made no real progress towards settling their differences, Communists and Social Democrats on the ground in Germany went much further in the direction of unity.[56] According to a number of scholars, this discrepancy in KPD–SPD relations inside and outside Germany led to a growing rift between SPD and KPD activists inside Germany and their respective party leaderships outside Germany. In the words of Hermann Weber, for example: 'Between the politics of the Communist emigration... and the practical politics of the [KPD] resistance groups, who were prepared to co-operate with all antifascists, there thus existed substantial differences.'[57]

In fact, the evidence suggests that each of these three interpretations contains elements of truth. Even before 1933, there were divisions inside both working-class parties on the issue of unity. For many rank-and-file Communists and Social Democrats, the threat posed by the Nazis was so pressing that it no longer made sense rigidly to apply the sectarian policies of their respective party leaderships. On the other hand, there were also many die-hard sectarians in both parties, for whom the rival left-wing party was as obnoxious as the NSDAP. In both parties, there were considerable tensions between the sectarians and the advocates of unity. The impact of the Nazi dictatorship was to cause these contrary tendencies in both parties to diverge even further. By 1945, there were serious divisions in the ranks of the KPD over the issue of working-class unity, whilst the SPD was hopelessly split on the matter.

Thus, in some parts of eastern Germany, Social Democrats and Communists did indeed begin to unite against the common Nazi enemy during the turbulent months leading up to Hitler's seizure of power. In Harthau, in the vicinity of Chemnitz, there was a joint anti-Nazi demonstration in which the KPD, SPD, League of Red Front Fighter (RFB) and *Reichsbanner* (a paramilitary organisation for the defence of the Weimar Republic, with close links to the SPD) jointly participated. On one occasion, the SPD and KPD co-operated to prevent the *Sturmabteilung* (SA) from distributing election leaflets and other propaganda material around working-class tenements. When the SA arrived at the buildings, they found only locked doors protected by groups of KPD and SPD workers. According to one account of the incident: 'Without discussion, they [the SA] retreated in a rage.'[58] In Chemnitz itself, joint KPD–SPD 'fighting committees' were being constructed as early as 1932, the purpose of which was to defend working-class districts from Nazi encroachment and to protect functionaries returning from meetings.[59]

A similar story is told by a *Reichsbanner* member from Chemnitz who reports that, in the period 1930 to 1933, both he and a number of his comrades established contacts with local Communists 'in order jointly to prosecute the struggle against the Nazi criminals'.[60] Another Social Democrat from Chemnitz recounts that there were many instances where SPD members co-operated with Communists to prevent the SA from marching through working-class districts. Two incidents, in particular, are recounted by the Social Democrat with particular vividness:

> I can still clearly remember one incident. One Sunday a band of Nazis... attempted to march through the Martinstrasse. Together with comrades of the KPD we taught the Nazis a lesson, and only two truck loads of policemen, who ruthlessly set about the workers with their rubber truncheons, were able to free the Nazis from their predicament.
>
> It also came to joint actions in Rossdorf, near Limbach. The *Jungbanner* [the youth wing of the *Reichsbanner*] had taken over the protection of the encampment of the SAJ [Socialist Workers' Youth, the youth organisation of the SPD] there. Already on the Friday night, the camp was fired upon several times. These provocations and the murder of the *Jungbanner* member L.R. was organised from the pub 'Heiterer Blick', which was at that time the headquarters of the SA in Rossdorf. Together with comrades of the KPD and the League of Red Front Fighters, the pub was stormed and the SA put to flight.[61]

In the months that followed the Nazi seizure of power, large numbers of clandestine KPD–SPD groups sprang up in working-class districts and workplaces throughout East Germany. According to one tram worker and SPD member from Chemnitz, co-operation between SPD and KPD workers on the trams began as soon as the Nazis seized power and lasted for twenty months, when the network was finally broken by the Gestapo. Sadly the tram worker records that: 'We on the trams had found each other only when it was too late.'[62] In Markranstädt, a small town just west of Leipzig, the local Communists claimed to have had 'strong connections with SPD-followers', and above all with younger Social Democrats who, before 1933, had been opponents of the moderate, anti-Communist policies of the SPD leadership.[63] In the Thuringian town of Mühlhausen, local Communists and Social Democrats built a 'working community' (*Arbeitsgemeinschaft*) in 1933, which was able to maintain its illegal activities until finally being smashed by the Gestapo in 1936.[64] Twenty miles south of Jena, in the medium-sized town of Pössneck, there emerged a similar joint KPD–SPD resistance cell. According to one young Social Democrat who became a member of this group: 'Immediately after the National Socialist seizure of power in 1933 we young comrades in the SPD got in touch with comrades of the KPD and together we discussed all necessary measures.' Together, the young Social Democrats and Communists built a *Kampfgemeinschaft*, which met in woods or, with the connivance of a sympathetic pastor, in a local church. The KPD–SPD network in Pössneck, if the testimony of the Social Democrat is to be believed, survived a wave of arrests in 1936, and was only finally broken apart by the call-up of its members into the Wehrmacht after 1939.[65]

According to the standard interpretation of East German historians, the will to unity emerged not only as a result of the joint resistance of Communists and Social Democrats, but also as a consequence of their shared suffering. Henry Krisch, by contrast, argues that in the prisons and concentration camps of the Third Reich, 'there was little activity pointing to a unification of political organisations'.[66] The evidence, however, suggests that, whilst the claims of the East German historians may be hugely exaggerated, Henry Krisch is wrong in his assertion that the shared experience of incarceration did not break down the barriers between SPD members and Communists. Even a moderate SPD functionary such as Erich Schilling, who in 1945 fell foul of the KPD and the Soviets for refusing to toe the line, and whose testimony is therefore highly credible, acknowledged that the experience of mutual suffering and incarceration had tended to bring SPD members and Communists closer together:

> For six years I sat in Buchenwald at the same table as a Communist. We discussed [political] problems. Here and there we concurred, here and there we could not agree. When that happened we did not shout at each other, we did not swear at each other, but we said: here we disagree. But we also did something else. During these six years we tried, in a brotherly and comradely fashion, to improve one another's lot. Neither took advantage of the other. We behaved during this time as comrades and proletarians...[67]

In the light of such testimony from a source as credible as Erich Schilling, it is all the more easy to given credence to the numerous other examples of a KPD–SPD rapprochement in the prisons and concentration camps of the Third Reich. According to one account from Annaberg in south-west Saxony, two leading functionaries, one from the SPD and one from the KPD, were given the task of cleaning the SA toilets. In the words of one of the functionaries: 'At that point we understood the common mistake we had made... We forged unity there in the concentration camp.'[68] A *Reichsbanner* member from Chemnitz reports that, whenever the opportunity presented itself, Communist and Social Democrat inmates of the local prison would engage in eager, and fraternal, discussions. During such moments it gradually dawned on the prisoners that 'whether SPD, KPD or *Reichsbanner*, we all belong together. In our case, too, the foundation stone of unity was laid in prison.'[69]

According to historians such as Hermann Weber, these trends towards unity amongst rank-and-file Communists and Social Democrats led to tensions with their respective party leaderships, which were by no means so enthusiastic about co-operating with the rival left-wing party. This interpretation is amply supported by the available evidence. Even before 1933, the paralysis of the KPD and SPD leaderships in the face of the increasing menace of the Nazis, and their failure to create a united front against Hitler, were a cause of anger and concern amongst large sections of the party memberships. According to one Social Democrat from Chemnitz, the city's *Reichsbanner* members were on a permanent state of alert and preparedness in the months leading up to the Nazi take-over of power. All preparations, however, had to made by middle-ranking functionaries, since:

> nothing was forthcoming from above. Of central leadership there was no trace, or at best a load of useless paperwork. I know from countless discussions during this time that the workers (whether organised in the SPD or KPD) were clear that the struggle against the fascists could only be carried on jointly. We were at that time all bitterly disappointed at how, after the March [1933] elections, everything fell apart, at how everybody had to rely on himself [or herself] alone, at how the party leaders only wanted to keep their posts and were prepared to do anything.[70]

Once the KPD and SPD had been proscribed, many rank-and-file activists became increasingly disenchanted by the reluctance of the leaderships-in-exile to set aside old scores. Whilst conditions on the ground in Nazi Germany often dictated that Socialist and Communist resistance cells collaborate with each other – for example by sharing information or by alerting each other to the presence of infiltrators or agents provocateurs – the KPD and SPD leaderships-in-exile were apparently far more interested in acrid doctrinal disputations than in practical, anti-Nazi unity. In the words of one Chemnitz Social Democrat:

> Already at this time it became evident that the majority of those SPD members who had emigrated to Czechoslovakia had learned nothing from the whole development. For this reason it came to bitter arguments between those of us who had stayed in Chemnitz and a section of those comrades who had

emigrated. The main reason was that comrades in Czechoslovakia did not want to abandon their old attitude, namely their campaign of hatred against the Communist Party.[71]

On the basis of such common experiences of resistance and persecution, many rank-and-file Communists and Social Democrats at Zero Hour believed the creation of a united left-wing party, or, at the very least, the closest possible relations between the SPD and KPD, to be an absolute priority. This pro-unity sentiment was particularly strong amongst Social Democrats, who proved rather more willing than their Communist counterparts to think critically about their past mistakes and to draw the appropriate conclusions.[72] Accordingly, throughout East Germany at Zero Hour, local Social Democrats approached their neighbourhood Communists with a view to the immediate establishment of one, united left-wing party. In some places, Communists proved amenable to these advances, and united party organisations were indeed established. Elsewhere, Social Democrats wanted to go straight into the ranks of the KPD, without bothering to set up a unity party.[73]

The Soviets, however, were at this stage not prepared to countenance any move towards the creation of a single left-wing party. Possibly, as Wolfgang Abendroth has argued, the Soviets wanted to restore order and discipline inside the KPD itself, before countenancing the creation of any united working-class party.[74] After all, if the Soviets and the KPD leadership were not yet securely in control of rank-and-file Communists, what hope would there be of being able to manipulate a left-wing party rendered even more unwieldy by the admission of tens of thousands of unschooled, undisciplined Social Democrats? Norman Naimark, meanwhile, asserts that the Soviets regarded not just the KPD, but also the SPD, as not being ready for political unity. According to Naimark: 'Not only were the social democrats too strong, but their politics were also too uncertain for... [SMAD's] purposes. If a socialist unity party were to be formed, then... [SMAD] wanted a more compliant and predictable SPD as one of its partners.'[75]

Whatever the reason might have been for their response, the Soviets and the KPD leadership set their faces resolutely against the demand for unity. The justification put forward for this was that if the two parties merged prematurely, before a common ideological foundation had been laid, the new party would contain within itself the seeds of future division. Thus, whilst claiming to be in favour of the closest possible fraternal relations between the SPD and KPD, the Communist leadership also demanded a period of 'ideological clarification'. Eventual unity was, according to the KPD leadership, a highly desirable goal, but it would have to wait until the ground had been sufficiently prepared.[76] Employing such arguments, the KPD leadership and the Soviets moved consistently and systematically to block any moves towards working-class unity.

In Dresden, for example, the newly appointed lord mayor (*Oberbürgermeister*), Rudolf Friedrichs, invited a number of Social Democrats and Communists for discussions at his private residence. The Communists present urged their Social Democratic colleagues immediately to refound the SPD in Dresden. The Social Democrats responded that they had not reckoned on the refounding of the SPD, and their preference would be for the immediate creation of a unity party. Only after lengthy discussions were the Social Democrats persuaded reluctantly to accept that unity was not yet a possibility.[77] Similarly, the majority of Social Democrats in Leipzig 'were, from the beginning, of the opinion that only one workers' party should be built, and they were, in part, disappointed when two workers' parties re-emerged'.[78] In Görlitz, according to one contemporary account, the first SPD party organisation was founded in July 1945, 'although the majority of former SPD comrades put forward the view that only one workers' party should be created'.[79]

In most cases, SPD attempts to create a united workers' party were blocked right at the outset. In a number of localities, however, where Social Democrats and Communists had proceeded further down the road to unity, energetic action on the part of the Soviets and KPD leadership was necessary to hold them apart. In Markranstädt, the local Communists reported that those functionaries and members of the SPD who were still present in the town were resolved to join the KPD as a block. Only through the intervention of the local Soviet commandant were they prevented from doing so.[80] In Eisleben, which had initially fallen to the Americans, the Communists and Social Democrats who participated in the local *antifa* had assumed that, upon their entry into the town, the Soviets would allow the foundation of a single unity party. When, at the beginning of July, the Red Army marched into the town and promptly forbade the founding of such an organisation, there was much 'surprise and disappointment' amongst the rank-and-file activists.[81] The Social Democrats, indeed, refused point-blank to refound their old party in Eisleben, and it was only with the greatest of effort that the more disciplined Communists could reconcile them to the situation.[82] As late as September 1945, Communist functionaries were still complaining about the continued existence – above all in remote localities – of such unity organisations.[83]

It is clear, then, that the view put forward by some western historians, and by all GDR historians, to the effect that there was between 1933 and 1945 a real rapprochement between rank-and-file Communists and Social Democrats, contains considerable elements of truth. It would, however, be thoroughly misleading to claim, as East German historians have done, that this was a general phenomenon, and that the only Social Democrats who resisted this process were die-hard reactionaries who were more willing to work with former Nazis than with the Communists. In many localities, there is no evidence of any co-operation between Communists and Social

Democrats whatsoever. Many Social Democrats were as hostile to the Communists in 1945 as they had been in 1933, whilst, even among the majority whose opinion of the KPD had softened somewhat, there was still a determination to refound the SPD rather than participate in the creation of a unity party.[84]

Thus, even in Chemnitz, where there were numerous examples of KPD–SPD collaboration both before and after 1933, there were also many instances of mutual hostility and friction. When Hitler was named chancellor, for example, the KPD in Chemnitz distributed leaflets calling for a general strike. Although the Nazis made no effort to intervene, a group of *Reichsbanner* men did try and stop the Communists from distributing their leaflets, no doubt because they regarded the call for a general strike as dangerous ultra-left nonsense. The result, according to one source, was a 'public set-to'.[85] The same Social Democrat who reports considerable friction between the SPD resistance in Chemnitz and the exiled SPD leadership in Prague, also concedes that some SPD members still in Chemnitz were no less hostile to the idea of KPD–SPD collaboration than was SOPADE. If his testimony is to be believed, most of these anti-Communist Social Democrats departed to the western zones after 1945.[86]

If, in 1945, there was a ground swell of support amongst large numbers of Communists – and especially Social Democrats – in favour of unity, it was equally true that very many Social Democrats – and even more Communists–had forgiven nothing and forgotten nothing. At an early meeting of the SPD in the Saxon village of Schönfeld, for example, the speaker, who had travelled for the occasion from Dresden, referred to the KPD as the 'degenerate daughter' of the SPD.[87] At another SPD meeting in the nearby village of Großhartmannsdorf, the speaker spoke at length about the events of 1918, when the SPD had received 'a stab in the back' at the hands of those (that is, the Communists) who had split away from the Party.[88] A Social Democrat from Klostermannsfeld records that in 1945 he viewed the local KPD with great suspicion, largely because the Communists who were now arguing that the KPD and SPD must co-operate in the tasks of reconstruction had, before 1933, maltreated his father.[89] In Leipzig, Stanislaw Trabalski, who was by no stretch of the imagination on the right of the Party, was from the very beginning resolutely opposed to unity with the Communists. In an interview which he gave in 1973, Trabalski commented that:

> Although, after the collapse in 1945, the union with the Communists was endorsed by some Social Democrats, I did not hold to this view even at that time, since my experiences with the Communists, even during the Nazi period and in imprisonment, had been generally negative and I could not imagine that it would be possible to co-operate with them.[90]

An even larger proportion of the KPD was hostile to any real co-operation between the two rival working-class parties. For many members of the KPD, the Social Democrats were still 'Social Fascists', whose perceived betrayals of the German working class could neither be forgiven nor forgotten. At Zero Hour, such Communists either ignored the message of proletarian brotherly love now being preached by the KPD leadership in Berlin, or regarded it purely as a tactical manoeuvre. For example, in a detailed internal KPD report on the activities of the party in Plauen in August 1945, the compiler conceded that many local Communists were displaying 'strong left tendencies' in their attitudes towards the SPD. Many rank-and-file Communists, the report continued, 'have not yet understood the sense of our policies and see these people [the Social Democrats] as absolute enemies whose political dealings are aimed at the open resumption of hostilities against our party'.[91] As has been seen, in localities where the Communists and Social Democrats were getting too friendly for the Soviets' liking, the SMAD intervened in order to keep them apart. In localities where Social Democrats and Communists were at loggerheads, the Soviets intervened to try and bring them closer together. Hard-line anti-Communist Social Democrats were pressured by the local Soviet authorities to become more co-operative and, in some cases, were even arrested. Hard-line Communist sectarians were brought to heel by the apparatus of the KPD itself, through schooling, through demotion, or through appeals to their sense of Communist discipline. These, however, are all matters which will be examined in Chapters 5, 6 and 7.

In view of the enormous diversity of opinion within both the SPD and the KPD, it is difficult to arrive at a definitive answer to the question of unity at Zero Hour. The approach of GDR historians, whilst greatly exaggerating the degree of KPD–SPD rapprochement, does indeed seem to be valid for many localities and many individuals. On the other hand, it is also true that in many parts of East Germany there was no move towards working-class unity in the period between 1933 and 1945. For many individual Social Democrats and Communists, their deep-seated prejudices against the rival working-class party were intensified, rather than ameliorated, by their experiences under the Nazi dictatorship. Thus, on the question of unity, the only general pattern which emerges from the evidence is that there was no general pattern. Cut off from the outside world, and isolated from their own comrades, individuals responded to developments in very different ways. Whether or not individual rank-and-file Communists or Social Democrats moved towards or away from the idea of working-class unity depended on their views on this matter before 1933, on local circumstances obtaining in their particular town or village in the period 1933 to 1945 and on their personal experiences of life under the Nazi dictatorship. When the Third Reich eventually collapsed in May 1945, all these differences and variations came bursting to the surface, with fateful consequences for the future of East German politics.

Notes

1 H. Weber, *Geschichte der DDR*, 3rd edition, Munich, 1989, p. 74.
2 D. Staritz, *Die Gründung der* DDR, 2nd edition, Munich, 1987, pp. 76–77.
3 For the text of the 'Appeal', see W. Ulbricht, *Zur Geschichte der neuesten Zeit*, [East] Berlin, 1955, pp. 370–79.
4 SStA Leipzig, KV, Nr. 158, 'Agitprop–Mitteilungen der Unterbezirksleitung Leipzig', 30.7.45.
5 Weber (n. 1 above), p. 81.
6 SStA Chemnitz, BPA Karl-Marx-Stadt, V/5/120, Bl. 24.
7 SStA Chemnitz, BPA Karl-Marx-Stadt, V/5/220, Bl. 67–68.
8 SStA Chemnitz, BPA Karl-Marx-Stadt, V/5/126, Bl. 52.
9 SStA Chemnitz, BPA Karl-Marx-Stadt, V/5/012, 'Meine illegale Tätigkeit', Bl. 8.
10 B. Bouvier & H. Schulz, '...*die SPD aber aufgehört hat zu existieren*', Bonn, 1991, p. 203.
11 SStA Chemnitz, BPA Karl-Marx-Stadt, V/5/120, Bl. 123–24.
12 SStA Chemnitz, BPA Karl-Marx-Stadt, V/5/219, Bl. 4–5.
13 SStA Chemnitz, BPA Karl-Marx-Stadt, V/5/220, Bl. 68.
14 Bouvier & Schulz (n. 10 above), pp. 265–67.
15 See, e.g., SStA Chemnitz, BPA Karl-Marx-Stadt, V/5/175, Bl. 4; V/5/026, Bl. 4.
16 SStA Chemnitz, BPA Karl-Marx-Stadt, V/5/219, Bl. 3.
17 A. Merson, *Communist Resistance in Nazi Germany*, London, 1985, p. 190.
18 SStA Leipzig, BPA Leipzig, I/3/17, 'Material zur Einschätzung der Lage beim Zusammenbruch des deutschen Faschismus'.
19 See, e.g., ThHStA Weimar, BPA Erfurt, AIV/2/4-138, 'Betr. Material "Die Illegalen"'.
20 W.S. Allen, 'Die sozialdemokratische Untergrundbewegung', in J. Schmädeke & P. Steinbach (eds.), *Der Widerstand gegen den Nationalsozialismus*, Munich & Zurich, 1986, p. 856.
21 SStA Chemnitz, BPA Karl-Marx-Stadt, V/5/022, Bl. 1.
22 SStA Leipzig, BPA Leipzig, II/2/02, 'Gründung der SPD im Bundesland Sachsen', Bl. 7.
23 N. Naimark, *The Russians in Germany*, Cambridge, MA., 1995, p. 254.
24 SStA Leipzig, BPA Leipzig, I/3/13, 'Protokoll zur Sitzung in Böhlen', 25.3.46, Bl. 13.
25 ThHStA Weimar, BPA Erfurt, II/1-001, 'Manifest der demokratischen Sozialisten des ehemaligen Konzentrationslagers Buchenwald', 13.4.45.
26 ThHStA Weimar, BPA Erfurt, II/1-001, 'Rede des Genossen Dr. Hermann Brill', 8.7.45, Bl. 2.
27 Bouvier & Schulz (n. 10 above), p. 255.
28 SStA Leipzig, BPA Leipzig, I/3/16, 'Bericht über die 1. Referenten-Zusammenkunft der Arbeitsgebiete, Stadtteile und Ortsgruppen Leipzig-Stadt und Leipzig-Land', 12.10.45.
29 See, e.g.: ibid.; SStA Chemnitz, BPA Karl-Marx-Stadt, I-4/33, Bl. 108–09.
30 SStA Leipzig, BPA Leipzig, I/3/27, '1. Versammlung der Kommunistischen Partei in Gräfenhainichen', 15.7.45, Bl. 6.
31 ThHStA Weimar, BPA Erfurt, I/1-001, 'Protokoll der 1. Funktionärkonferenz der KPD Thüringen in Weimar', 15.7.45, Bl. 13.

32 SStA Chemnitz, BPA Karl-Marx-Stadt, V/5/198, Bl. 41.
33 ThHStA Weimar, BPA Erfurt, II/1-001, 'Wie kommen wir zur sozialistischen Einheit der deutschen Arbeiterklasse?', Bl. 23–24.
34 Naimark (n. 23 above), p. 255.
35 SStA Chemnitz, BPA Karl-Marx-Stadt, V/5/198, Bl. 31.
36 SStA Chemnitz, BPA Karl-Marx-Stadt, I-4/26, Bl. 125.
37 SStA Leipzig, BPA Leipzig, I/3/23, 'Bericht von der Parteiarbeiterversammlung der KPD Leipzig in den Köllenwerken'.
38 SStA Leipzig, BPA Leipzig, I/3/01, 'Protokoll der Unterbezirks-Partei-Delegiertenkonferenz', 18-19.8.45, Bl. 72.
39 For examples, see G. Pritchard, *German Workers under Soviet Occupation* (doctoral thesis, University of Wales, 1997), pp. 102–03.
40 SStA Leipzig, BPA Leipzig, I/3/27, '1. Versammlung der Kommunistischen Partei in Gräfenhainichen', 15.7.45.
41 ThHStA Weimar, BPA Erfurt, I/1-002, Bl. 107 & 109.
42 SStA Leipzig, BPA Leipzig, I/3/17, 'Information Nr. 14', 28.4.45.
43 SStA Leipzig, BPA Leipzig, I/3/27, '1. Versammlung der Kommunistischen Partei in Gräfenhainichen', 15.7.45.
44 Naimark (n. 23 above), p. 255.
45 SStA Chemnitz, BPA Karl-Marx-Stadt, V/5/057, Bl. 40.
46 SStA Chemnitz, BPA Karl-Marx-Stadt, V/5/126, Bl. 74. For further examples, see V/5/002, Bl. 13 & V/5/170, Bl. 5.
47 SStA Chemnitz, BPA Karl-Marx-Stadt, I-4/21, Bl. 119.
48 SStA Leipzig, BPA Leipzig, I/3/23, letter from the KPD Arbeitsgebiet Nord to the KPD Unterbezirksleitung in Leipzig, 30.7.45.
49 SStA Chemnitz, BPA Karl-Marx-Stadt, I-4/25, Bl. 270.
50 G. Sandford, *From Hitler to Ulbricht*, Princeton, NJ, 1983, p. 44.
51 SStA Leipzig, BPA Leipzig, I/3/28, 'Bericht der erweiterten Leitungssitzung', 15.9.45, Bl. 2.
52 Bouvier & Schulz (n. 10 above), p. 25.
53 O. Hippe, *...And Red is the Colour of our Flag*, London, 1991, p. 210.
54 J. Heise & J. Hofman, *Fragen an die Geschichte der DDR*, [East] Berlin, 1988, p. 38.
55 H. Krisch, *German Politics under Soviet Occupation*, New York, 1974, pp. 17–20.
56 G. Stuby, 'Die SPD von der Niederlage des Faschismus bis zur Gründung der Bundesrepublik (1945–49)', in J. von Freyberg et al. (eds.), *Geschichte der deutschen Sozialdemokratie von 1863 bis zur Gegenwart*, Cologne, 1989, p. 266.
57 H. Weber, 'Die Ambivalenz der kommunistischen Widerstandsstrategie bis zur "Brüsseler" Parteikonferenz', in Schmädeke & Steinbach (n. 20 above), p. 80.
58 SStA Chemnitz, BPA Karl-Marx-Stadt, V/5/002, Bl. 10–11.
59 SStA Chemnitz, BPA Karl-Marx-Stadt, V/5/170, Bl. 1.
60 SStA Chemnitz, BPA Karl-Marx-Stadt, V/5/028.
61 SStA Chemnitz, BPA Karl-Marx-Stadt, V/5/113.
62 SStA Chemnitz, BPA Karl-Marx-Stadt, V/5/022, Bl. 1.
63 SStA Leipzig, BPA Leipzig, I/3/23, 'Genosse Major Eserski'.
64 ThHStA Weimar, BPA Erfurt, AIV/2/4-138, 'Darstellungen der illegalen Betätigung der ehemaligen kommunistischen und sozialdemokratischen Partei-Ortsgruppen Mühlhausen', 4.3.47.

65 ThHStA Weimar, BPA Erfurt, AIV/2/4-138, letter from the SED Ortsgruppe Pössneck, 12.5.47.
66 Krisch (n. 55 above), p. 18.
67 SStA Leipzig, BPA Leipzig, II/2/05, 'Zentrale Mitgliederversammlung der Sozialdemokratischen Partei Leipzig', 7.2.46, Bl. 22.
68 SStA Chemnitz, BPA Karl-Marx-Stadt, III-4/01, 'Gemeinsame Konferenz der SPD und KPD', 30.3.46, Bl. 55.
69 SStA Chemnitz, BPA Karl-Marx-Stadt, V/5/028.
70 SStA Chemnitz, BPA Karl-Marx-Stadt, V/5/175, Bl. 2.
71 SStA Chemnitz, BPA Karl-Marx-Stadt, V/5/026, 'Der illegale Kampf von einigen Genossen im damaligen Chemnitz', Bl. 2–3.
72 Stuby (n. 56 above), p. 266.
73 See, e.g., SStA Chemnitz, BPA Karl-Marx-Stadt, I-4/17, Bl. 50.
74 Stuby (n. 56 above), p. 291.
75 Naimark (n. 23 above), p. 273.
76 Krisch (n. 55 above), Chapters 3 & 4.
77 SStA Leipzig, BPA Leipzig, II/2/02, 'Gründung der SPD im Bundesland Sachsen', Bl. 1.
78 Ibid., Bl. 8.
79 Ibid., Bl. 5.
80 SStA Leipzig, BPA Leipzig, I/3/23, 'Genosse Major Eserski'.
81 Naimark (n. 23 above), p. 265.
82 Staritz (n. 2 above), pp. 90–91.
83 StA Leipzig, BPA Leipzig, I/3/28, letter from the secretariat of the KPD Kreisleitung Döbeln to the secretariat of the SPD Döbeln, 14.9.45.
84 A. Malycha, *Partei von Stalins Gnaden?*, Berlin, 1996, pp. 42–43.
85 SStA Chemnitz, BPA Karl-Marx-Stadt, V/5/170, Bl. 81.
86 SStA Chemnitz, BPA Karl-Marx-Stadt, V/5/026, 'Der illegale Kampf von einigen Genosssen im damaligen Chemnitz', Bl. 3.
87 SStA Chemnitz, BPA Karl-Marx-Stadt, I-4/18, letter from the KPD Ortsgruppe Pfaffroda-Schönfeld to the KPD Kreisleitung in Freiberg, 25.10.45, Bl. 9.
88 SStA Chemnitz, BPA Karl-Marx-Stadt, I-4/28, 'Bericht über die SPD-Versammlung', 3.10.45, Bl. 3.
89 Bouvier & Schulz (n. 10 above), p. 192.
90 Ibid., p. 209.
91 SStA Chemnitz, BPA Karl-Marx-Stadt, I-4/26, 'Politischer Bericht für Monat August 1945 von der Kreisleitung Plauen', Bl. 124.

4

Denazification
and reconstruction

Between the late summer of 1945 and the spring of 1946, the Soviet zone of occupation witnessed a whole series of 'reforms', such as land reform, denazification and the reconstruction of the state apparatus, which transformed the political and economic landscape of East Germany. In the GDR, it was always argued that the Soviets during this period were not imposing their political system on the East Germans, but, on the contrary, were simply helping the Germans find a peaceful and progressive road to self-determination. According to East German scholars, the people of the Soviet zone seized this opportunity to implement what was habitually referred to as the 'antifascist democratic transformation'. In the West, by contrast, it has often been argued that the concept of the 'antifascist democratic transformation' was simply a piece of camouflage behind which the Soviets concealed their true goal, namely systematically to absorb East Germany into the Soviet Bloc. According to Michael Klonovsky and Jan von Flocken, for example, the real goal of Stalin was always 'the annexation of East Germany with the purpose of extending the reach of Soviet–Communist power to the Elbe.' The so-called 'antifascist democratic transformation' was no more than a 'disguise' for this process.[1]

But the prevailing view in recent historiography has been that the Soviets during the immediate post-war years possessed 'no clearly thought-out plan for the future of Germany and indeed could not have had unless the Red Army had been able to occupy the whole country'.[2] According to this interpretation, the possibility of incorporating the eastern zone of occupation into the Soviet Bloc was just one of the alternatives which the Soviets were considering, and not necessarily the preferred one. Soviet occupation policy during the 'antifascist democratic transformation' should therefore be seen, not as part of some fixed and definite master plan, but as flexible and multilayered. In the words of Norman Naimark:

> the evolution of Soviet thinking on Germany did not follow a clear trajectory...
> Part of the problem was that the Soviet leadership pursued a number of

parallel policies for a German settlement that were fundamentally inconsistent. Another problem was that Soviet policy in Germany was, at its core, opportunistic, which left plenty of room for tactics and diplomacy.[3]

Which of these views comes closest to the truth will remain in doubt until scholars have full and unrestricted access to the Russian archives, if, indeed, even that would allow us definitively to solve the problem. What is beyond doubt, however, is that whatever the Soviets' long-term intentions may have been, their short-term goals are clear from the policies which they implemented. First, the Soviets were determined to exploit their zone of occupation by seizing as much German scientific knowledge, weaponry and military technology as possible and, above all, by exacting an enormous quantity of reparations. Second, the Soviets were intent on neutralising Germany as a threat to the Soviet Union, partly through reparations and territorial annexations, but mainly through the implementation of a whole series of reforms, the purpose of which was to destroy once and for all the political and economic roots from which they believed Nazism and German militarism had sprung. In the view of the Soviets, these roots were to be found above all in the reactionary character of the German state apparatus and in the entrenched power of the *Junkers* and the 'monopoly capitalists'.

The role which the Soviets were expecting the labour movement to play in all this was spelt out by General I.S. Kolesnichenko, the commandant of Thuringia, at a meeting with representatives of the antifascist parties in August 1945. According to Kolesnichenko, the newly founded workers' parties should devote themselves to six central tasks, namely: raising the political level of the masses; re-educating the masses away from Nazism and towards democracy; co-operating in the denazification of industry and the state apparatus; co-operating in the practical tasks of reconstruction; defending the Potsdam agreements on reparations and territorial alterations; and studying and reacting to the mood of the masses.[4] Put more simply, the Soviets were demanding that the two left-wing parties play a key role in the accomplishment of both of their principal short-term goals. On the one hand, the KPD and SPD were being expected to implement the various political reforms which the Soviets considered to be necessary. On the other hand, the KPD and SPD were to assist in the exploitation of the Soviet zone by explaining and justifying it to the population.

Land reform

The Soviets, the SPD and the KPD were all agreed that the *Junker* had for centuries played a reactionary role in German politics and were thoroughly implicated in the crimes of the Nazis. It was generally accepted, even by the two 'bourgeois parties', that land reform was necessary if the malign influence of the large landowners was to be for ever broken. In accordance with its moderate political orientation, however, the KPD leadership argued that the land of the *Junker* should not be nationalised or collectivised, but should instead be divided amongst the hundreds of thousands of small farmers, landless labourers and refugees.

In its wartime planning for the post-war occupation of Germany, the exiled leadership of the KPD in Moscow had envisaged that the land reform would take place in the spring of 1946 at the earliest.[5] However, in accordance with the general quickening of tempo which followed the Soviets' discovery that the Germans were not quite so politically inert as they had expected, the land reform was eventually brought forward to the autumn of 1945. It was an enormous administrative undertaking, involving the redistribution of no fewer than 2,743,306 hectares of land: 398,080 hectares to poor farmers, 740,704 to landless farmers and farm labourers and 567,366 to refugees. In all, some 7,000 *Junker* were expropriated, whilst 504,000 small farmers, labourers and refugees received land from the commissions which had been set up to administer the reform.[6]

From the point of view of the Soviets and the KPD leadership, the land reform was, in some senses at least, a tremendous success. Large numbers of Social Democrats and Communists were enthusiastic about the reform and were prepared to play an active part in its implementation. Indeed, given their lack of personnel, local knowledge and relevant experience, it would have been quite impossible for the Soviets to execute the land reform without the active participation of the many thousands of Communists and Social Democrats who constituted the backbone of the land commissions. According to contemporary KPD and police reports from the autumn of 1945, the land reform was also a success in the sense that it seems to have been well received by the small farmers and landless labourers.[7]

However, despite these successes, the land reform also encountered a number of serious problems and difficulties. Amongst the rank-and-file membership of the KPD, for instance, there was a widespread dissatisfaction with the apparent moderation of the reform. Many Communist activists and functionaries believed that it would have been much better had the great estates been kept intact and run as state farms or collectives, for, in their opinion, the parcelisation of the land would make it more difficult to apply efficient farming techniques and use agricultural machinery. In some places, Communist officials appear to have deliberately dragged their feet when it came to dividing the expropriated estates amongst the farmers and refugees. Edwin Hoernle, the leading agricultural expert of the KPD, complained that in November 1945 some 25 per cent of the available large holdings in Thuringia had still not been divided up. In Grimma, a medium-sized town near Leipzig, local Communist authorities were so opposed to parcelisation that, by January 1946, they had permitted the breaking-up of only three of twenty-seven estates.[8] In Plauen, the local KPD agitprop department was compelled to conclude in its monthly report for September that 'our campaign for the land reform was very weak'.[9]

If anything, discontent with the moderation of the land reform was even more prevalent in the ranks of the SPD. Many Social Democrats considered the reform to be 'un-Marxist', for, in terms of Marx's historical schema, to split up the great estates amongst the small farmers was a step backwards to small-scale and inefficient production.[10] Unrestrained by 'Communist discipline', many Social Democrats proved more willing than their KPD counterparts to criticise the land reform in public, a breach of the 'unity front' which irritated many Communists and infuriated the Soviets. One Social Democrat, for example, reports that in his home town of Klostermansfeld there had initially been excellent relations between the KPD and SPD. On the issue of the land reform, however, the first serious cracks began to appear. To a man, the local Social Democrats regarded the splitting up of the great estates as 'economic nonsense', and demanded instead that the land of the *Junker* should be turned into agricultural co-operatives. Indeed, so opposed was the local SPD chief to the land reform that he refused to implement it, as a result of which he was arrested and detained for three days by the Soviets.[11]

Underlying this hostility to the land reform amongst many Communists, Social Democrats and unaffiliated workers was more than a concern with the impact it would have on agricultural production. Within the German labour movement, there was a deep-seated tendency to regard the farmer as 'reactionary and unusable for the revolutionary class struggle of the workers', and this tradition of hostility to the farmer did not suddenly disappear in 1945.[12] On the contrary, the conditions of post-war Germany greatly exacerbated the tensions between town and countryside. In order to survive, the average worker was compelled to travel into the countryside to buy or barter food from the farmers. There soon emerged a general but probably justified feeling that the farmers were exploiting their relatively advantageous position to rob the desperate workers of whatever money and valuables they still possessed. In the words of one Leipzig woman: 'The era had dawned when the farmer in the countryside no longer even needed a "carpet for the cow stall". The starving city dwellers exchanged everything they had for food.'[13]

Not surprisingly, this perception of the farmers as rapacious exploiters aroused deep and bitter resentment amongst the industrial workers, and hence amongst the ranks of the working-class parties. According to a report from Leipzig: 'The worker is being dragged along by a campaign of hatred against the farmers, which in part is a result of the farmers' profiteering.'[14] In a report from the Thuringian town of Pössneck, it was noted that the workers were now so hostile to the farmers that they were arguing that farmers should hand over 100 per cent of their produce, and in return receive wages and ration cards just like the urban workers.[15] In the Saxon town of Falkenhain, local Communists complained bitterly that 99 per cent of farmers were Nazis, so that while anti-Nazis were going hungry, Nazi farmers were growing fat.[16]

Thus, for many activists the great problem with the land reform was that it simply made too many concessions to the despised farmers. For the time being, a combination of party discipline and Soviet pressure was sufficient to ensure that, for all the reservations of the rank-and-file activists, the reform was pushed through in the manner desired by the KPD leadership. However, the tensions aroused by the land reform revealed the fragility of the so-called 'antifascist popular front' which the Soviets and the KPD leadership were attempting to construct. In order to conciliate the conservative farmers at one end of the political spectrum, the authorities had risked alienating their own party activists at the other.

Denazification

At the same time as the land reform, the Soviet military authorities also implemented a far-reaching programme of denazification. Many Red Army officers no doubt felt a deep-seated repugnance for Nazism and a desire to revenge themselves on the violators of their motherland. However, even if viewed purely in terms of Realpolitik, Nazism had clearly proved itself to be a threat to the security and territorial integrity of the Soviet Union, and it was therefore entirely logical that the Soviets should want to extirpate it.

However, if the Soviets were intent on purging industry and the state apparatus of former Nazis, they were also clear that they did not want this purge to cut too swiftly or bite too deep, lest it jeopardise other Soviet interests in East Germany. Too savage a purge might irredeemably alienate the millions of small-time Nazis or Nazi sympathisers whom the Soviets and KPD leadership wanted to win over to the unity front. More importantly, if thousands of skilled workers, technicians and managers were dismissed from their jobs, this might well have a deleterious effect on production, and hence upon the ability of the Soviets to exploit the economy of the eastern zone. As Fritz Selbmann, a leading KPD functionary in Saxony, attempted to explain to the workers, their desire to rid their factories entirely of former Nazis 'would mean that we would be completely unable to bring them [the factories] back into production'.[17]

Yet, despite these reservations, denazification still came high on the Soviets' list of priorities, and the most important instruments through which the Soviets sought to implement this policy were the KPD and SPD. The tribunals which were established to judge the extent to which former Nazis should be punished were largely staffed by, and almost entirely under the control of, reliable Communists and Social Democrats.[18] In the state apparatus, Communists and Social Democrats were appointed by the Soviets as *Bürgermeister*, police chiefs and senior officials, and they were entrusted with the task of clearing out their new departments. Similarly in the so-called masterless' factories, the trustees appointed by the authorities, whose responsibility it was to implement denazification procedures, were drawn largely from the two left-wing parties. Though the Soviets kept a watchful eye on proceedings, the burden of denazifying the state apparatus thus largely devolved upon the German anti-Nazis.

The willingness of the Soviets to utilise the services of Germans to implement the denazification process made possible a much more systematic purge of Nazis than occurred in the western zones, where the anti-Nazi activists were generally regarded with great suspicion by the military authorities. In Leipzig, for instance, the Americans, during the three months in which they occupied the city, dismissed some 1,251 former Nazis from the city administration. In the three months following the entry of the Soviets into Leipzig, 2,732 Nazis were kicked out of the apparatus of local government. Thus, more than twice as many Nazis were sacked in the three months following the Soviets' entry into Leipzig than in the three preceding months.[19] In Halle, 45 per cent of all tenured officials and 32 per cent of junior officials in the city administration had been members of the NSDAP, and most of these were still in place when the Soviets took control of the city in July 1945. Yet, by the end of 1945, every single one had been dismissed.[20] According to official statistics, in the Soviet zone as a whole no fewer than 520,000 Nazis were ejected from their posts in the state apparatus, more than in the other three zones of occupation put together.[21]

Nonetheless, as with the land reform, the apparent success of the Soviets' approach to denazification concealed underlying weaknesses and problems. As one police report from the Thuringian town of Frankenheim noted, the majority of the population had either been members of the NSDAP, or had friends or relations who had been members. Outside the ranks of the organised working class, therefore, there was little public enthusiasm for a sweeping programme of denazification.[22] In Waldheim, the local Communists noted that, whilst the sacking of Nazi school-teachers was greeted warmly by the anti-Nazi section of the population, there were also many voices raised in opposition.[23] According to a report from the KPD local group in Pausa: 'If a Nazi or SS leader is arrested in the locality, nowhere does this produce joy, but, on the contrary, regret.'[24]

If the denazification process in the Soviet zone was regarded by many ordinary Germans as being too harsh, many rank-and-file Communists and Social Democrats wanted to see an even more radical purge and were dissatisfied with what they perceived to be the slow pace of denazification. Indeed, judging by the frequency with which they complained, this was one of their most significant concerns and most prominent grievances. In Plauen, the leadership of the local KPD complained that large numbers of Nazis who had been dismissed from the police or local government were being directed into responsible jobs by the local labour office.[25] In Freiberg, the local SPD bemoaned the fact that too many low-ranking Nazis 'are still too much entrenched in today's economic process'. Accordingly, the Freiberg Social Democrats demanded 'that in this area we should take yet more vigorous action in order to be able to eliminate reactionary forces from this field of activity'.[26] The authorities were also inundated with letters from individual antifascists, complaining bitterly about the privileges and perquisites which so many of their former Nazi tormentors continued to enjoy.[27]

In some places, anti-Nazi activists went beyond simply complaining, and took matters into their own hands. In such cases, the civilian or military authorities had to intervene to keep the activities of the anti-Nazi radicals within acceptable limits. In the Vogtland town of Mylau, the local Communists wanted to compel all former members of the NSDAP, including minor and purely nominal members, to attend a showing of a film about Auschwitz, and were only prevented from doing so by the timely inter-vention of the authorities. According to the local KPD secretariat, the mistake of the Mylau Communists was typical of the many KPD members who had not yet properly understood the party line.[28] In Plauen, the local KPD complained that many of its own members were implementing de-nazification measures with far too much ruthlessness and without distinguishing between high-ranking Nazis and the small fry. This was leading to numerous undisciplined actions such as the unlicensed expulsion of Nazis from their houses, from their jobs and even from their allotments. In one instance, radical Communists interned leading Nazis in a former hotel on the outskirts of the town. When the local commandant learnt of this, he intervened to close down this unofficial internment camp and allowed the Nazis to return to their homes. According to the leadership of the KPD in Plauen, this was interpreted by the radicals as a triumph for the Nazis, which 'naturally got the Left up in arms'.[29]

Occasionally, this dissatisfaction with the pace of denazification led to open clashes between the lower party organs and the regional party leader-ships. In one part of Plauen, the local KPD group refused to obey their instructions to help organise voluntary rubble clearing on the grounds that it was intolerable that there were still Nazis in positions of responsibility.[30] In Pockau, the KPD *Bürgermeister*, S.N., wanted to expropriate a local entrepreneur who had behaved appallingly during the Nazi period and who was hated by the workers. Permission for this, however, was refused by the local authorities on the grounds that the man had never actually belonged to the NSDAP. S.N. then travelled to Dresden in a vain attempt to persuade the regional (*Land*) government to overturn the decision to spare the entrepreneur. On his return to Pockau, S.N. thereafter refused to co-operate in the expropriation of smaller Nazis, justifying this act of defiance with the comment: 'I will not allow myself to become a laughing-stock by expropriating the small proprietors whilst the big exploiters remain untouched.' As a result, the whole process of confiscating the property of Nazi entrepreneurs in Pockau was greatly delayed.[31]

The state apparatus

In order to replace the Nazis who had been thrown out of their jobs, thousands of working-class people, many of whom were Communists or Social Democrats, took up positions in local government, the education system, the civil service, the police and the judiciary. In Dresden, forty-three out of fifty-eight 'leading staff members' in the city administration were either Social Democrats or Communists.[32] In the *Bezirk* of Leipzig, forty-seven of the sixty-four *Bürgermeister* came from one or other of the left-wing parties.[33] In the city of Leipzig, 90 per cent of the police force consisted of newly recruited workers, most of whom were SPD and KPD members.[34] Of the 445 new appointments to posts in the city administration of Leipzig in the first two months of 1946, some 282 (63 per cent) were Social Democrats or Communists, overwhelmingly from working-class backgrounds.[35]

In terms of personnel, this represented something of a revolution. Since the days of the Kaisers, the German civil service and state apparatus had been dominated by middle- or upper-class men of conservative, sometimes reactionary, views. This stratum had survived the overthrow of Imperial Germany and had, by and large, continued to serve under the Third Reich. In the western zones of occupation, many such individuals survived the early post-war denazification purges and remained in office into the 1950s and 1960s. According to Barbara Marshall, the typical post-war civil servant in West Germany proved to be 'indistinguishable from his [or her] anti-republican ancestor during the Weimar Republic'.[36] In the Soviet zone, by contrast, the conservative, middle-class traditions of the tenured officials (*Beamtentum*) were smashed. In the words of one Communist report on the political and class composition of the city administration in Leipzig: 'For the first time in the history of Germany, thousands of working-class elements, who had not grown up in the conventional education system, entered the administration.'[37]

In many places, the new Social Democratic and Communist officials seem to have worked together quite harmoniously. During the Nazi period, long-standing differences between local SPD and KPD groups had often been forgotten in the desperate struggle for political and physical survival. Now that the Nazis had been overthrown, Communists and Social Democrats were often united in their efforts to meet the pressing demands of reconstruction. This tendency was particularly evident in many of the smaller towns and villages, where rank-and-file activists and functionaries knew little or nothing about the tensions which were emerging elsewhere. According to one Social Democrat from the Thuringian town of Saalfeld: 'At first, co-operation with the Communists went fairly well, for we knew our local

Communists from before 1933.'[38] The KPD group in the small Saxon town of Zug-Langenrinne reported that 'in general the two workers' parties in our locality co-operate well', and that 'the suggestions of the KPD always meet with the unanimous approval of the SPD'.[39] In Zwenkau, the local KPD group reported: 'Co-operation with the SPD is good, and, even where there are hitches, these are only superficial'.[40] Similarly in Markranstädt, the local Communists asserted: 'The unity in action with the SPD can be described as good throughout the district. In this matter, Markranstädt gives a very good example. From the day of the entry of the Americans there has been a very positive collaboration.'[41]

In numerous localities, however, the SPD and KPD did not co-operate well in the tasks of reconstruction, and bitter conflicts and tensions between Communists and Social Democrats soon began to emerge. This was particularly the case in the many localities where the Nazi years had not brought the two parties together, but, on the contrary, had deepened the divisions which had already existed in 1933. Without question, the main source of friction between the two parties was competition for influence in the re-emerging apparatus of government. There were, for example, numerous instances of local SPD groups complaining that the Communists were hogging posts in the new administrations, and using their control of local government to hamper the organisational development and political activities of the SPD. Typical is the case of Großvoigtsberg in Saxony, where the local SPD group protested about the KPD *Bürgermeister*, T.R., 'on account of his dictatorial behaviour, indeed open hostility to our party'. According to the disgruntled Social Democrats, not only had T.R. refused to give the Social Democrats any posts in local government, but his whole bearing towards the SPD was so intimidating and threatening that the local SPD accused him of employing 'fascist-Nazi methods'.[42] In Seiffen, a large village on the border between Saxony and (the then) Czechoslovakia, the newly founded SPD group had tried to obtain permission from the KPD *Bürgermeister* to hold a rally. The *Bürgermeister*, however, placed so many bureaucratic obstacles in the way of the Social Democrats that the latter broke off negotiations in disgust and complained to the local authorities in Freiberg.[43] In Großhartmannsdorf, ten miles south of Freiberg, the local SPD group was incensed by the refusal of the local KPD *Bürgermeister* to honour an agreement to appoint an SPD member as his deputy. According to the Großhartmannsdorf Social Democrats: 'Many similar examples could be mentioned. In this fashion, a course is being steered which is reminiscent of the inglorious days of division of the pre-1933 period.'[44]

Many Social Democrats were also incensed by the tendency of their local Communists to revert to the destructively militant and underhand political methods in which they had been so skilled during the Weimar period. In the state apparatus, for example, it was not uncommon for SPD officials to complain that their Communist colleagues, who had been foisted on them by the Russians, were good at making rabble-rousing speeches but had 'no idea' of practical administrative work.[45] There were numerous complaints from Social Democrats about the personal slanders with which ultra-left Communists were trying to undermine their credibility.[46] Typical is the case of Mühlhausen in Thuringia, where the Communists had promised to support the SPD *Bürgermeister*, but had then denounced him both to the civilian authorities in Weimar and to the Soviet military government. According to the Mühlhausen Social Democrats, the KPD's letter of denunciation was so vitriolic 'that one must assume it was composed by an hysteric. All the events described [in the letter] are grotesquely distorted and not one of the accusations contains the tiniest particle of truth.' So blatant an act of provocation, the Mühlhausen SPD concluded, could not be tolerated, and they called upon the *Kreisleitung* of the KPD 'to ascertain the identity of the author and publicly to bring him to account'.[47]

Just as many Social Democrats became increasingly disenchanted with their local Communist counterparts, so did many Communists begin to nurture resentments against their supposed class brothers in the SPD. In some localities, Communists protested that SPD *Bürgermeister* and officials were using their powers to frustrate and hinder the development of the KPD, whilst packing the organs of local government with Social Democrats.[48] In very many places, Communist functionaries complained that their SPD colleagues were only interested in securing positions for themselves in the state apparatus, and were making little or no contribution to the political donkey-work of organising meetings, distributing leaflets and visiting workers in their homes and factories. The KPD in Plauen, for example, complained in December 1945 that the SPD had managed to install one of its members as the leader of the local 'antifascist women's committee', despite the fact that the bulk of the practical work of the committee was conducted by Communists. According to the Plauen Communists: 'The consequence is the regrettable fact that, although the activity of the women's committee is largely carried by us, in the eyes of the world the credit is reaped by the SPD.'[49]

There was also a widespread perception amongst many Communists that their local SPD colleagues had learned nothing from the experiences of the past and were still addicted to the reformist policies which, in Communist eyes, had led to disaster so often in Germany's recent history. In a number of localities, KPD groups protested that 'arrogant' SPD officials, who were stuck in 'Weimar thinking', were frustrating the reform process with their bureaucratic quibbling and behind-the-scenes machinations.[50] Many of these SPD functionaries were accused by their KPD counterparts of being more willing to work with the two 'bourgeois' parties than with the KPD, and even, on occasion, of forming alliances with the LDP and CDU in order to undermine the position of the Communists in industry and the state apparatus. In the Saxon town of Rackwitz, for instance, the KPD accused the SPD of having formed an unofficial electoral pact with the two 'bourgeois' parties in order to ensure that the Communists did badly in trade union elections.[51]

However, the most serious charge made against local SPD functionaries was that, true to their reformist antecedents, they were seeking to gain an electoral advantage over the KPD by pandering to the unrealistic hopes and backward, recidivist ideas of the population. In Leubnitz, the Communists complained that, whereas the KPD was truthful with the population about the gravity of Germany's plight and about the huge sacrifices which the situation demanded, the local SPD was trying to play 'Father Christmas' by making all kinds of unrealistic and irresponsible promises.[52] In Mulda, the KPD accused the local SPD of seeking to exploit the anti-Communism of the population in order to curry favour with the electorate. The Mulda Social Democrats, it was alleged, were not only failing to challenge the widespread view that the KPD, rather than the Nazis, were to blame for the population's travails, but were cynically encouraging and manipulating this dangerous and reactionary sentiment.[53] Most seriously of all, a number of KPD local groups claimed that the Social Democrats in their localities were so obsessed with stealing a march on the KPD that they were even prepared to recruit former Nazis to the SPD, and actively to seek to win the favour of the pro-Nazi section of the population.[54]

Clearly, then, many towns and villages across East Germany witnessed a serious deterioration in KPD-SPD relations during the summer and autumn of 1945. It is important to note, however, that the causes of this deterioration were primarily local and personal, and beyond the direct control of either the SPD or KPD party leaderships or of the Soviets. Not surprisingly, difficulties were most likely to occur in places where there was a history of bad relations between the two parties, or where the local SPD happened to be under the control of right-wing and anti-Communist Social Democrats. More often, problems arose because the local KPD was dominated by die-hard, ultra-left sectarians who, far from acting on instructions from the KPD party apparatus, often incurred the wrath of their leaders on account of their provocative and sectarian behaviour. The KPD leadership in Plauen, for example, frankly acknowledged that the majority of problems with the SPD were largely caused by 'the too limited political maturity of our own comrades', who could not overcome their old antipathy towards the SPD, and whose sectarian and dictatorial behaviour 'naturally produces on the other side a feeling of anger and suspicion'.[55] The Communists at the Espenhain plant near Leipzig were reprimanded by their own party leadership for having seized all the leading posts at the factory for themselves, thereby jeopardising the unity front which the KPD was attempting to build with the Social Democrats. According to the KPD district leadership, the Espenhain Communists had 'pursued a false policy towards the SPD from the start... They have simply taken all the posts for themselves. The SPD feels itself cheated and slighted. We are of the opinion that it is only possible for

Communists to work with the Social Democrats if we let them share responsibility and in general encourage them to play their part.'[56]

Coping with the Russians

Of the two tasks allotted to them by the Russians, the KPD and SPD coped with the first (reform and reconstruction) with at least some degree of success. However, the second task assigned to the East German labour movement (justifying reparations, the new eastern borders and the other unpleasant aspects of Soviet rule) proved to be far more problematic. This is hardly to be wondered at, for, on the issues of reconstruction and anti-Nazi reform, Soviet policy and the interests and aspirations of the labour movement largely coincided. On issues such as reparations and territorial annexations, by contrast, the interests of the Soviets were directly opposed to those of East German workers. From this simple fact arose numerous tensions and conflicts within the labour movement which were to have a considerable impact on the course of political developments.

Before considering the many problems and dilemmas which Russian rule created for the SPD and KPD, it is important to note that there were also positive sides to the Soviet occupation. These, too, should be considered, for workers' attitudes to the Soviet authorities were conditioned, not just by the innumerable acts of cruelty and despoliation which the Russians perpetrated in Germany, but also by their occasional kindness and constructiveness.

In particular, it would be quite wrong to depict the behaviour of Red Army soldiers as having been uniformly barbaric. In some places, for example Waldheim, it was reported that local Red Army units were orderly and disciplined, and that this had a very favourable impact on public opinion.[57] Elsewhere, it was noted that by no means all Red Army soldiers were habitual looters. According to one report from Weimar: 'A proportion of the soldiers of the Red Army only concerned themselves with the population when they wanted to confiscate pocket or wrist watches, whilst another section paid for everything they purchased in the shops and private houses in an orderly fashion, even paying more than the asking price.'[58] In another report from Weimar, it was noted that Red Army officers were often very disciplined and well behaved, and that this, too, was having a positive effect on public attitudes to the Russians.[59]

The Russians were also capable of showing great generosity, particularly towards children. In this respect, the Russian occupation of Germany differed greatly from the Nazi occupation of Russia in the period 1941 to 1944. During the latter, the bestial behaviour of many German soldiers had been part of a deliberate and conscious official policy of intimidating, exploiting and, in many cases, of physically liquidating the 'sub-human' Slavonic or Jewish inhabitants of the Soviet Union. The brutalities committed by Red Army soldiers in Germany, by contrast, were spontaneous and unplanned, and were perpetrated, not as part of any official policy, but on the initiative of ordinary soldiers. However, just as the Russians indulged in innumerable acts of spontaneous cruelty, they also often demonstrated much spontaneous kindness. According to one foreign journalist who witnessed the onslaught of the Red Army on Germany, the Russian soldiers behaved: 'In part like pigs, in part like angels... In single apartments it often came to wild scenes with women and girls. One woman died from being misused by the soldiers. In other houses, the Russians acted more like friends... They are like a hailstorm that only destroys part of the harvest.'[60] In the words of Klaus Bölling, who at that time was a teenager: 'The Russian occupation was gruesome, especially the rapes... but I also experienced a great deal of spontaneous kindness at Russian hands.'[61]

These enormous variations in the behaviour of the Russians, and hence also the experiences of the Germans, were extremely significant. As Norman Naimark has pointed out: 'Russian–German relations in the zone were influenced as much, if not more, by the everyday interactions of Soviet soldiers and German civilians as they were by formal administrative arrangements.'[62] Individual Germans who were raped or assaulted or robbed often never forgave the Russians for what had happened to them, and their whole attitude to the Soviet occupation was irreparably poisoned. As for those who encountered the kindness and generosity of which the Russians were capable, their positive experiences often left a lasting impression and helped to influence their subsequent political attitudes. In this area, as in so many others, personal experiences and local circumstances were the dominant factor in determining later opinions and political behaviour.

A good example of how an act of Russian kindness could shape the whole political perspective of the German who benefited from it is furnished by Lothar Loewe, who in 1945, as a young Hitler Youth member, was sent into battle against the Red Army. He and his comrades had been led to believe that, should they be captured by the Russians, they would be brutally mistreated or summarily executed. In fact, however, after their capture they were neither mishandled nor abused, but, on the contrary, they were treated by their captors with consideration and sympathy. Those who had been wounded received medical attention, and they were given cigarettes and something to eat. One Red Army soldier even lent his mess kit and spoon to Loewe, so that he could eat the food he had been given. According to Loewe:

> I had seen many Soviet POWs during the war. And I had also seen how they were treated... The Soviets were always beaten, really, and they never got anything to eat. They were made to look like the subhumans we imagined them to be. The idea that a German soldier would give a Russian prisoner his mess kit and spoon to eat from was simply unimaginable to me. And the fact that this Soviet gave me his, voluntarily, happily, because he felt sorry for me, shook the foundation of my image of them.

That's when I told myself that maybe the Soviets were much different from what they [the Nazis] had told us to believe. This was my first encounter with the Soviet people, and I'll never forget it for the rest of my life. And it has continued to influence my feelings towards the Soviet Union.[63]

The fact that the behaviour of Russian soldiers upon their entry into East Germany was by no means entirely barbaric was thus one important circumstance which had a positive influence on subsequent attitudes. However, it should also be borne in mind that, for the inhabitants of the more westerly parts of the Soviet zone, their first experience of invasion and occupation was brought to them, not by the Red Army, but by the British and Americans. When the Russians finally marched into this territory at the beginning of July, many eastern Germans discovered, no doubt to their great surprise, that in some ways life under Russian rule was actually better than it had been under the Western allies.

The US military government, for example, had issued strict instructions to American soldiers to refrain from fraternising with the civilian population, and, as a result, the Americans were often perceived to be arrogant and aloof. The Russians, by contrast, mixed freely with the Germans, often with positive results. Where, for instance, Russian officers were billeted upon German families, very warm personal relations often developed.[64] In Weimar, the fact that Russian soldiers shared the public baths with the civilian population had a generally favourable impact on public opinion. Whilst a number of Germans refused to use the baths on the grounds that they would not bathe 'where the dirty Russian soldiers bathe', many others were impressed by the contrast between the gregarious Russians and the cold and aloof Americans.[65]

Similarly, the measures the Americans had taken to normalise daily life had been rather lacklustre, partly because they knew they would soon be leaving the area anyway, and partly because they were most reluctant to enlist the services of German antifascists. This contrasted very strongly with the attitude of the Soviet authorities, who were both far less restrictive in their approach and far more willing to allow the Germans to assume a modicum of responsibility for their own affairs. As a result, the entry of the Red Army in July 1945 produced a noticeable increase in the tempo of normalisation. In Werdau, the Russians had opened two cinemas within just seven days of having taken over control of the town from the Americans. In Leubnitz, the arrival of the Red Army was followed, within a few days, by the arrival of the first trains, the restoration of the local telephone network and the return of a local postal service.[66] In Weimar, the energetic measures of the Russians to clear the streets of rubble were acknowledged, albeit rather grudgingly, by the town's population.[67] In Leipzig, a woman who had previously dreaded the arrival of the Russians, confided to her diary:

I had expected only bad things of the Russians. But so far their arrival has had only positive consequences, in that they have removed all the signs put up by the Amis [Americans]: 'No Loitering!' – 'Bus Stop Removed' – 'No Entry' – 'Military Personnel Only'. Also, curfews were lifted, public baths and cinemas were opened, one might once again sit on all public benches, and even public meetings might once again take place.[68]

By the end of 1945, the more energetic approach of the Russians to the tasks of reconstruction, and, more importantly, their willingness to allow the Germans to get on with the business of restoring some degree of normality to their daily lives, had led to a noticeable discrepancy with the western zones and this, too, had a positive impact on people's attitudes to the Soviet occupation. In Waldheim, a KPD report of December 1945 noted that a rumour was circulating amongst the population that the area would soon be taken over by the British, but that most Waldheim citizens were saying that they would rather remain under Soviet occupation.[69] In Plauen, a report, also of December 1945, stated that many Germans could now be heard making comments such as: 'One can say what one likes, but the Russians are first in everything!' Moreover, given the energetic reconstruction now taking place in the Soviet zone, many of Plauen's citizens were coming to the conclusion that perhaps, after all, they were fortunate to have been occupied by the Russians. According to the report: 'It is dawning on many that we have order, whereas across the border everything happens on the basis of disorder.'[70]

However, for all these more positive aspects of the Russian occupation, most people's experiences of the Soviets were, on balance, either negative or extremely negative, and this fact created numerous problems and dilemmas for both the KPD and the SPD. For most German civilians, the most obvious disadvantage of living in the Soviet zone was the lack of personal security. Especially during the first chaotic weeks of occupation, but also in the subsequent months and years, many tens of thousands of the inhabitants of the Soviet zone were raped or assaulted or robbed by Red Army soldiers. To a large extent, attacks by Red Army soldiers on German civilians were a legacy of wartime hatreds, coupled with the bitterly anti-German character of Soviet wartime propaganda. According to Norman Naimark, the problem was also partly caused by 'the ignitable combination of aggressiveness and defensiveness that was associated with first-time occupation duty'. To some extent, such attacks on civilians were also occasioned by the fact that Red Army troops were often very poorly provided for in logistical terms, and therefore sought to supplement their meagre incomes or rations by theft and robbery.[71]

Perhaps rather surprisingly, the German authorities often scrupulously recorded such attacks, and, as a consequence, a vast amount of documentation on this subject is available to the historian in the East German archives.

The reports make distressing reading, but they nonetheless permit the scholar to gain an insight into both the range and the brutality of Russian attacks on German civilians. Typical is the case of A.D., an elderly farmer who lived near the Thuringian village of Lehesten. In the night of 26 March 1945, a drunken Soviet officer turned up at A.D.'s house, and demanded that he fetch his nineteen-year-old granddaughter. When A.D. informed the officer that his granddaughter had gone into town, and was not expected back that night, the officer demanded that A.D. immediately go out to fetch her, so that she might be brought to him. When, however, A.D. failed to obey this request with sufficient alacrity, the officer shot him in the throat, as a result of which A.D. subsequently died.[72]

Very often, German civilians were attacked, wounded or killed when Red Army soldiers stationed in rural districts went hunting for food or alcohol in nearby farms or villages. Late in the evening of 16 April 1946, for example, one such raid on the Thuringian village of Ehrenstein got out of hand with tragic consequences. After having robbed an innkeeper, the soldiers became involved in an altercation with the village *Bürgermeister*, during the course of which he was 'severely mistreated'. They then drove to a neighbouring village where they attacked a refugee family, beating up the father and raping the daughter.[73] On another similar raid in the village of Rockhausen, a drunken Russian soldier managed to start a fire which consumed a barn, pigsty and stable, along with the farmhouse itself and much agricultural machinery.[74]

Generally speaking, the urban population did not suffer to quite the same extent from attacks by Red Army personnel, partly because so many attacks occurred during raids for food, which for obvious reasons happened more often in the countryside than in the towns, and partly because the general discipline of soldiers stationed in towns seems to have been better. Even in the major urban centres, however, civilians were by no means safe from the attentions of drunken and aggressive Soviet soldiers. At the beginning of May 1946, for example, the population of Gotha was much distressed by an incident when, in broad daylight, a Russian soldier shot an architect on the Reinhardsbrunnerstrasse and raped his female companion.[75] On 10 March 1946, a young man was shot by a Soviet soldier in the middle of Saalfeld.[76] According to one Red Army report from Leipzig, the city witnessed five or six acts of thievery, assault or rape every day.[77]

Such attacks generally cast a shadow of fear over the population, and irreparably damaged relations between a large part of the population and the Soviet occupiers. According to the chief public prosecutor in the Thuringian town of Rudolstadt: 'The mood of the population towards the occupying power is, in view of the numerous excesses against women and other outrages, in particular drunkenness, thoroughly negative.'[78] Similarly, a political report compiled by the Thuringian Ministry of the Interior commented that: 'The incessantly occurring capital crimes perpetrated by persons in Russian uniform are detrimental to good relations between the population and the occupying power. This has put the population so greatly under pressure that above all women, but even stout-hearted men, avoid going out on to the street after twilight.'[79]

Of all the negative features of the Soviet occupation, the assaults and rapes perpetrated by Red Army personnel on German civilians were the most obvious, tragic and distressing. On many occasions, however, the population suffered as a result of stupid and overbearing behaviour by Red Army commandants. In some places, for example, local commandants foisted *Bürgermeister* on the population who were manifestly unfit to perform their duties.[80] Elsewhere, Soviet commandants issued senseless or harmful directives. In Dresden, the Soviet commandant issued the order to cut down the trees of a local, much-loved park, in order to provide fuel for the city's bakers, despite the fact that the wood was far too damp to burn.[81] In one locality in the vicinity of Plauen, farmers were ordered to bring in the harvest, even though the crops had not yet had time to dry out after a recent spell of wet weather. In another village, the commandant instructed the local farmers to bring in the potato crop in the middle of August, despite the fact that in Vogtland potatoes are not normally ready for harvesting until October. Even those farmers who were good antifascists were unable to persuade the commandant to rescind his nonsensical order.[82]

Many functionaries and rank-and-file activists found it difficult to come to terms with the command mentality which was so much a feature of the Soviet tradition of Marxism, but which had little or nothing to do with the native traditions of the German labour movement. One disgruntled Social Democrat from Dresden commented that the typical Soviet commandant 'was always giving out ambitious orders, but never asked "can this be realised, is it possible?" And when he discovered that it was not possible, the blame was laid on the shoulders of the person who had undertaken the task.'[83] On occasion, the irrational demands of local commandants bordered on the farcical. In the Saxon village of Ruppertsgrün, the Communist *Bürgermeister*, C.K., was summoned to see the local commandant, who demanded that the villagers shear their sheep and deliver the wool to the Red Army. When C.K. objected that it was still the middle of winter, and that it was impossible to shear the sheep when there were ten degrees of frost, the commandant replied that the farmers would just have to take the shorn sheep into their houses. Taken aback by this bizarre demand, C.K. was imprudent enough to burst out laughing. Unfortunately, the commandant was apparently a man with little sense of humour, for his response was to have C.K. imprisoned overnight in a cold cellar without blankets. So shaken was C.K. by his experience that he had to spend the next eight days in bed.[84]

If the attacks and rapes were the most distressing aspect of Soviet occupation, and if the irrational demands of Red Army commandants were often the most ludicrous, the most damaging in material terms were the border changes imposed by the Soviet Union and the enormous quantities of reparations which the Russians extracted from East Germany. As a result of the annexation of East Prussia, eastern Pomerania and Silesia, millions of what the East German authorities euphemistically called 'resettlers', and what many West Germans called 'expellees', flooded into the Soviet zone. Usually, these refugees from the east arrived exhausted and destitute. Often, they had been brutally mistreated by the Poles, Czechs or Russians who had driven them from their homes. According to many contemporary reports, these refugees proved to be the most apolitical and cynical section of the population, and it was no accident that localities or workplaces where there were large concentrations of 'resettlers' became, in later years, centres of opposition to the Ulbricht regime.[85]

From the point of view of the working class as a whole, however, the single most threatening aspect of Soviet occupation policy was reparations, for the removal of so much plant and material by the Russians threatened the material base of the workers' survival. From the very beginning of the occupation, the Soviets had made it clear that one of their most important goals was the economic exploitation of Germany. Originally, the Soviets had hoped that the western allies would allow the Soviets access to the economic potential of the whole of Germany, including the Ruhr basin. At the Potsdam conference, however, the British and Americans proved unwilling to accede to Stalin's wishes, and, as a consequence, the Soviets began to concentrate on fulfilling their reparations requirements entirely from their own zone of occupation. In the following months, special reparations teams, answerable directly to Moscow rather than to Karlshorst (the headquarters of SMAD), roamed hither and thither through the zone seizing enormous quantities of material. By the end of 1946, some 1,400 enterprises had been wholly or partially dismantled and sent to the Soviet Union.[86] In all, it has been estimated that approximately 25 per cent of the productive capacity of the zone was thus removed by the Russians.[87]

Not surprisingly, workers in East Germany were shocked, dismayed and angered by the wholesale official plundering of their factories and workplaces. What many workers found particularly frustrating was that, no matter how hard or skilfully they worked in order to repair their machinery and put their factories back into operation, their efforts were nullified by the rapacious activities of the Soviet reparations squads. In his memoirs, Peter Bordihn, who at that time was a worker in an engineering factory, recalls:

> We employed all our skills to get old machines going again. In this way, we put together vertical and horizontal borers and moulding cutters, grinding machines and lathes came into being under our hands. But as soon as a machine was finished, it was packed away in a crate marked with Russian letters and put on transport heading east. We workers were very indignant

about this, because what little we had with which to get production going was being taken away from us![88]

For the KPD and the SPD, the aspect of Soviet occupation policy which was most divisive was Soviet interference in the political process itself. In particular, the Soviets intervened consistently and systematically to promote the Communists at the expense of the Social Democrats. On many occasions, the interference of local Soviet commanders in the political process was not officially sanctioned by Karlshorst, and was more an expression of the low political level of many Soviet officers, and their failure to understand their own army's occupation policy. In August 1945, for example, a Soviet observer in the zone complained that many commandants were relying exclusively on local Communists for help and were ignoring Zhukov's order to allow the establishment of political parties. In the Thuringian town of Eisenach, the commandant either wilfully ignored or hopelessly misunderstood official SMAD policy by refusing to allow local Social Democrats to engage in any political activities.[89]

Notwithstanding such deviations by local Soviet commandants, there can be no doubt that there was also an official SMAD policy of favouring the Communists over the Social Democrats. The aim seems to have been, not to drive the SPD out of politics altogether, for it was still performing a useful role in terms of providing a political home, within the 'popular front', for workers who were not yet ready to join the Communists. Rather, the intention of the Soviets seems to have been to try and nudge political developments onto a different and, for the KPD, more favourable trajectory.

The military authorities, for example, went to great lengths to ensure that the KPD always had adequate supplies of paper, office space and transport. The SPD, by contrast, was given nothing like the same degree of logistical support. In November 1945 the district area executive (*Bezirksvorstand*) of the SPD in Weimar complained that the party's activities were being seriously hampered by a chronic shortage of paper. In particular, the lack of paper was affecting the numbers of newspapers the SPD could produce, and, hence, the ability of the SPD to convey its message to the masses.[90] This problem was exacerbated by the activities of SMAD's censorship offices, which were often staffed by German Communists, and which made it yet more difficult for the party leadership to communicate with its members.[91] Even in Berlin, the epicentre of political activity in the zone, the main KPD paper *Deutsche Volkszeitung* was able to have 50 per cent more copies printed than the SPD paper *Das Volksblatt*, in a larger format, and with more pages.[92] According to Otto Buchwitz, the leader of the SPD in Saxony, the Social Democrat *Land* executive did not have a single car available to it, and it was therefore extremely difficult for leading functionaries to visit or keep in contact with towns and villages.[93]

The logistical support which the Soviets gave the KPD, and their lack of generosity in giving support to the SPD, had a significant impact above all in the smaller towns and villages. In the major towns and cities, it was easier for the Social Democrats to maintain contact both with their own party apparatus and with the masses. However, given the chaotic material conditions and the poor state of the transport network, it was almost impossible for the SPD party apparatus to reach the smaller localities. As a result, in many such places there was either no SPD political activity of any kind, or the local Social Democrats had virtually no contact with their own party apparatus. The KPD, by contrast, was not only able to reach such outlying localities, but was often the only party able to do so, and was hence much more dominant than in the major towns and cities. In Markranstädt, the local Communists reported that the countryside was the 'one area where we can report positive successes'.[94] As one Communist functionary frankly acknowledged at an internal party meeting in Leipzig: 'The influence of the KPD is strong in the countryside, but in the towns the SPD is the leading force.'[95]

The Russian question in KPD–SPD relations

All these negative features of the Soviet occupation created numerous dilemmas for both the KPD and the SPD, though, in the event, the two parties responded very differently to the problem of how to cope with the Russians. This fact was to have fateful consequences for KPD–SPD relations in the zone, and for the whole course of subsequent political developments.

In public, and at the higher levels of the party organisation, the KPD responded to the problems created by the Soviets either by pretending that these problems did not exist, or by attempting to justify them. With regard to the issue of rapes and attacks by Red Army soldiers on German civilians, leading KPD functionaries variously failed to mention the subject,[96] or argued that the level of attacks was massively exaggerated,[97] or pretended that the attacks were carried out by German 'bandits' dressed up as Russian soldiers,[98] or argued that the Germans were now only reaping the whirlwind which they themselves had sown through the bestial behaviour of the Wehrmacht and the SS in Russia.[99] Similarly, leading KPD functionaries justified the reparations and territorial annexations on the grounds that the German people as a whole could not escape a share of the guilt for the crimes of the Nazis, and that it was therefore only right that the Germans should make restitution to the countries they had so brutally attacked and exploited.[100] Anybody who protested too much at the level of rapes and assaults committed by Red Army soldiers, or who criticised the reparations and border changes, was, at best, politically misguided and, at worst, reactionary. In a speech of 12 October 1945, Ulbricht argued that:

Had those people who today are always talking about all sorts of after-effects of the war, fought as hard against the Hitlerite war as did our party, then...[we] would now have no territorial losses or other unpleasantnesses. If there are those... who feel compelled to seek political advantage in the unpleasantnesses which are bound up here or there with the occupation, I can only say to them: Such manoeuvring signifies nothing so much as support for fascist forces of disruption.[101]

This was the official, public response of the KPD. However, behind the scenes things were often very different. Especially at the lower levels of the party organisation, Communists complained bitterly about the policies of the Soviets and did what they could to ameliorate them. In Sonneberg, for example, the local KPD earnestly begged the Thuringian government to try and persuade the Soviets to refrain from blowing up a number of former munitions factories.[102] At the Vomag plant in Plauen, the KPD factory director was sacked from his post for attempting to frustrate the activities of a Soviet reparations team.[103] In the countryside south of Plauen, the fact that the Soviets were making it difficult for German refugees to cross the nearby border into Bavaria was causing huge problems, for it resulted in a bottleneck of people who were trying to travel to the west but were being turned back at the zonal frontier. The Plauen KPD vigorously attempted to persuade the Red Army to relax its grip on the border, appealing in turn to the local Red Army authorities, the KPD district leadership in Chemnitz and eventually Marshal Zhukov himself. As the Plauen Communists repeatedly pointed out, the local authorities simply could not cope with the burden of housing and feeding these thousands of refugees, and if the situation was not remedied soon there would be a catastrophe.[104]

Rank-and-file Communist activists and functionaries were particularly worried by the behaviour of Red Army soldiers, not least because of the devastating impact which the excesses of Soviet troops were having on the attitude of the population towards the USSR and also towards the KPD. The Communists in Weimar reported that there was a widespread feeling, both in the population and inside the party, that the future of the KPD 'is in part dependent on the behaviour of the Red Army towards the population'. Unfortunately, however, the fact 'that soldiers break into houses at night and rape the women ... causes general head-shaking even amongst that part of the population which sympathises with us, and it requires the greatest eloquence... to overcome this impression'.[105] In Norman Naimark's view: 'There can be little question that the communists suffered an almost immediate loss of prestige and popularity as a result of the behaviour of the Red Army before and after the capitulation.'[106]

It is hardly surprising, then, that the issue of looting and rape by Red Army soldiers was often raised by KPD members and low-ranking functionaries. In Leipzig, the KPD functionaries from the northern part of the city wrote to the *Unterbezirksleitung* (sub-district leadership) demanding that something be done to protect food supplies from Red Army plundering.[107] In Erfurt, the Communist police chief wrote to the Thuringian interior ministry to demand that the Red Army do more to bring its troops under control.[108] The Communists in Düben, meanwhile, appealed to the KPD *Bezirksleitung* to do something to about the behaviour of local Red Army troops, who were not only imposing a reign of terror on the population as a whole, but seriously hampering the work of the KPD itself. According to the Düben Communists:

> All the work which we have hitherto undertaken has been continually hampered by the confiscation of trucks, which cost us great efforts to repair, through the requisitioning of materials which are absolutely necessary to us for reconstruction... Above all, agriculture and the rural population are suffering terribly from the perpetual pressure of the Red Army, which oppresses the population through its attacks, rapes and plundering.[109]

All this, however, was hidden from public view, leaving the general population with the impression that the KPD seemed to justify and excuse every detested policy which the Soviets were implementing and, worse still, the barbaric behaviour of the Soviet soldiers. This in turn had a very deleterious effect on the popularity of the KPD, for, as far as the majority of Germans were concerned, the Soviets and the KPD were one and the same thing. The Communists were therefore held responsible for all the hardships and problems which the Soviet occupation brought with it. Already by July, rank-and-file Communists, who had just two months before been confident of winning mass support in post-war Germany, were having to admit that the popularity of the party was rapidly diminishing.[110] In the later summer and early autumn of 1945, the first trade union and workplace council elections seemed to confirm that the KPD was losing support even amongst the industrial working class. At the giant Leuna factory south of Halle, for example, there were elections in August 1945 in order to choose thirty-two trustees. The Communists launched an intensive propaganda campaign, during the course of which the plant was inundated with leaflets, posters, and KPD agitators. The other parties, meanwhile, lacking the organisational and logistical strength of the Communists, were able to do little more than ensure that their candidates' names appeared on the ballot slips. Yet, despite the fact that the KPD had far more resources at its disposal, only one Communist was elected, compared to five 'bourgeois' candidates and twenty-six Social Democrats.[111]

As a direct result of its diminishing popularity, the KPD in the summer and autumn of 1945 and the spring of 1946 found itself in a vicious circle. As the population increasingly blamed the KPD for its troubles, the KPD became more dependent on the Soviets to maintain its pre-eminent position. In private, if not in public, the Communists frankly acknowledged 'the power that we have rests on the bayonets of the Red Army'.[112] At the same time, the Communists themselves became increasingly frustrated and angry at what they perceived to be the unfairness of the view that they were to blame for everything. As one frustrated KPD functionary from Böhlen ruefully exclaimed: 'Who is actually doing all the work? We are! We are the ones who have ensured that there is something to eat! And yet we are held responsible for everything.'[113] According to another functionary from Leubnitz: 'The only thing that is still missing is that we are pronounced guilty for losing the war.'[114] In Leipzig, the KPD issued a leaflet pointing out to the population that it was only thanks to the ceaseless efforts of the Communists that an outright catastrophe had been avoided. 'Every honest person', the leaflet asserted, 'should be grateful to the men of the KPD... But is this gratitude present? For the most part, no.'[115]

The failure of the KPD publicly to criticise the harsher aspects of Soviet occupation policy, and to condemn the brutal behaviour of the Red Army troops, confirmed the Communists and the bulk of the German population in their mutual antagonism. For the majority of Germans, the KPD was demonstrating that it was simply a slavish apologist for Russian barbarism. For the Communists, by contrast, the fact that the population blamed them rather than the Nazis for their troubles was proof, if more proof were needed, that the German people as a whole were still sunk in bigotry, reaction and self-pity. According to the Communists in the Saxon town of Pausa:

> As unbelievable as it may sound, one scarcely ever hears the people holding the Hitler regime responsible for Germany's present unhappy situation. Incomprehensibly, they seek to put the blame on the Communist Party. This may be because the KPD alone is in favour of the occupation by the Red Army, because in this way the severe persecution of the Communists came to an end and the building up of the party became possible.[116]

The response of the Social Democrats to the problems of Russian rule was very different. Like the Communists, the Social Democrats attempted behind the scenes to alleviate the harshness of the Soviet occupation by, for example, intervening on behalf of factories which were scheduled to be dismantled, or by pleading the case of individuals who had been arrested by the Soviet military authorities.[117] Unlike the Communists, however, the Social Democrats were also prepared to bring up such issues in public. Given the Soviet stranglehold on the media, it was of course impossible for the SPD to raise its criticisms of the Russians in its newspapers and party literature or on the radio. However, at their party and public meetings, Social Democrats were still able to speak with relative freedom, and much of what they had to say concerned their grievances with the Soviet occupiers. Moreover, it was not just rank-and-file Social Democrats who took the opportunity to condemn the occupation policies of the Soviets, but even the foremost figures of the SPD were prepared to make trenchant criticisms.

At the first district party conference of the SPD in Leipzig in August 1945, for instance, the two main speakers were Stanislaw Trabalski, the local SPD chief, and Otto Grotewohl, the head of the SPD in the whole of the Soviet zone. Both men made speeches which were astonishingly candid. Grotewohl openly denounced those soldiers in the Red Army 'who believed that they have the right to violate our women where and when they please, who believe they are entitled to hold up people on the street, take away their bicycles, rob them and leave them half naked'. He was equally blunt in his criticisms of the territorial changes imposed by the Soviets, arguing that so much land had been taken away from Germany, and so many expellees were arriving in the Soviet zone from the east, that it was a complete mystery to him how the people of East Germany could be expected to feed themselves.[118]

Such opinions were almost guaranteed to be well received, not just be Social Democrats, but also by the German public. In the minutes of SPD meetings, it is striking that, whenever an SPD speaker criticised the behaviour of Red Army troops or reparations or the territorial changes, his comments were almost invariably followed by applause or cries of 'Quite right!' Fritz Schenk, who at that time was a young Social Democrat from the Mansfeld region, heard Otto Grotewohl speak to a rally in the Volkspark in Halle. Grotewohl roundly condemned a whole range of Soviet policies, and his comments were rapturously received both by Schenk himself and by the thousands of other people at the rally:

> In the Volkspark, all the hardships of our journey were forgotten. We no longer noticed the grumbling of our stomachs. In his speech, Grotewohl tackled precisely those problems that preoccupied us. Without pulling any punches, he condemned the coercive measures of the Soviets. It was music to our ears when he said that, although the German people could not expect to be treated leniently, the SPD would resist any attempt to present black as white or hunger as prosperity. One should call a spade a spade. What did the word 'resettler' mean? For us they were and would always remain 'expellees'.[119]

The assertiveness of the SPD towards the Russians did wonders for the party's popularity. The Soviets and KPD dominated the press and the radio, and the two other parties were too small and badly organised to make a significant impact. However, the SPD was a genuine mass party with an organisation which was second only to that of the KPD, and it was possible to say and hear things at SPD meetings and rallies which one could neither hear nor say elsewhere. Under these circumstances, many Germans increasingly came to see the SPD as the best guarantor of the freedom and sovereignty of Germany and the best defence against the Soviets. Accordingly, the party grew at a spectacular rate and soon outstripped the KPD, despite the massive logistical advantages enjoyed by the Communists. Significantly, the SPD grew particularly rapidly in precisely those towns and cities in which it was putting up the stiffest resistance. In the whole of Saxony, for example, no local SPD organisation proved more troublesome to the Russians than that of Leipzig. It was therefore no accident that the SPD in the district (*Bezirk*) of Leipzig grew far more rapidly than anywhere else in the *Land* of Saxony.[120]

Whereas the KPD's response to the problems of Soviet occupation had brought the party into a vicious circle, the SPD's response produced precisely the opposite effect. As the popularity of the Social Democrats increased, so did their confidence and hence their assertiveness. As the SPD became more assertive, so did it gain in popularity. By the autumn of 1945, the Social Democrats were beginning to ask themselves whether they might become strong enough to assume the primary responsibility for the future of the country. At the first district conference of the Leipzig SPD in August, Grotewohl, to the delight of his audience, proclaimed that it would be the Social Democrats who would become the leading force in the new German state: 'And, comrades, we must be clear about something else as well: The only party and the only stratum within the German people which is at all capable of bringing the administrative apparatus into order... is Social Democracy.'[121]

From the point of view of the Soviets and the KPD leadership, something was clearly going badly wrong. They had always wanted the participation of the SPD in the 'popular front', but only as junior partners. At first, the Social Democrats had been sufficiently traumatised by their experiences of Nazism placidly to accept this role. Now, however, heartened and encouraged by their own success, the Social Democrats were beginning to get out of hand.

Where this process might have led, had the Soviets not intervened, is difficult to say. Possibly, relations between the KPD and SPD would have fallen back into the bitter divisions of the Weimar period. Alternatively, it is possible that the harsh lesson of the Nazi period – that disunity brings defeat – would have prevented KPD–SPD relations from deteriorating too far. In the event, however, the Soviets evidently decided that they had better intervene to halt these degenerative processes before they went too far. If political forces were driving the SPD and KPD apart, thereby endangering the whole system of political transmission belts through which the Soviets sought to shape the destiny of the zone, then an administrative means would have to be found of keeping them together. Consequently, in another major policy reversal, the Soviets began, in the late autumn of 1945, to press for the most rapid possible merger between the SPD and the KPD. After thirty years of division, the campaign to create a single, united working-class party had begun.

Notes

1   M. Klonovsky & J. von Flocken, *Stalins Lager in Deutschland*, Munich, 1993, pp. 11–12.

2   M. McCauley, *The Origins of the Cold War*, New York, 1983, p. 31.

3   N. Naimark, *The Russians in Germany*, Cambridge, MA, 1995, p. 9.

4   ThHStA Weimar, BPA Erfurt, II/2-003, minutes of a sitting of the SPD Bezirksvorstand Thuringia, 21.8.45.

5   W. Leonhard, *Die Revolution entläßt ihre Kinder*, Frankfurt/M, 1961, p. 269.

6   D. Childs, *The GDR: Moscow's German Ally*, 2nd edition, London, 1988, p. 15.

7   G. Pritchard, *German Workers under Soviet Occupation* (doctoral thesis, University of Wales, 1997), pp. 135–36.

8   Naimark (n. 3 above), p. 153.

9   SStA Chemnitz, BPA Karl-Marx-Stadt, I-4/25, Bl. 170–71.

10 ThHStA Weimar, BPA Erfurt, II/1-001, 'Wie kommen wir zur sozialistischen Einheit der deutschen Arbeiterklasse?', Bl. 41–43.

11 B. Bouvier & H. Schulz, '...*die SPD aber aufgehört hat zu existieren*', Bonn, 1991, pp. 118–19. See also SStA Chemnitz, BPA Karl-Marx-Stadt, I-4/33, Bl. 37 & V/5/321, Bl. 2.

12 SStA Leipzig, BPA Leipzig, I/3/01, 'Protokoll der Unterbezirks-Partei-Delegiertenkonferenz', 18-19.8.45, Bl. 77.

13 U. Oehme, *Alltag in Ruinen*, Dresden, 1995, p. 122.

14 SStA Leipzig, KV Leipzig, 382, Bl. 4.

15 ThHStA Weimar, MdI, 142, Bl. 55.

16 SStA Leipzig, BPA Leipzig, I/3/30, 'Bericht an das Instrukteurbüro der KPD Falkenhain', 26.9.45.

17 F. Selbmann, 'Die sowjetischen Genossen waren Freunde und Hilfer', in F. Rosner et al., *Vereint sind wir alle*, [East] Berlin, 1966, p. 356.

18 G. Schaffer, *Russian Zone*, London, 1947, pp. 59–60.

19 SStA Leipzig, BPA Leipzig, I/3/03, 'Die Personalpolitik der Stadt Leipzig', 10.3.46, Bl. 2–3.

20 H. Siegel, *Der Kampf um die Schaffung antifaschistisch-demokratischer Selbstverwaltungsorgane in Halle, 1945–46*, SED Stadtleitung Halle, 1965, p. 24.

21 M. Dennis, *German Democratic Republic*, London & New York, 1988, p. 14.

22 ThHStA Weimar, MdI, 142, Bl. 7.

23 SStA Leipzig, BPA Leipzig, I/3/29, 'Stimmungsbericht Waldheim', 3.12.45.

24 SStA Chemnitz, BPA Karl-Marx-Stadt, I-4/26, Bl. 204.

25 SStA Chemnitz, BPA Karl-Marx-Stadt, I-4/27, Bl. 173.

26 SStA Chemnitz, BPA Karl-Marx-Stadt, II/3-05, Bl. 23.

27 For examples, see Pritchard (n.7 above), pp. 173 & 174, n. 44 & 48.

28 SStA Chemnitz, BPA Karl-Marx-Stadt, I-4/29, Bl. 22.

29 SStA Chemnitz, BPA Karl-Marx-Stadt, I-4/26, Bl. 124.

30 Ibid., Bl. 7.

31 SStA Chemnitz, BPA Karl-Marx-Stadt, V/5/220, Bl. 78–79.

32 G. Sandford, *From Hitler to Ulbricht*, Princeton, NJ, 1983, p. 30.

33 M. Unger, 'Herausbildung revolutionär-demokratischer Staatsorgane in Kreisen des Bezirks Leipzig', in K. Schöneberg et al., *Revolutionärer Prozeß und Staatsentstehung*, [East] Berlin, 1976, p. 35.

34 Schaffer (n. 18 above), p. 62.

35 SStA Leipzig, BPA Leipzig, I/3/03, 'Die Personalpolitik der Stadt Leipzig', 10.3.46, Bl. 4.

36 B. Marshall, *The Origins of Post-War German Politics*, London, 1988, pp. 169–70.

37 SStA Leipzig, BPA Leipzig, I/3/03, 'Die Personalpolitik der Stadt Leipzig', 10.3.46, Bl. 4.

38 Bouvier & Schulz (n. 11 above), p. 281.

39 SStA Chemnitz, BPA Karl-Marx-Stadt, I-4/21, Bl. 13.

40 SStA Leipzig, BPA Leipzig, I/3/23, letter from the KPD Ortsgruppe Zwenkau to the KPD Kreisleitung Leipzig, 4.3.46.

41 SStA Leipzig, BPA Leipzig, I/3/23, 'Tätigkeitsbericht vom Arbeitsgebiet Markranstädt für den Zeitraum 25.2.46–25.3.46'. For further examples, see Pritchard (n. 7 above), p. 175, n. 71.

42 SStA Chemnitz, BPA Karl-Marx-Stadt, I-4/21, letter from the SPD Ortsgruppe Großvoigtsberg to the Landrat in Freiberg, 10.2.46.

43 SStA Chemnitz, BPA Karl-Marx-Stadt, II-3/05, Bl. 3.

44 SStA Chemnitz, BPA Karl-Marx-Stadt, II-3/05, Bl. 11. For further examples, see Pritchard (n. 7 above), p. 176, n. 76.

45 Bouvier & Schulz (n. 11 above), p. 19.

46 See, e.g.: SStA Leipzig, BPA Leipzig, II/2/10, Bl. 90; ThHStA Weimar, BPA Erfurt, II/1-001, resolutions passed by the first Landesparteitag of the Thuringian SPD, Bl. 1–2.

47 ThHStA Weimar, MdI, 268, letter from the SPD Mühlhausen to the SPD Landesverband, 13.3.45.

48 For examples, see Pritchard (n. 7 above), p. 176, n. 80.

49 SStA Chemnitz, BPA Karl-Marx-Stadt, I-4/25, Bl. 315.

50 See, e.g., SStA Chemnitz, BPA Karl-Marx-Stadt: V/5/198, Bl. 61; I-4/21, Bl. 47; I-4/25, Bl. 315.

51 SStA Leipzig, BPA Leipzig, I/4/34, letter from the KPD Betriebsgruppe at the 'LLW' Rackwitz to the KPD Kreisleitung, Delitzsch, 29.12.45. For similar examples, see Pritchard (n. 7 above), p. 176, n. 84.

52 SStA Chemnitz, BPA Karl-Marx-Stadt, V/5/198, Bl. 61.

53 SStA Chemnitz, BPA Karl-Marx-Stadt, I-4/18, Bl.202. For similar examples, see Pritchard (n.7 above), p.176, n.86.

54 See, e.g., SStA Chemnitz, BPA Karl-Marx-Stadt: I-4/18, Bl. 175; I-4/26, Bl. 205; I-4/33, Bl. 108–9.

55 SStA Chemnitz, BPA Karl-Marx-Stadt, I/3/33, Bl. 320.

56 SStA Leipzig, BPA Leipzig, I/3/13, Bl.320. For further examples, see Pritchard (n. 7 above), p. 177, n. 89.

57 SStA Leipzig, BPA Leipzig, I/3/29, 'Stimmungsbericht, Waldheim', 12.1.46, Bl. 1.

58 ThHStA Weimar, MdI, 273, Bl. 15–16.

59 Ibid., Bl. 20–21.

60 Naimark (n. 3 above), p. 82.

61 J. Steinhoff et al. (eds.), *Voices from the Third Reich*, New York, 1994, pp. 482–85.

62 Naimark (n. 3 above), p. 5.

63 Steinhoff (n. 61 above), pp. 469–74.

64 Naimark (n. 3 above), pp. 92–93.

65 ThHStA Weimar, MdI, 273, Bl. 20-21.

66   SStA Chemnitz, BPA Karl-Marx-Stadt, V/5/198, Bl. 39.
67   ThHStA Weimar, MdI, 273, Bl. 20–21.
68   Oehme (n. 13 above), p. 21.
69   SStA Leipzig, BPA Leipzig, I/3/29, 'Nachrichtenamt Waldheim, Bericht', 27.12.45.
70   SStA Chemnitz, BPA Karl-Marx-Stadt, I-4/29, Bl. 3.
71   Naimark (n. 3 above), pp. 72–22 & 90.
72   ThHStA Weimar, MdI, 954, Bl. 24.
73   Ibid., Bl. 9.
74   Ibid., Bl. 3.
75   Ibid., Bl. 2.
76   Ibid., Bl. 8.
77   Naimark (n. 3 above), p. 89.
78   ThHStA Weimar, MdI, 954, Bl. 17–18.
79   Ibid., Bl. 14.
80   See, e.g.: SStA Chemnitz, BPA Karl-Marx-Stadt, I-4/18, Bl. 4 & I-4/29, Bl. 16; ThHStA Weimar, MdI, 274, Bl. 110.
81   Bouvier & Schulz (n. 11 above), p. 231.
82   SStA Chemnitz, BPA Karl-Marx-Stadt, I-4/26, Bl. 122.
83   Bouvier & Schulz (n. 11 above), pp. 230–31.
84   SStA Chemnitz, BPA Karl-Marx-Stadt, V/5/198, Bl. 48.
85   See, e.g., SStA Chemnitz, BPA Karl-Marx-Stadt, IV/2/4/62, Bl. 125–30.
86   V. Berghahn, *Modern Germany*, 2nd edition, Cambridge, 1987, p. 193.
87   H. Turner, *The Two Germanies since 1945*, New Haven & London, 1987, p. 13.
88   P. Bordihn, *Bittere Jahre am Polarkreis*, Berlin, 1990, pp. 16–17.
89   Naimark (n. 3 above), pp. 14–15.
90   ThHStA Weimar, BPA Erfurt, II/2-003, minutes of the meeting of the SPD Bezirksvorstand, 24.9.45.
91   For examples, see Pritchard (n. 7 above), p. 179, n. 134.
92   SStA Leipzig, BPA Leipzig, II/1/01, 'Protokoll des 1. Bezirkstages der SPD Bezirk Leipzig', 26.8.45, Bl. 54–55.
93   Sandford (n. 32 above), p. 65.
94   SStA Leipzig, BPA Leipzig, I/3/23, 'Arbeitsgebiet Markranstädt, Tätigkeitsbericht', 26.9.45, Bl. 3.
95   SStA Leipzig, BPA Leipzig, I/3/23, '3. Schulungsabend', 25.3.46.
96   Naimark (n. 3 above), pp. 132–40.
97   See, e.g., SStA Leipzig, BPA Leipzig, I/3/28, 'Bericht von der Parteiarbeiter- und Arbeiterräte-Versammlung', 9.8.45.
98   See, e.g., SStA Chemnitz, BPA Karl-Marx-Stadt, V/5/323.
99   See, e.g., SStA Leipzig, BPA Leipzig, I/3/06, 'Niederschrift über die erste öffentliche Versammlung der KPD', 17.7.45.
100 See, e.g., ThHStA Weimar, MdI, 273, Bl. 4–5.
101 H. Krisch, *German Politics under Soviet Occupation*, New York, 1974, p. 32.
102 ThHStA Weimar, BdM, 659, Bl. 142.
103 SStA Chemnitz, BPA Karl-Marx-Stadt, I-4/33, Bl. 39.
104 SStA Chemnitz, BPA Karl-Marx-Stadt, I-4/26, Bl. 121–22. For further examples, see Pritchard (n. 7 above), p. 179, n. 148.
105 ThHStA Weimar, MdI, 273, Bl. 15–16 & 21–22.

106 Naimark (n. 3 above), pp. 119–20.
107 SStA Leipzig, BPA Leipzig, I/3/23, letter from the KPD Arbeitsgebiet Nord to the KPD Unterbezirksleitung Leipzig, 30.7.45.
108 ThHStA Weimar, MdI, 1010, Bl. 3.
109 SStA Leipzig, BPA Leipzig, I/3/27, letter from the KPD Unterbezirk Düben to the KPD Bezirksleitung, 26.6.45.
110 See, e.g., SStA Leipzig, BPA Leipzig, I/3/23, letter from the KPD Arbeitsgebiet Nord to the KPD Unterbezirksleitung Leipzig, 30.7.45.
111 SStA Leipzig, BPA Leipzig, II/1/01, 'Protokoll des 1. Bezirkstages der SPD', 26.8.45, Bl. 48.
112 SStA Leipzig, BPA Leipzig, I/3/27, '1. Versammlung der KPD in Gräfenhainichen', 15.7.45, Bl. 10.
113 SStA Leipzig, BPA Leipzig, I/3/13, Bl. 320–21.
114 SStA Chemnitz, BPA Karl-Marx-Stadt, I-4/39, Bl. 11.
115 SStA Leipzig, BPA Leipzig, I/3/27, 'Warum KPD?'.
116 SStA Chemnitz, BPA Karl-Marx-Stadt, I-4/26, Bl. 203.
117 For examples, see Pritchard (n. 7 above), p. 180, n. 164.
118 SStA Leipzig, BPA Leipzig, II/1/01, 'Protokoll des 1. Bezirkstages der SPD', 26.8.45.
119 F. Schenk, *Im Vorzimmer der Diktatur*, Cologne & [West] Berlin, 1962, pp. 13–14.
120 SStA Leipzig, BPA Leipzig, II/2/02, 'Gründung der SPD im Bundesland Sachsen', Bl. 5.
121 SStA Leipzig, BPA Leipzig, II/1/01, 'Protokoll des 1. Bezirkstages der SPD', 26.8.45, Bl. 47.

5

The Socialist Unity Party

The first signs that the Soviets and the KPD leadership were considering changing tack on the issue of the unification of the KPD and SPD came in September 1945, when Wilhelm Pieck, the chairman of the KPD, began to speak of the necessity of creating a united working-class party, 'in order to bring the tasks we have begun to a conclusion'.[1] Not until November 1945, however, did the systematic campaign to create a unity party begin in earnest. By December 1945, the Central Committee (ZA) of the SPD in the Soviet zone had been persuaded to agree to a number of far-reaching measures which prepared the ground for unity, although, at this stage, the ZA still insisted that unification itself could not be carried through in one zone alone, but would have to be sanctioned by a national conference of the entire German SPD. In February 1946, the ZA finally abandoned this proviso and, by a majority of eight votes to three, agreed to a merger of the SPD and the KPD in the Soviet zone only. On 21 April 1946, with great pomp and ceremony, the Social Democrats and the Communists united to form the so-called Socialist Unity Party of Germany (SED).

The unity campaign, and the subsequent foundation of the SED in April 1946, have received more attention than any other aspect of the Soviet occupation. At the time, the foundation of the SED was seen by West German politicians as representing the de facto partition of Germany and the imposition of a Soviet puppet regime on its eastern half. For the British and American governments, the creation of the SED was a major factor in persuading them that Soviet policy in East-Central Europe was basically hostile and expansionist, and that Stalin was a man with whom they could not do business.[2] According to many scholars, the foundation of the SED was thus a prominent milestone on the road to the Cold War.

Given the centrality of the SED to subsequent developments in East Germany, the manner and significance of its creation has never ceased to be a subject of intense debate amongst historians and politicians. In the GDR, it was always argued that the creation of the SED was, for the vast majority of Social Democrats and Communists, 'a simple, self-evident truth', which was opposed only by a small rump of reactionary SPD functionaries.[3] In the west, by contrast, it was often maintained that the creation of the SED represented a forced union (*Zwangsvereinigung*), which was imposed on an unwilling SPD at the point of Russian bayonets.[4] In particular, Social Democrats in the western zones, keen to distance their own tradition from that of the Communists, argued that the SPD had fiercely resisted being swallowed up by the KPD, and that this resistance had only been broken by means of deception, intrigue and violence.[5] By East German scholars, however, all such arguments about there having been a forced union were denounced as 'fiction', and as a 'West German manipulation of history'.[6]

There has also, however, been an important current in western historiography which stresses the ambiguous nature of the union between KPD and SPD. For historians of this school, the creation of the SED was neither a love-match, nor a shotgun wedding, but something between the two. Hermann Weber, whilst accepting that much coercion and violence was used to bring the SPD to the altar, also asserts: 'at least as important was the... will to create a single workers' party, which many Social Democrats continued to show in 1945'.[7] Gerhard Stuby has argued that 'the majority of SPD members in the Soviet zone agreed with the union, even if they did not always approve of all the details'.[8]

Yet, despite the hundreds of books and articles which have been written on this subject, the whole discussion, for all its heat and vitriol, proceeded on the basis of woefully insufficient data. To begin with, the poor communications and chaotic circumstances which still prevailed in the Soviet zone as late as the spring of 1946 made it extremely difficult to build up a general picture of the mood inside the SPD. More seriously, the debate about the foundation of the SED was hindered by the inaccessibility of the relevant archival sources. For scholars in the GDR, any objective examination of the unification was out of the question, for the whole legitimacy of the SED, and hence of the GDR, would have been undermined by any suggestion that the unification had not been genuine and voluntary. Since the relevant archives contained numerous unpleasant secrets which would inevitably challenge the official orthodoxy, the East German authorities denied access even to their own hagiographers.

Western scholars, of course, had even less access to the sources, and were hence obliged to make the best use of whatever material was available. For this reason, accounts written in the west focused almost entirely on Berlin, which, by virtue of its special status as a city under four-power occupation, was far more open to western eyes than the rest of the Soviet zone. Similarly, western scholars tended to concentrate their attention very much on the Berlin Central Committee and the SPD leadership, partly because it was based in Berlin and was therefore more visible, and partly because of the revelations of leading SED functionaries, such as Erich Gniffke and Wolfgang Leonhard, who subsequently defected. Very little, however, was known

about the situation in the provinces of East Germany, for the only information available to western historians on this subject came from the memoirs
and reports of Social Democrats from provincial towns and cities who, at a
later date, had managed to escape to the west.

All these sources of information, whilst unquestionably useful, were also
problematic and allowed western historians to construct only a very partial
picture of what was going on in the Soviet zone. There was no particular
reason to assume that Berlin was representative of the whole of the Soviet
zone, nor did information about developments in the Central Committee
necessarily tell historians very much about the lower levels of the party
organisation. Similarly, Social Democrats who escaped the zone had their
own stories to tell, and although western historians were absolutely right to
listen to them, there was no justification for assuming that those who had
fled were representative of those who had stayed behind.

The collapse of the GDR, however, threw open the vaults in which the
relevant archives had been imprisoned. On the basis of the huge amounts of
evidence which was previously hidden away, it is now possible for scholars
to look again at the question of the SED, not just from the point of view of
Berlin, or from that of self-professed opponents and critics of the regime, but
from the standpoint of the thousands of ordinary functionaries and members
in the provinces, who, for whatever reason, remained in the Soviet zone of
occupation.

The unity campaign

Before the unity party could be created, the members of the KPD and SPD
had to be persuaded or coerced into agreeing to the merger. Unfortunately
for the Soviets, however, many members of both left-wing parties did not
seem to view the proposed union with any degree of enthusiasm. Even
Walter Ulbricht had doubts about the policy the Soviets were expecting him
to execute, for, as late as December 1945, he was arguing 'that the unity of
the working class will only be possible if the KPD imparts Marxist–Leninist
theory to our Social Democratic comrades and succeeds in persuading them
of its [correctness]'. According to (Wilfried Loth), however, the Soviets were
more interested in creating an instrument with which to shape the future of
Germany than they were in the creation of a 'flawless Marxist–Leninist
party', and Ulbricht was obliged to put aside his reservations.[9]

At the grass roots of the party, meanwhile, many Communists were even
more reluctant than Ulbricht to live under the same roof as the Social
Democrats. For many veteran Communists, the opening of the doors of the
party to the masses during the first months of occupation had been bad
enough. Now they were being expected to give up their independent
organisation altogether. According to one report from Plauen, there were
large numbers of Communists, 'who could not shake off the feeling that it

would be better to retain our old Communist party, and who all too easily get goose pimples when the words Socialist Unity Party are mentioned'.[10] In Zwenkau, it was reported that above all the older members 'are very suspicious of the unity party, though they do not express this openly in meetings. But when one discusses with them in person, then it comes to the surface.'[11]

Even amongst Communists who accepted the desirability of organisational unity with the Social Democrats, there was a widespread concern lest the entry of so many unschooled 'reformists' into the unity party should lead to an unacceptable dilution of political standards. In Zug-Langenrinne in Saxony, the local KPD group complained about the low political level of most Social Democrats and stressed that, even after unification, Communists in the new party should never forget their revolutionary traditions. Moreover, the Zug-Langenrinne Communists advocated a long period of discussion in the period leading up to unification, during which time something at least could be done to raise the political consciousness of SPD members. After the unification, they insisted, responsible political positions in the new party should be held only by Communists or by Social Democrats who were deemed by the KPD to be reliable. Finally, they also demanded that immediately after the foundation of the unity party there should be a purge of 'dishonest elements, i.e. of those who consciously attempt to dilute the goals of the party'.[12]

For all these worries and concerns amongst Communists, there seem to have been very few examples of open resistance to the party line. In Berlin, approximately 10 per cent of Communists refused to join the new party on the grounds that it was 'opportunistic',[13] but there do not seem to have been many instances of such open defiance in the provinces. However, if most Communists were prepared to swallow their doubts, no matter how disagreeable a taste it might leave in their mouths, most Social Democrats proved to be rather less tractable.

As we have already seen, large numbers of Social Democrats had, at Zero Hour, been very much in favour of an immediate merger with the KPD. In the ensuing months, however, their experiences of the KPD had by no means been uniformly favourable. Consequently, when the unity campaign began in the autumn of 1945, very many Social Democrats viewed the creation of a unity party with far less enthusiasm than they had just a few months previously. This is not to say that they had entirely abandoned the idea of a united working-class movement. On the contrary, despite all their negative experiences, many Social Democrats remained deeply convinced that the division of the labour movement had been one of the root causes of all the setbacks and defeats suffered in the period 1918 to 1933, and that the *principle* of unity was as desirable and as worthy as ever. Nonetheless, this acknowledgement of the theoretical desirability of unity was now tempered by numerous practical doubts and reservations.

For example, at a joint meeting of Communist and Social Democrat functionaries in Leipzig in February 1946, Stanislaw Trabalski, the chairman of the SPD *Bezirksvorstand*, reminded his Communist colleagues that, in April and May 1945, the SPD's attempt to build a united working-class party had been brusquely rejected. For this reason, Trabalski continued, the Communist decision 'that a united party should so suddenly be manufactured' had provoked a great deal of suspicion in the ranks of the SPD. Moreover, the 'party egoism' which the KPD had displayed in recent months had given rise to the fear that the Communists now desired not to unite with the SPD, but to crush it. In the words of Trabalski, most Social Democrats were afraid 'that our party comrades will be put under pressure in this new united party, that the fundamental democratic rights of the members will be lost, that the new party will then be completely under Soviet influence'.[14]

In order to overcome this reluctance on the part of Social Democrats to agree to a merger with the Communists, the Soviets and the KPD leadership employed four main tactics. First, the Soviets went to considerable lengths to cultivate the goodwill and gratitude of SPD functionaries. For example, on a number of occasions the Soviet military authorities arranged the release of family members of SPD functionaries from the Soviet POW camps in which they were incarcerated.[15] Elsewhere, the Soviets attempted to win the friendship of Social Democrats by placing them in well-paid, desirable posts in industry or the state administration. It was quite common for the Soviets to treat SPD functionaries to what would nowadays be called 'corporate hospitality', social occasions which would be lavishly supplied with food and alcohol. One particularly common method of gaining the loyalty of SPD functionaries were the so-called 'payoks', special parcels containing foodstuffs, chocolate, cigarettes and other scarce commodities.[16] There can be little doubt that the Soviet charm offensive did help to undermine the resistance of some SPD functionaries, either because they were indeed corrupted, or because the receipt of so many perks and privileges had placed them in a compromised position.

SPD functionaries who, for whatever reason, were willing to speak ardently in favour of unification were treated by the Soviets with special solicitousness. In Saxony and Thuringia, the two most prominent and important examples of this were Otto Buchwitz, the chairman of the Saxon SPD, and Heinrich Hoffmann, a member of the executive committee of the Thuringian SPD. Both men were vigorous advocates of unity, and, as a result, they enjoyed the exceptional favour of the Soviet authorities and the KPD leadership. Hoffmann, for example, was invited to attend Wilhelm Pieck's birthday party in Berlin, whereas his boss, Hermann Brill, who was a determined opponent of unification, was pointedly left off the invitation list.[17] On several occasions, Hoffmann was summoned by the Soviet authorities for political discussions whereas Brill was ignored. When Brill managed to obtain a special telephone for long-distance calls, the Russians intervened to ensure that Hoffmann should have one too.[18] When Brill was eventually forced to flee the Soviet zone in December 1945, it was therefore no surprise that it was Heinrich Hoffmann who was appointed as his successor.

Such partisan treatment led to considerable tensions within the SPD, for favoured individuals such as Buchwitz and Hoffmann were often regarded by anti-unity Social Democrats as little more than the paid lackeys of the Soviets. According to one SPD member who fled to the west in 1956, Hoffmann, during the unity campaign, cut a 'miserable figure'.[19] At a meeting of the Thuringian regional excutive committee (*Landesvorstand*) in November 1945, there were angry exchanges between Brill and Hoffmann after the former accused the latter of being the 'SMAD candidate' for the leadership of the SPD in Thuringia.[20] In Saxony, meanwhile, serious tensions emerged between the *Land* leadership, under the staunchly pro-unity Buchwitz, and the Leipzig leadership, under the anti-unity Trabalski. The Dresden Social Democrats, and above all Buchwitz himself, continually intervened to try and pressurise the Leipzig leadership into abandoning its resistance to unity.[21] In response, Trabalski and the Leipzig Social Democrats asserted that the *Land* leadership in Dresden had no right to tell the Leipzig SPD what to do, for in their view they were answerable solely to the Central Committee in Berlin.[22] Furthermore, as in the cases of Hoffmann and Brill, these political differences spilled over into personal animosities. As far as one Social Democrat was concerned, Buchwitz

> was a renegade. When, for the first time... he spoke in favour of unity in pompous and pretentious words, we, his former party friends, were quite appalled and would have liked to give him a piece of our minds... That was a heavy blow for us, we could have spat at him.[23]

Clearly, the Soviet policy of fostering pro-unity functionaries was causing fissures to emerge inside the ranks of the SPD, which further undermined the resistance of the Social Democrats to the unity campaign. It is important to note, however, that whilst the Soviets manipulated and exploited these tensions, and whilst they opened them up for all the world to see, they did not create them. Even during the Weimar period, there had been deep divisions inside the SPD over the issue of whether or not to co-operate with the Communists, and the experience of Nazi dictatorship and Soviet occupation had done nothing to attenuate, and a great deal to aggravate, these divisions. By the time the unification campaign began in the autumn of 1945, the pro-Communist and anti-Communist extremes of the SPD could no longer be contained within the same party, a fact which the Soviet policy of fostering the pro-Communists made manifestly obvious.

If the first tactic of the Soviets and the KPD leadership was to try and cultivate the allegiance and gratitude of SPD functionaries, their second tactic was to put pressure on those functionaries who withstood the Soviet charm offensive and who remained resolutely opposed to unification. Often, the Soviets and Communists would grub around in the past or private lives of recalcitrant SPD functionaries in search of any compromising details which might be used against them. In Leipzig, for example, the members of the secretariat of the KPD *Kreisleitung* discussed whether or not to use the information which they had collected against both Trabalski and the SPD *Oberbürgermeister*, Erich Zeigner. One member of the secretariat argued that the SPD 'should use the available material against the enemy Zeigner in order to put him under pressure'. Interestingly, however, such underhand methods did not meet with the unanimous approval of the members of the secretariat. In the words of one of the Communists present: 'I do not agree with the way you want to deal with Zeigner. We are strong enough politically and we don't have to get involved in such things.'[24]

It is difficult to gauge the extent to which the Soviets and the KPD leadership employed such measures, for blackmail is a plant which always flourishes best in the shadows. Many anti-unity Social Democrats, however, harboured the suspicion that their most outspoken pro-unity colleagues were acting under duress. According to Stanislaw Trabalski, for instance, the sudden conversion of Otto Grotewohl to immediate unification in February 1946 was prompted, not by a genuine change of heart, but by Soviet threats to reveal an affair he was allegedly having with his secretary. 'In my opinion', asserted Trabalski, 'they were able to use this affair to break Grotewohl's back.'[25]

Alongside such methods, the Soviets also made liberal use of intimidation, that less underhand but more brutal twin brother of blackmail. SPD functionaries who proved too stubborn in their opposition to unification were liable to find themselves being browbeaten and threatened by the Soviet military authorities. On one occasion, Stanislaw Trabalski was visited by two Soviet officers, who ordered him to speak in favour of unity at the next meeting of the Leipzig *Bezirksleitung*. Trabalski refused and sent the two officers away. Shortly thereafter, Trabalski was telephoned by the chief political officer of the Red Army in Saxony, who abused him as an 'enemy of unity' and threatened 'to crush him like a piece of dirt'.[26] On another occasion Trabalski was 'dragged off by military policemen with submachine guns', and taken to the Red Army administration to be hectored and bullied.[27] In January 1946, the whole of the Leipzig *Bezirksvorstand* was threatened that, if it maintained its negative attitude to working-class unity, it could reckon with 'considerable difficulties from the side of the Russian commandant and perhaps with prohibition'.[28]

Unfortunately for the SPD, the Soviets were quite prepared to carry out their threats and many Social Democrats were arrested, though it is difficult to assess how frequently this happened. Erich Ollenhauer, the leader of the West German SPD from 1952, estimated that, between December 1945 and April 1946, some 20,000 Social Democrats were imprisoned for longer or shorter periods, or even killed.[29] Possibly this is an exaggeration, for references to such arrests either in the reports of Social Democrats who fled to the West, or in the SPD archives in East Germany, are somewhat rare. On the other hand, it is possible that Social Democrats shied away from broaching such delicate subjects even in their own party meetings.[30] However many Social Democrats were actually arrested, the *fear* of arrest and imprisonment was certainly widespread. During the unity campaign, and in the immediate aftermath of the unification, hundreds if not thousands of Social Democrats fled to the western zones because they feared for their safety. No doubt this, too, was a factor which substantially undermined the resistance of the SPD to being merged with the Communist Party.

The third, rather more subtle tactic employed by the Soviets and the KPD leadership to break SPD resistance to unification, was to demand that Social Democrat leaders make public speeches in favour of the closest possible relationship between the two left-wing parties, or conclude agreements with the Communists in which co-operation between the SPD and KPD was given organisational expression. Such demands placed SPD functionaries in a very difficult situation. Even firm opponents of unity such as Hermann Brill still desired a good relationship with the Communists, and were therefore reluctant to jeopardise that relationship by brusquely rejecting KPD overtures. Moreover, SPD functionaries could hardly fail to be aware that a blank refusal to go along with KPD demands for joint public statements would be likely to incur the wrath of the Soviet authorities.

In most cases, SPD leaders tried to resolve their dilemma by agreeing to speak in public in favour of the principle of unity, and to sign agreements intended to increase the level of co-operation between the two parties, whilst seeking to avoid making any specific commitments. Throughout the Soviet zone, SPD functionaries stood on platforms alongside Communists, and made speeches about how the divisions of the past had allowed the Nazis to come to power, and how the KPD and SPD needed to work shoulder to shoulder in tackling the pressing tasks of reconstruction. All these sentiments were, however, couched in vague and general terms, and any mention of the creation of a united party was scrupulously avoided, except as a noble but still distant goal.[31]

The Communists often interpreted the divergence between the public statements and the private sentiments of SPD functionaries as evidence of their duplicity. In Reichenbach and Pausa, for instance, KPD members complained that local SPD leaders only pretended to be in favour of unity, but behind the scenes employed all kinds of strategies to sabotage unity.[32] In Leipzig, the Communists asserted that, whilst Trabalski and his associates publicly advocated a united front between the KPD and SPD, in private 'they have used every means to torpedo the unity of the German working class'.[33] In reality, the discrepancy between the public and private statements of Social Democrats probably arose, not so much from duplicity, but from a sense of discipline. Many SPD functionaries remained deeply convinced that the division of the German labour movement during the Weimar period had been a fundamental prerequisite of the rise to power of the Nazis, and that such a 'fraternal struggle' should at all costs be avoided in the future. In the words of one SPD functionary, on no account should the two parties 'conduct an open battle, which would give the [fascist] enemy courage and hope'.[34] For this reason, many SPD functionaries were extremely reluctant to parade their differences with the KPD in public, but rather sought to settle their disagreements behind closed doors.

Whatever the reason for the SPD tactic of guarded public endorsements of the principle of unity, coupled with vigorous self-defence in private, the results were almost entirely counter-productive. The subtle distinction which SPD speakers sought to make in public between the *principle* of unity, which they accepted, and *organisational* unity, which they did not, was often lost on the rank-and-file. Moreover, the Soviet stranglehold on the press ensured that all such KPD-SPD agreements were so presented as to give the impression that the decisive steps towards unity had already been taken, with the full approval of the SPD leadership. Ignorant of the battles which were raging behind the scenes, pro-KPD Social Democrats saw no reason to reject the advances of their local Communist counterparts.[35] Anti-unity activists, by contrast, were often shocked and dismayed by the apparent willingness of their leaders to go along with KPD plans, which further tended to undermine their confidence and their will to resist.[36]

The fourth and possibly most important tactic of the Soviets and the KPD leadership was to undermine the resistance of SPD functionaries from below, by 'capturing' grass-roots SPD groups in the localities and the factories. In Leipzig, for example, where the local SPD leaders were proving particularly obdurate, the KPD deliberately and systematically set about trying to turn rank-and-file Social Democrats against their own leaders. According to one KPD report of November 1945:

> There is only one way to force the SPD executive in Leipzig on to the path towards unity; the KPD must educate all local SPD associations to unity through joint activities and meetings. Only through this method will the local SPD associations be brought into conflict with their party executive, i.e. the [SPD] party executive will be recognised by the ordinary SPD workers as blockers and as saboteurs of the united front.[37]

In this task, the Communists were considerably aided by a number of important factors. Of great significance was the fact that the KPD party apparatus, thanks to Russian sponsorship, was far more developed than that of the SPD. Whereas the Social Democrats were always desperately short of paper, offices, transport facilities and, above all, full-time functionaries, the KPD was amply provided for in every respect. It was hence able to maintain a presence in every district of every town, in every village and on every shop-floor. This enabled the Communists to build a closer relationship with many rank-and-file Social Democrats than the latter had with their own party apparatus, which in turn made it easier for the Communists to win them over. Furthermore, many of the newer members who had flooded into the SPD were not politically sophisticated and had joined the party, not on the basis of any refined political analysis, but out of a visceral hatred of Nazism and an equally nebulous desire for a better and more egalitarian society. As Franz Walter has pointed out: 'These political greenhorns were easy prey for the Communists.'[38]

Of particular importance in this regard were the SPD factory groups. Unlike the KPD, the Social Democrats had traditionally been organised on a geographical, rather than on an industrial, basis and the SPD party apparatus was hence even less able to influence developments on the shop-floor than it was in the more remote towns and villages. Consequently, the KPD issued instructions to all its own factory groups to do everything in their power to develop the closest possible relations with the SPD groups in their workplaces. Where SPD factory groups were not yet in existence, Communists were instructed to find one or two sympathetic SPD workers who should be encouraged to establish a cell. This, it was hoped, would change the organisational character of the SPD, rendering it more receptive to Communist advances. According to one circular, issued by the KPD to all Communist factory groups in Leipzig, 'the best opportunity to work together and create the conditions for the unification of the two workers' parties exists only in the workplace'.[39]

The efforts of the Communists to win over rank-and-file SPD workers met with no small measure of success. In the East German archives there are literally hundreds of examples of local KPD organisations reporting that it was above all the links built with SPD workers on the shop-floor which provided the lever with which to overcome resistance at the higher levels of the SPD party organisation. In the words of one Communist from Chemnitz: 'The organisation of the two [parties] in the workplaces was of great significance in the process of unification. They developed above all the initiative to the acceleration of unification and the rejection of elements hostile to unity.'[40] According to one KPD report from Reichenbach, the tide of pro-unity sentiment in many local factories was now so powerful that even right-wing SPD functionaries, in order to avoid becoming isolated from their own members, were being compelled to make statements in favour of unification.[41] In Leipzig, the obdurate local leadership of the SPD was inundated with angry letters from pro-unity party groups in the localities and workplaces. Significantly, the vast majority of these communications were submitted by SPD groups from the environs of Leipzig, rather than from the city itself, which once again illustrates that it was always easier for the KPD to manipulate political developments in the smaller towns and villages than it was in the larger towns and cities of the Soviet zone.[42]

The SPD attempts to defend itself

The four tactics of the Soviets and the KPD leadership were pursued with vigour and cunning, and were ultimately successful in bringing the SPD to heel. It would, however, be misleading to present the contest between the Social Democrats and the Communists as having been entirely one-sided. On the contrary, members of the SPD put up a vigorous resistance to the tactics being employed by their Soviet and Communist adversaries. Some braver rank-and-file Social Democrats risked their freedom, and possibly their lives, by producing and distributing illegal anti-Communist leaflets, with which they sought to alert the masses to the machinations and skulduggery which the SPD leadership disdained to mention in public. In Leipzig, for example, hard-line SPD opponents of unity produced a leaflet, which was distributed in great numbers in the city, and which called upon all Social Democrats to refuse to have anything to do with the KPD's unity campaign, and not to allow themselves to be betrayed by the SPD leadership.[43]

Whilst many SPD functionaries, particularly in a city such as Leipzig, no doubt entertained a degree of sympathy for such sentiments, only very rarely did they follow the leaflet's injunction by refusing even to discuss unity with their Communist counterparts. By and large, even committed opponents of unity such as Hermann Brill and Stanislaw Trabalski turned up to the conferences to which the Communists invited them. Once there, however, they tried, as best they could, to counter the arguments with which the Communists sought to persuade them to agree to organisational unity. The determination of their ideological resistance to unification is attested to by the fact that it took many months of intense discussions and negotiations before their opposition finally collapsed.

Precisely because these discussions between KPD and SPD functionaries lasted so long, and went into such depth, they provide a very rich seam of information for the historian. The minutes of these meetings survive in great abundance and furnish us with a most revealing insight into the thinking of SPD functionaries, the arguments with which they sought to ward off the Communists, and the means by which the Communists attempted to disprove and discredit these arguments. What is very striking, however, when one reads the minutes of such joint conferences, is that, in the ideological debate between the KPD and SPD, whilst the latter may have argued with greater passion and conviction, it was the KPD which held all the trump cards.

To begin with, SPD functionaries, in their discussions with the Communists, were hampered by the fact that they did not speak with one voice. Amongst the Social Democrats, the divisions were so deep that, even in front of their KPD rivals, they could not be prevented from coming to the surface.[44] The Communists, by contrast, whatever their private thoughts and feelings about unification, generally managed to present a united front in public. Before important meetings with the SPD, it was common practice for the Communists to meet up beforehand to discuss (or be told) exactly what tactics they were to adopt and what arguments they would use.[45] Also of significance was the fact that many SPD functionaries were beset by feelings of self-doubt, which arose out of their perception that the SPD before 1933 had been guilty not just of making enormous blunders but also of cowardice and pusillanimity.[46] The Communists, by contrast, whilst accepting that the KPD had made tactical errors during the Weimar period, were nonetheless far more critical of the SPD than they were of themselves, and were not borne down by the same feelings of guilt and remorse.

However, the most important advantage which the KPD possessed during its long debate with the SPD on the issue of unification was one particular intellectual weakness which lay at the heart of all the arguments with which the Social Democrats sought to defend themselves. The majority of SPD functionaries could not bring themselves to acknowledge that it would never be possible to construct a truly fraternal relationship with a Stalinist organisation such as the KPD. On the other hand, they were suspicious of Communist motives and feared that the proposed unity party would become an undemocratic instrument of Soviet domination. Caught between the devil of working-class disunity and the deep red sea of Communist dictatorship, the Social Democrats sought to wriggle out of their dilemma by putting forward a whole range of pretexts for postponing unification. Only rarely did SPD functionaries acknowledge to themselves that their arguments and objections to immediate unification were no more than pretexts, but pretexts they were nonetheless. In the course of the unification debate, the Communists systematically and ruthlessly demolished them.

Thus, one important pretext on the basis of which the SPD attempted to ward off the Communists was the argument that, whilst unity in the long term was desirable, it would be premature and counter-productive to implement it before there had been a long period of ideological discussion and clarification. As one Social Democrat from Görbersdorf put it, the unity party could not 'be created overnight'.[47] Sometimes, Social Democrats justified this call for delay by arguing that the middle classes had not yet been sufficiently re-educated, and that immediate unification would therefore frighten them away from the 'progressive' parties (meaning the KPD and SPD) and into the arms of the 'bourgeois' parties (the CDU and LDP), which in turn could become collecting points for disaffected and potentially reactionary elements.[48] Sometimes, Social Democrats argued that before any unification there should be elections in the Soviet zone to determine the relative strengths of the KPD and SPD.[49] On many occasions, Social Democrats asserted that, since there were still so many problems besetting KPD-SPD relations, in particular on personnel issues, unity should be delayed until such tensions, disagreements and problems had been resolved.[50] Finally, many SPD functionaries attempted to argue that they did not have the right to take any decisive steps towards unity, for they were, after all, only representatives of their members and, in a larger sense, of the working class as a whole. It followed, many SPD functionaries concluded, that, before any definitive measures could be agreed upon, not only would the rank-and-file membership of the SPD have to be consulted, but the working class as a whole would have to be persuaded of the necessity of unification.[51]

Faced by such arguments for delay, the Communists were able to muster some convincing rebuttals. To begin with, they pointed out that the arguments with which the SPD were seeking to delay unification would have been equally true in April and May 1945, when the very Social Democrats who were now seeking to postpone the merger had been enthusiastic advocates of immediate organisational unity.[52] Moreover, the Communists argued, the relatively minor reservations on the basis of which the SPD was seeking to justify delay were as nothing compared to the historical responsibility of the two parties to ensure, through their unity, that Nazism could never happen again. In 1918, petty divisions between Communists and Social Democrats had allowed the reactionaries to recover from defeat in the First World War, with disastrous consequences for Germany and the world. In 1945 and 1946, as in 1918, the Communists continued, the forces of reaction had again been temporarily paralysed, but were already, in the western zones of occupation, beginning to recover, and would soon be stretching out their tentacles to the Soviet zone. If the mistakes of 1918 were to be avoided, then surely the KPD and SPD must learn the lesson of history and unite, before it was too late, in order to crush the arch-enemy of German reaction for ever. As one KPD functionary pointed out to his SPD colleagues at a joint meeting in Seiffen: 'We cannot afford to lose any more time in the discussion of petty reservations or organisational questions. Too much is at stake.' In the words of another KPD functionary at the same meeting:

> Any reservations must lead to ruin. It must at long last be understood that the great goals of the working class are at stake, and it is highly dangerous to mix up petty local matters with the creation of the unity party... Today, the only slogan can and must be: All our united strength in the interests of the working class.[53]

Many Social Democrats, weighed down by their sense of past failure, worried by the apparent re-emergence of reactionary tendencies in the western zones, and full of hope for a united and Socialist future, were convinced by such arguments. With increasing frequency through the autumn of 1945 and the spring of 1946, many Social Democrats began to repeat the arguments which they had learned from their Communist counterparts. This, in turn, widened the gap between the anti-unity and pro-Communist wings of the SPD, as the latter became increasingly frustrated at the delaying tactics and stalling of the former.[54] Once again, the

Communists, through their tactics, were able to exploit the divisions inside the SPD which had been present during the Weimar years, and which had been widened still further by divergent experiences during the Nazi and immediate post-war periods.

Of particular interest are the arguments which the KPD deployed against the Social Democrats' objection that no decisive moves could be made towards unity until the membership of the SPD had been consulted, and until the working masses had been won over to the necessity of unity. At this time, the official political line of the KPD was still grounded in the moderate 'Appeal' of 11 June 1945, in which the KPD had claimed to be striving, not towards a workers' dictatorship, but towards 'a parliamentary-democratic republic with all democratic rights and freedoms for the people'.[55] However, the response of KPD functionaries to SPD concerns about winning over the rank-and-file membership revealed clearly that, at root, the KPD was grounded as firmly as ever in the Leninist concept of the vanguard party.

The unification of the SPD and KPD, the Communist argument ran, was an objective necessity determined by the interests of the entire working class. Since, in Communist orthodoxy, the definition of a 'class conscious' worker was a worker who has understood where his or her objective interests lie, it therefore followed that, from the point of view of the KPD, all workers who were in favour of unity were ipso facto 'class conscious' and 'progressive', whereas anybody who stood against unity was objectively siding with the interests of the reactionaries, for whom the unification of the KPD and SPD would sound the death-knell. Therefore, the KPD functionaries concluded, to worry overmuch about those sections of the SPD membership or of the working class who were against unity was to allow 'backward' and possibly 'reactionary' elements to have a decisive say in the formation of a crucial aspect of KPD and SPD policy.

This kind of Leninist thinking underlay many of the statements made by KPD functionaries during the course of their long debate with their SPD counterparts on the issue of unification. According to the Communists in Leipzig, the vast majority of SPD members were new to the party, did not possess a high level of political consciousness and, in many cases, were still infected by backward and reactionary ideas:

> Do we want to leave to this section of the party the decision as to whether there will be a union of the Socialist parties? Do we want to hand over to them this opportunity... of taking a political decision which will mean another setback for the working class? That would be an abdication of power. He who is not hidebound by the rules of formal democracy, who rather recognises the political will of the class conscious workers, who are alone justified and able to be the bearers of the future, knows, that they have long since decided in favour of unity.[56]

Such assertions seem to have made considerably less impression on Social Democrats than KPD arguments about the necessity of uniting to ensure that the mistakes of 1918 should not be repeated. There appear to be no examples of Social Democrats arguing that the rank-and-file membership, or the working class as a whole, should be excluded from any influence on the decision as to whether or not to unify the KPD and SPD. In the end, however, this particular delaying tactic of the SPD was undermined, not by argument, but by the course of events. For all their assertions that the masses of new and inexperienced SPD members had no right to influence such important decisions, the Communists had no reservations about exploiting the inexperience and naivety of rank-and-file Social Democrats in order to win them over to the slogan of working-class unity. This, in turn, helped to undermine the resistance of SPD functionaries, who could no longer plausibly demand that the reservations of the membership be taken into account, when the membership was inundating the functionaries with pro-unity letters and resolutions. Ironically, by arguing that it was important to consider the views of their rank-and-file members, the SPD functionaries merely made themselves more vulnerable to the KPD tactic of 'capturing' rank-and-file Social Democrats in the local and factory groups.

Once their other pretexts and excuses had been subverted, either by argument or by the course of events, the last remaining line of defence for SPD functionaries was to insist, first, that only the Central Committee in Berlin could make the final decision about whether or not to agree to unification in the Soviet zone alone, and, second, that it was the view of the ZA that, in order to avoid splitting Germany irreparably, the unification of the two left-wing parties should take place in all the zones of occupation or not at all. To this end, the East German SPD demanded that an all-German national conference be convened in order to discuss the issue, and that, in the meantime, whilst it was permissible to make preparations for organisational unity, the merger itself would have to wait. This argument, to which the SPD leaders in Berlin continued to cling once all other pretexts had been stripped from them, was also vigorously propounded by SPD functionaries at lower levels of the party. [57]

To counter these final objections of the SPD, Communist functionaries pointed out that there was also a widespread desire for a united working-class party in the western zones of occupation, that numerous unity committees had already been set up in West Germany, and that a unity party in the Soviet zone would provide a good example to the West German working class.[58] In the end, however, the last redoubt of the East German SPD was overrun as a result neither of KPD argument nor of any Soviet measure, but by Kurt Schumacher, the leader of the SPD in the western zones of occupation. Schumacher steadfastly refused to countenance any national conference until a unified German state had been constructed and there had been democratic elections in all the zones of occupation. On 8 February 1946, Grotewohl met Schumacher to plead with him one last time to support the delaying tactics of the SPD by agreeing to the convocation of a national conference. Schumacher, however, remained adamant that the SPD in the Soviet zone had only two alternatives: 'The conquest of the Social Democratic Party of Germany [by the KPD] or its dissolution.'[59] According to Schumacher, it would be better for the SPD to expose the dictatorship which now existed in the Soviet zone by refusing to play along with it, than to provide it with a veneer of democratic legitimacy by continuing to exist.[60]

Schumacher's reaction effectively shattered the SPD's last line of defence. Once he had made it clear that there was no possibility of there ever being a national conference, the ZA in Berlin could no longer predicate its delaying tactics on the future convocation of such a national conference. Accordingly, on 11 February, following a demand by the KPD leadership that unity be achieved by 1 May 1946 at the very latest, the Central Committee resolved 'immediately to lay before the membership the question of the unity of the two workers' parties'.[61] The method by which the SPD would 'decide' on this issue would not be a general referendum, but a series of local and *Land* conferences leading up to a zonal conference to be held in Berlin in April. From this moment on, the resistance of SPD functionaries at lower levels of the party apparatus crumbled, for, having insisted for so long that only the ZA could make a final decision on unity, they could hardly now turn around and refuse to implement the ZA's change of policy. Throughout March and April, founding conferences of the SED were held in all East German villages, towns and states, culminating, on 21 April 1945, in a joint conference of 507 KPD delegates and 548 SPD delegates from all corners of the Soviet zone of occupation.[62] Accompanied by 'thunderous applause' and 'enthusiastic cheers', the assembled delegates duly, and unanimously, voted the SED into existence.[63]

Voluntary or forced union?

An analysis of the tactics used by the KPD against the SPD during the unity campaign, and of the methods used by the Communists and Soviets to over-come the objections of Social Democrats, can reveal *how* unity was achieved. Such an analysis, however, can provide only a partial answer to the question of whether the creation of the SED constituted a voluntary or forced union of the two parties. To resolve that issue, one would also have to try and build up a picture of how SPD members, at all levels of the party and in all parts of the Soviet zone, felt about the dissolution of the SPD and the foundation of the SED. This is no easy task, for, with the exception of Berlin, no referenda or opinion polls were conducted to ascertain how the membership of the SPD viewed what was happening to their party. In Berlin, where a referendum was organised by the West Berlin SPD, 82.2 per cent of Social Democrats who participated voted against the immediate organisational unification of the KPD and SPD.[64] By those who argue that the SED did indeed come into being as the result of a forced union, it is this statistic, above all else, which is put forward as conclusive proof of the undemocratic and coercive character of the unification.[65]

There are, however, all kinds of problems with using the Berlin referendum as evidence of the opposition of the overwhelming majority of Social Democrats to the creation of the SED. To begin with, only 23,000 of Berlin's 66,000 registered SPD members took part in the referendum. The low turn-out was in no small measure due to the fact that the polling stations in East Berlin were closed down almost immediately by the Soviet authorities. However, since it was at that time possible for Berlin residents to move freely across zonal boundaries, there was nothing to prevent SPD members from East Berlin from participating in the ballot had they chosen to do so. Moreover, even in West Berlin, where there were no restrictions of any kind, only about 70 per cent of SPD members turned out to vote.[66] Given the fact that the ZA had called upon Social Democrats not to participate in the referendum, it is at least conceivable that many of the SPD members who abstained were in fact supporters of unification who were obeying the ZA's instructions to boycott the ballot. Furthermore, it should be noted that the referendum also asked voters whether or not they were in favour of a close working relationship with the KPD, and no fewer than 62.1 per cent of those who participated voted in the affirmative.[67]

More revealing than the referendum, perhaps, is the statistic that of Berlin's 66,000 Social Democrats, some 24,000, or 36 per cent, made the decision to join the SED, rather than remain in the SPD.[68] Even here, how-ever, it would be extremely dangerous to assume that, since only 36 per cent of Berlin Social Democrats in Berlin chose to join the SED, only 36 per cent of SPD members in the zone as a whole joined the SED voluntarily. For reasons which are dealt with shortly, there are good grounds for doubting that Berlin was representative of East Germany as a whole.

With the opening-up of the East German archives, it is now possible for the historian to build up a much more accurate picture of how SPD members in the provinces felt about the merger of their party with the KPD. Despite the fact that no referenda were carried out in the provinces, both the KPD and the SPD assiduously compiled reports on public opinion (*Stimmungs-berichte*) on the issue of unification. What these reports demonstrate is that the situation on the ground with regard to the issue of unification was ex-traordinarily complex and contradictory.

In very many localities, the evidence suggests, the vast majority of Social Democrats were hostile to the unity campaign from the very beginning and, once it had become clear that the two parties would be merged, either dropped out of politics, or fled to the western zones, or entered the SED only with the greatest reluctance. In Reichenbach, the majority of SPD members decided to reject unification with the KPD 'as long as dictatorial measures are applied'.[69] In Pockau, almost the entire SPD group was hostile to unity, only took part in joint meetings because it was forced to, and dropped out of political activity rather than enter the SED.[70] At a joint KPD–SPD meeting in Großvoigtsberg, during the course of a bitter argument about unity, a KPD speaker demanded that all those who were against unity should rise from their seats. According to one account of what happened next, 'all the SPD comrades present in the room... rose up as a bloc', and it was only with the greatest difficulty that they were prevented from storming out of the hall en masse.[71] At joint KPD–SPD meetings in the vicinity of Großhartmannsdorf, only a very small minority of those who participated (about 20 per cent) were Social Democrats,[72] whilst in Großhartmannsdorf itself it was reported that: 'The members have, in their meeting, unanimously decided that, under the circumstances which obtain here, there can be no thought of united party built on a democratic basis.'[73] At joint KPD–SPD meetings in Leipzig, it was noted that, even on the left wing of the SPD, only a very small number of functionaries and members 'adopted a clear line in the spirit of the united front' and that pro-unity speakers received only very little applause from the Social Democrats in the audience.[74]

In an equal, or possibly even larger number of localities, however, local SPD groups were reported as being enthusiastic about the prospective merger of the KPD and SPD. In Oelsnitz, the local KPD reported that there was an excellent relationship between the KPD and SPD, and that there were 'no serious difficulties from which one might conclude that the union of the two parties will not come about'.[75] In Ruppertsgrün, a public meeting on the issue of unity was packed to capacity, and the speaker received stormy and continued applause. According to one report of the meeting: 'Probably not one of those present did not understand that the fulfilment of this task of joining the two workers' parties must be achieved.'[76] In Steinpleis, the local KPD noted that on the issue of unity one 'only had good things to report. The will to unity is good even on the side of the SPD. Locally we shall have no difficulties with the merger.'[77] Amongst the Social Democrats in Markranstädt, there were, according to one report, only very few voices raised against unity, but these were being 'dismissed by the good functionaries of the SPD itself'.[78]

Significantly, such reports of excellent KPD–SPD relations leading to a harmonious unification were filed, not just by local Communists, but also by local SPD groups. The SPD group in Freiberg, for example, reported that its members were strongly in favour of unity, for they believed not merely that a united working-class party would be a mortal danger to the forces of reaction, but also that 'only unity can ensure for all time the security of the proletarian masses in a united German workers' party and the peace of Europe and the entire world'.[79] In Colmnitz, the local SPD group declared that its members were without exception in favour of unification and, in an interesting reversal of the normal pattern, complained that locally it was the Communists who were insufficiently enthusiastic about the creation of the SED.[80]

Thus, a considerable part of the SPD was enthusiastically in favour of unity, just as an equally significant section was resolutely opposed to it. Overall, however, the largest single group inside the SPD was made up of people who, whilst being in favour of organisational unity, nonetheless entered the new party with all kinds of worries and reservations.[81] In Crimmitschau, the mood at a mass meeting of 1,000 local Social Democrats was generally in favour of unity, but numerous doubts were raised about whether the leadership of the new party would fall too much under Communist influence. According to the minutes of the meeting, L.R., who was the main SPD speaker, asserted: 'The rights of both parties must be safeguarded in the new party. According to L.R., the KPD claimed too much for itself in the new party, for the SPD was also a great party and should not be disadvantaged.'[82] In Leubnitz, the KPD reported that, whilst unity was generally seen in a positive light by local Social Democrats, it was also the case that an 'immediate union is very desirable, since every day brings with it new points of friction between the two parties.'[83] In Seiffen, a joint members' meeting of the SPD and KPD resolved unanimously to press ahead with building a unity party, but the Social Democrats present nonetheless stressed that the new party must not be called the KPD, and that former members of the KPD and SPD would have to have equal representation in local government.[84] If one had to choose a single town which, more than any other, was representative of the mood inside the SPD as a whole, a good candidate would be Klostermansfeld, where, according to one local Social Democrat, approximately 10 to 15 per cent of SPD members were against unity, whilst a similar proportion was enthusiastically in favour. However, in the words of the Social Democrat: 'The larger part was made up of those who waited on events – we'll see how things turn out, and if needs be we have a majority after all. That was how the majority thought.'[85]

Amidst this bewildering array of responses inside the SPD on the issue of unity it is possible to see only the vaguest of patterns. Generally speaking, SPD veterans of Weimar vintage seem to have been marginally more inclined to be hostile to unity than younger and newer members.[86] Generally speaking, though by no means always, the higher up the hierarchy of the SPD, the more scepticism there was about the proposed unity party. Similarly, there was often more pro-unity sentiment in SPD groups in villages and smaller towns than there was in the major towns and cities. Normally, for reasons which will be detailed shortly, there was more resistance in those parts of East Germany which had initially been captured by the British or Americans, than there was in the territory which was taken by the Red Army. To all these general rules, however, there were numerous exceptions, and the only universal pattern, in this matter as in so many others, was that political responses were determined, not primarily by general or national, or even regional considerations, but by local and individual circumstances and experiences.

All of the above leaves one vital and perplexing problem still to be resolved. If so many Social Democrats harboured grave reservations about the merger of the KPD and SPD, what persuaded them to swallow their doubts and enter the SED? Even more puzzling is the question of why so many Social Democrats, who had been staunch opponents of unity, nonetheless went on to become members or functionaries, or even local or regional leaders, of the SED? Erich Schilling, for example, the moderate and resolutely anti-Communist trade union leader from Leipzig, was elected as a delegate to attend the founding conference of the SED in Berlin, where he no doubt participated in the 'thunderous applause' which accompanied that event. Stanislaw Trabalski, who had been in the very forefront of the resistance to unification in Leipzig, subsequently became the joint chairman of the SED in the *Bezirk* of West Saxony and, eventually, the secretary of the SED in Saxony. What motives can such men possibly have had for participating in a united party against which they had campaigned so bitterly and for so long?

Fear of persecution no doubt played a part, though this can only serve as a very partial explanation. Many of the Social Democrats who in 1946 entered the SED only with reluctance had been active in the anti-Nazi resistance. It is simply not credible that men and women who had braved the terrors of the Gestapo would wilt before the lesser oppression which the Russians and the KPD leadership imposed on the Soviet zone. Moreover, at that time it was still relatively easy to escape to the western zones, and, in any case, the evidence suggests that there was no pressure on former Social Democrats to remain inside the SED.[87] Why, then, did Social Democrats who entertained strong reservations about the SED choose neither to flee the zone nor to drop out of politics altogether?

It is likely that, as Trabalski asserts, personal ambition played some part in persuading reluctant members of the SED either to swallow their reservations or abandon their opposition.[88] In Plauen, for example, it was noted that many SPD functionaries who appeared unenthusiastic about the merger of the SPD and KPD were nonetheless energetically seeking posts in the new party.[89] However, this explanation, too, can only provide us with a very partial answer. No doubt the Soviets did corrupt many SPD functionaries, and no doubt many SPD functionaries were in any case corrupt or self-serving. However, again, it would hardly be tenable to suppose that men and women who had risked their lives in the struggle against Hitler, and who had risked the wrath of the Soviets by speaking out against the unification of the two left-wing parties, were the sort of people who were motivated primarily by personal gain.

A more credible explanation, at least with regard to a section of the membership, is that large numbers of Social Democrats clung to the belief that the KPD really had changed its spots, and that it would not attempt to dominate the new party. This, at least, was the argument put forward by the Soviets, by the Communists themselves and, after 11 February, by the SPD leadership. Social Democrats who wanted to convince themselves that the KPD was a reformed party could also take comfort from the thought that the statutes of the SED had been drawn up jointly by their own leaders and the KPD, and were scrupulously democratic. Furthermore, the leading party theoretician of the KPD, Anton Ackermann, had in February 1946 published a thesis on the 'German road to Socialism', in which he had explicitly endorsed the idea that it would be possible, in Germany, to proceed gradually to Socialism along a parliamentary and democratic, rather than a revolutionary path.[90] Finally, and most importantly, the SPD and the KPD had agreed that positions of responsibility in the SED, at all levels of the party organisation, would be distributed on the basis of strict 'parity', that is, equally between former Social Democrats and Communists. For some Social Democrats, such organisational guarantees were sufficient to calm their doubts and reservations. As one Social Democrat commented at a meeting in Leipzig, unity with the KPD was now possible 'because the Communists have now realised that democracy is necessary'.[91] According to another Social Democrat speaking at a meeting in Görbersdorf, both the workers' parties were now striving for democracy, and that even 'our Russian brothers have recognised that dictatorship is a bad thing'.[92]

However, the most important reason why so many Social Democrats swallowed their doubts and became members of the SED was that, for all their reservations, at heart they still remained passionately convinced that unity was necessary. The only alternative was to admit to themselves that real co-operation with the KPD was not a possibility, and that the divisions of the Weimar period could never be replaced by genuine fraternal solidarity. During the course of the unity campaign, many Social Democrats sought to run away from this painful truth by inventing all kinds of pretexts to justify their opposition to immediate organisational unity. By February 1946, however, all these pretexts had been demolished, and, with no room left in which to manoeuvre, the SPD was confronted with a stark choice of either giving way to the demand for unity or moving into outright and quite possibly illegal opposition to the Communists.

Confronted with this fateful dilemma, the majority of Social Democrats decided that it was better to sacrifice the organisational independence of the SPD than to risk a renewal of the 'fraternal struggle' of the Weimar period, for that, in turn, might once again lead to the triumph of reaction and of Nazism. Moreover, for people who had lived through the horrors of the Third Reich, no task seemed more important, more necessary or more sacred, than ensuring that such barbarism never happened again. However many reservations they might have had about the unity party, most Social Democrats saw it as their historical duty to put the interests of the working class as a whole, and those of the anti-Nazi united front, above the narrow party interests of the SPD itself. Thus, at a meeting in Markranstädt, one veteran Social Democrat stressed 'that he had always been an enemy of the KPD, but that we must now bite into the sour apple in the interests of the working class'.[93] In the words of another Social Democrat, speaking at the last SPD meeting to be held in Leipzig until the revolution of 1989: 'We are sacrificing our party for the freedom of Germany.'[94]

Working-class unity and allied occupation policy

Clearly, then, the creation of the SED should be seen neither as a voluntary expression of the desire of Communists and Social Democrats for unity, nor as the result of Soviet policy alone, but as a result of the interaction between the two. To understand the full significance and character of this inter-action, however, it is necessary to look at the creation of the SED, not just in the light of developments in the Soviet zone of occupation, but in the context of developments in Germany as a whole. At Zero Hour, the SPD in the western zones of occupation was no less divided on the issue of whether or not to collaborate with the Communists than was the East German SPD. In Hanover, for example, there were tensions from the very beginning between the re-emerging KPD and SPD.[95] In Bremen, by contrast, Communists and Social Democrats did not merely work shoulder to shoulder in the local *antifa*, they also proclaimed the 'immediate bringing about of unity' to be one of their primary goals.[96]

However, for all these differences in terms of political orientation, there was one characteristic which almost all rank-and-file Social Democrats in all the zones had in common. In 1945, after having lived through twelve long years of Nazi terror and political isolation, the majority of Social Democrats emerging from the rubble were confused and lacking in confidence. Whilst displaying a spontaneous, almost elemental hatred of Nazis, and whilst entertaining powerful but nonetheless nebulous hopes about a Socialist future, they did not normally possess any coherent or confident set of political ideas. Moreover, most ordinary SPD workers had for twelve years lived in a political system in which any independent thought was dangerous, and where the principle of blind obedience to authority was enforced with brutal savagery. Even amongst anti-Nazi workers, the wounds left by such experiences did not heal instantaneously, and it took time for them to learn once again how to develop their own ideas in free and open debate with others. As a consequence of all these factors, there was a very strong tendency amongst rank-and-file Social Democrats (and, for that matter, amongst trade unionist and workplace council members as well) to be very dependent on their local functionaries. According to one report from

Chemnitz, SPD members tended to be 'very reserved in their political attitude. They orientated themselves at first according to the opinions of the former leading members.'[97] Gordon Schaffer, who visited the Soviet zone in 1947, noted that: 'From the trade unions, the co-operatives and the political parties alike, I heard the same story of meetings where men and women influenced by years of Nazi propaganda were still ready to say "Yes" automatically to the proposals put by their elected officials.'[98]

This dependence of ordinary SPD workers on their functionaries was of profound significance, for it made the political development of the SPD peculiarly sensitive to intervention by the various military governments. In all the zones of occupation, the military authorities possessed not just sovereign power, but also an almost total control over the supply of paper, petrol, travel permits and, most importantly, over the appointment of Germans to public office. In all the zones of occupation, it was therefore relatively easy for the military governments to use these extraordinary powers to foster those SPD functionaries of whom they approved, whilst isolating and marginalising those of whom they disapproved. This in turn shaped the whole political character of the SPD in a given town or region, for the bulk of the membership tended to follow whatever functionaries emerged as dominant.

Thus, in the British zone of occupation, the British Military Government (BMG) systematically promoted moderate and anti-Communist SPD functionaries. In one BMG intelligence report, for example, Karl Germer, a moderate SPD functionary from Berlin, was praised for arguing that the SPD should 'get away from the old dogmas and must in the present situation concentrate on building up the idea of tolerant democracy'. In order to allow Germer to spread his moderate views more widely, the BMG arranged for him to travel from Berlin to the British zone of occupation.[99] In Hanover, the right-wing and bitterly anti-Communist SPD leader Brachte was appointed as chief-of-police, granted considerable powers and showered with privileges.[100] Most importantly of all, the British went to great lengths to promote the work of Schumacher by arranging transport for him, providing him with facilities and helping him to maintain contact with Social Democrats throughout the western zones of occupation.[101] Of course, Schumacher should in no way be regarded as a mere tool of British occupation policy, for he was an enormously courageous and principled individual who was no man's poodle. Nonetheless, as one foreign official frankly commented, the whole position of Schumacher and his associates rested 'on the extent to which they can rely on the effective continuance of British occupation, just as much as that of the Communists in the East depends on the Russian occupying forces'.[102]

With such strenuous British support, Schumacher and his colleagues were able to exert a decisive influence in pulling the SPD in the western zones away from any dangerous liaisons with the despised Communists. The

KPD activist Emil Carlebach, for example, records that in his home town of Frankfurt, Communists and Social Democrats in the immediate post-war period enjoyed excellent relations, and were united in the view that 'the deadly internecine struggle should never be allowed to begin again'. Once Schumacher had established contact with Frankfurt, however, local SPD functionaries became gradually less friendly until eventually there was a complete rupture of relations.[103] Raymond Ebsworth, meanwhile, has argued that: 'In the west the decision [of whether or not to merge with the KPD] was far from clear until the Social Democrat leader Kurt Schumacher rallied the party members against amalgamation.'[104]

In the Soviet zone, by contrast, the military authorities and KPD leadership tried very hard to promote and foster SPD functionaries who seemed to be favourably disposed towards the Communists. On many occasions, the SPD leaders whom they fostered did not, in fact, turn out to be as pro-Communist as the Soviets had hoped. In Chemnitz, for example, the SPD functionary H.H., who had been installed by the Russians, turned out to be a staunch opponent of unity. As a result, the members whom H.H. represented also became resolute critics of the unification campaign. In the words of H.H.: 'Amongst us there was only permanent rejection, and that certainly emanated from me, for there had definitely also been pro-unity sentiments.'[105] On numerous other occasions, however, SPD functionaries who had been fostered by the Russians or appointed to public office did indeed pull their members behind them into the SED. According to P.H., whose father was a leading SPD functionary in Klostermansfeld, it was above all else the pro-unity sentiments of his father which persuaded local rank-and-file Social Democrats voluntarily to enter the SED. If, P.H. asserts, his father 'had said no, we won't do that, then the overwhelming majority of Social Democrats would have said no, we won't do that. My father had a very considerable following behind him.'[106] Perhaps more frequently, it was not so much that SPD functionaries were in favour of unity that proved to be the decisive factor, but that they refrained from voicing their doubts and reservations in public. Unaware of the increasing tensions at higher levels of the party organisations, many Social Democrats trustingly followed their own functionaries into the ranks of the SED.

It is in this light that the significance of the temporary British and American occupation of parts of East Germany should be seen. During the three months in which western armies were present in the region, a whole series of SPD functionaries and leaders – such as Hermann Brill in Weimar, and Stanislaw Trabalski and Erich Schilling in Leipzig – who were staunchly anti-Communist came to the forefront. Between April and July 1945, such leaders and functionaries were able to consolidate their position, build up networks of supporters and, in general, determine the whole political coloration of their local SPD organisations. For this reason, it was precisely in places like Thuringia and Leipzig that the unity campaign encountered the most determined resistance. Similarly, it was no accident that in places such as Freiberg and Dresden, which had been under Soviet control from the very beginning, the SPD was always a rather deeper shade of red, and hence had fewer inhibitions about setting up home with the Communists.

It is also in this light that the decision of only 36 per cent of the SPD membership in Berlin to join the SED should be viewed. In Berlin, even more than in Thuringia and western Saxony, it was possible for anti-Communist functionaries to flourish and – with the energetic support of the British, French and Americans – to spread their propaganda. For this reason, Berlin cannot be considered as representative of the Soviet zone as a whole, for, unlike their counterparts in the rest of the Soviet zone, the Social Democrats in Berlin were being pulled in two opposite directions simultaneously.

In conclusion, it can be stated without any reservations that the contention of the East German historians that the unification of the SPD and KPD was almost entirely voluntary is false. The newly available archival records clearly demonstrate that point. The western historians who argued that the creation of the SED came about purely as the result of a forced union are also wrong, for the same archival records which disprove the official GDR orthodoxy clearly demonstrate that only a minority of the SPD was opposed in principle to unification. Closest to the truth are those historians, such as Weber and Stuby, who argue that the unification was something between a voluntary and a forced union. Even this position, however, is rather misleading, for to place the merger of the SPD and KPD at any point on a two-dimensional scale between 'voluntary' at the one extreme and 'forced' at the other, is to ignore the extraordinarily complex interaction between Soviet occupation policy and domestic German conditions.

For, in the Soviet zone, no less than in the western zones, the policies pursued by the military governments functioned as a catalyst, which interacted with domestic German circumstances to determine the whole pattern of KPD-SPD relations. In the western zones, the military governments used their powers to foster moderate and anti-Communist functionaries who, in turn, pulled their members along behind them. In the Soviet zone, the military authorities used exactly the same methods to encourage and nurture left-wing and pro-Communist SPD leaders and functionaries, who in turn tended to pull the whole of the SPD onto a more leftward path of development. In all the zones of occupation, military governments did not 'impose' a desired shape on the SPD. Rather, they utilised their dominant position to manipulate and develop political currents which were already there.

In one crucial respect, however, the interaction between occupation policy and SPD politics in the Soviet zone differed markedly from that in the other three zones of occupation. In the western zones, the military authorities did not employ intimidation and violence to help shape the development of the SPD. In the Soviet zone, by contrast, intimidation and violence were regularly used to crush those elements of the SPD of which the Soviets disapproved. Ironically, the Soviets' willingness to resort to violence was probably counter-productive, for the revulsion which such measures elicited only increased the doubts and reservations which had prompted Social Democrats to resist the unification campaign in the first place.[107] Nonetheless, coercion was only one weapon amongst many in the Soviets' armoury, and by no means the most important. Yet more significant was the Soviets' ability to manipulate the genuine hopes and pro-unity aspirations of large sections of the SPD. Hence, when unity eventually came in April 1946, most Social Democrats saw the SED, not just as a potential threat to their freedom, but also as a promise of a united working class and a better, Socialist future. Only bitter experience would show the Social Democrats how justified their doubts were, and how groundless their hopes.

Notes

1   W. Loth, *Stalins ungeliebtes Kind*, Berlin, 1994, p. 45.
2   R. Pommerin, 'Die Zwangsvereinigung von KPD und SPD zur SED', in *Vierteljahrshefte für Zeitgeschichte*, 36:2, April 1988, pp. 319–25.
3   O. Gotsche, 'Unser gemeinsamer Kampf in der Antifaschistischen Arbeitergruppe Mitteldeutschlands', in F. Rosner et al. (eds.), *Vereint sind wir alle*, [East] Berlin, 1966, pp. 413–14.
4   See, e.g.: Pommerin (n.2 above), pp.319-25; U. Rühmland, *Mitteldeutschland: 'Moskaus westliche Provinz'*, Stuttgart, 1959, pp.36-7; K.W. Fricke, *Selbstbehauptung und Widerstand in der sowjetischen Besatzungszone Deutschlands*, Bonn & [West] Berlin, 1964, p. 28.
5   F. Walter, 'Die Einheit der Arbeiterklasse', in *Die Zeit*, 15.3.96, p. 46.
6   Günter Benser, quoted in Pommerin (n. 2 above), p. 319.
7   H. Weber, *Geschichte der DDR*, 3rd edition, Munich, 1989, pp. 120–21.
8   G. Stuby, 'Die SPD von der Niederlage des Faschismus bis zur Gründung der Bundesrepublik (1945–49)', in J. von Freyberg et al. (eds.), *Geschichte der deutschen Sozialdemokratie von 1863 bis zur Gegenwart*, Cologne, 1989, p. 308.
9   Loth (n. 1 above), pp. 48–49.
10 SStA Chemnitz, BPA Karl-Marx-Stadt, I-4/29, Bl. 72.
11 SStA Leipzig, BPA Leipzig, I/3/23, letter from the KPD Ortsgruppe Zwenkau to the KPD Kreisleitung Leipzig, 4.3.46.
12 SStA Chemnitz, BPA Karl-Marx-Stadt, I-4/21, Bl. 13-14. For further examples, see: SStA Chemnitz, BPA Karl-Marx-Stadt, I-4/33, Bl. 47 & I-4/39, Bl. 14; SStA Leipzig, BPA Leipzig, I/3/13, Bl. 316–17.
13 N. Naimark, *The Russians in Germany*, Cambridge, MA, 1995, p. 283.
14 SStA Leipzig, BPA Leipzig, III/01, 'Gemeinsame Besprechung', 12.2.46, Bl. 9–10. For similar examples, see G. Pritchard, *German Workers under Soviet Occupation* (doctoral thesis, University of Wales, 1997), p. 218, n. 16.
15 B. Bouvier & H. Schulz, '...die SPD aber aufgehört hat zu existieren', Bonn, 1991, p. 206.

16   Weber (n. 7 above), p. 121.
17   ThHStA Weimar, BPA Erfurt, II/2-003, 'Protokoll zur Sitzung des Landesvorstandes Thüringen der SPD', 29.12.45, Bl. 3.
18   ThHStA Weimar, BPA Erfurt, II/1-001, 'Wie kommen wir zur sozialistischen Einheit der deutschen Arbeiterklasse?', Bl. 52–57.
19   Bouvier & Schulz (n. 15 above), p. 280.
20   ThHStA Weimar, BPA Erfurt, II/1-001, 'Wie kommen wir zur sozialistischen Einheit der deutschen Arbeiterklasse?', Bl. 52–57.
21   See, e.g., the numerous letters sent by Buchwitz to Trabalski in SStA Leipzig, BPA Leipzig, II/2/10.
22   SStA Leipzig, BPA Leipzig, II/2/10, letter from the SPD Bezirksvorstand Leipzig to the Zentralausschuß of the SPD, 30.1.46.
23   Bouvier & Schulz (n. 15 above), pp. 103–04.
24   SStA Leipzig, BPA Leipzig, I/3/05, 'Sekretariatssitzung', Bl. 6–7.
25   Bouvier & Schulz (n. 15 above), pp. 212–13.
26   Ibid., p. 213.
27   ThHStA Weimar, BPA Erfurt, II/1-001, 'Wie kommen wir zur sozialistischen Einheit der deutschen Arbeiterklasse?', Bl. 3–4.
28   SStA Leipzig, BPA Leipzig, II/2/10, letter from the SPD Bezirksvorstand Leipzig to the SPD Zentralausschuß, 30.1.46.
29   Fricke (n. 4 above), pp. 29–30.
30   See, e.g., G. Grunder & M. Wilke (eds.), *Sozialdemokraten im Kampf um die Freiheit*, Munich & Zurich, 1981, p. 146.
31   For examples, see Pritchard (n. 14 above), p. 219, n. 39 & 40.
32   SStA Chemnitz, BPA Karl-Marx-Stadt, I-4/25, Bl. 313.
33   SStA Leipzig, BPA Leipzig, I/3/14, 'Ergänzung zum Generalarbeitsplan', Bl. 2–3.
34   ThHStA Weimar, BPA Erfurt, II/1-001, 'Bericht der gemeinsamen Konferenz der KPD und der SPD, Weimar', 6.1.46, Bl. 4–5.
35   See, e.g., F. Schenk, *Im Vorzimmer der Diktatur*, Cologne & [West] Berlin, 1962, pp. 14–15.
36   See, e.g., Bouvier & Schulz (n. 15 above), p. 41.
37   SStA Leipzig, BPA Leipzig, I/3/16, 'Bericht von dem KPD-Schulungsabend im Büssingwerk Leipzig', 22.10.45.
38   Walter (n. 5 above), p. 46.
39   SStA Leipzig, BPA Leipzig, I/3/14, circular from the KPD Kreisleitung Leipzig, Kaderabteilung, to all KPD Betriebsgruppen, 27.11.45.
40   SStA Chemnitz, BPA Karl-Marx-Stadt, V/5/126, Bl. 79.
41   SStA Chemnitz, BPA Karl-Marx-Stadt, I-4/32, Bl. 53. For further examples, see Pritchard (n. 14 above), p. 220, n. 50.
42   See, e.g., SStA Leipzig, BPA Leipzig, III/05.
43   SStA Leipzig, BPA Leipzig, II/2/10, letter from the SPD Bezirksvorstand Leipzig to the SPD Landesvorstand, 30.1.46 & the leaflet 'Der Kampf um die Freiheit!'.
44   For examples, see Pritchard (n. 14 above), p. 220, n. 54.
45   H. Prauss, *Doch es war nicht die Wahrheit*, [West] Berlin, 1960, p. 24.
46   P. von zur Mühlen, 'Die SPD zwischen Anpassung und Widerstand', in J. Schmädeke & P. Steinbach (eds.), *Der Widerstand gegen den Nationalsozialismus*, Munich & Zurich, 1986, pp. 96–97.

47 SStA Chemnitz, BPA Karl-Marx-Stadt, III/4/03, Bl. 19. For further examples, see Pritchard (n. 14 above), p. 220, n. 59.

48 See, e.g., SStA Chemnitz, BPA Karl-Marx-Stadt, I-4/27, Bl. 168–70.

49 See, e.g., SStA Chemnitz, BPA Karl-Marx-Stadt, I-4/33, Bl. 52 & II-3/05, Bl. 10.

50 For examples, see Pritchard (n. 14 above), p. 221, n. 62.

51 For examples, see ibid., p. 221, n. 63.

52 See, e.g., SStA Leipzig, BPA Leipzig, III/01, 'Gemeinsame Besprechung', 12.2.46, Bl. 20–22.

53 SStA Chemnitz, BPA Karl-Marx-Stadt, I-4/17, Bl. 133–37. For further examples, see Pritchard (n. 14 above), p. 221, n. 65.

54 For examples, see Pritchard (n. 14 above), p. 221, n. 66.

55 R. Badstübner et al., *DDR: Werden und Wachsen*, [East] Berlin, 1975, p. 27.

56 SStA Leipzig, BPA Leipzig, I/3/14, 'Ergänzung zum Generalarbeitsplan', Bl. 6. See also SStA Chemnitz, BPA Karl-Marx-Stadt, I-4/17, Bl. 135.

57 For examples, see Pritchard (n. 14 above), pp. 221–22, n. 71.

58 For examples, see ibid., p. 222, n. 72.

59 E. Gniffke, *Jahre mit Ulbricht*, Cologne, 1966, p. 138.

60 Stuby (n. 8 above), pp. 305–06.

61 D. Staritz, *Die Gründung der DDR*, 2nd edition, Munich, 1987, p. 120.

62 Weber (n. 7 above), p. 132.

63 W. Leonhard, *Die Revolution entläßt ihre Kinder*, Frankfurt/M, 1961, pp. 359–64.

64 Stuby (n. 8 above), p. 307.

65 See, e.g., Rühmland (n. 4 above), pp. 36–37.

66 Staritz (n. 61 above), p. 122.

67 Stuby (n. 8 above), p. 307.

68 Bouvier & Schulz (n. 15 above), p. 44.

69 SStA Chemnitz, BPA Karl-Marx-Stadt, II-3/05, Bl. 7.

70 SStA Chemnitz, BPA Karl-Marx-Stadt, V/5/220, Bl. 73.

71 SStA Chemnitz, BPA Karl-Marx-Stadt, I-4/18, Bl. 157.

72 SStA Chemnitz, BPA Karl-Marx-Stadt, I-4/21, Bl. 147.

73 SStA Chemnitz, BPA Karl-Marx-Stadt, II-3/05, Bl. 11.

74 SStA Leipzig, BPA Leipzig, I/3/16, 'Bericht von den mit der SPD gemeinsam durchgeführten Schulungsabenden und Massenversammlungen am 7. und 9. Oktober'. For further examples, see Pritchard (n. 14 above), p. 223, n. 90.

75 SStA Chemnitz, BPA Karl-Marx-Stadt, I-4/24, Bl. 15–17.

76 SStA Chemnitz, BPA Karl-Marx-Stadt, letter from the KPD Ortsgruppe Ruppertsgrün to the *Sächsische Volkszeitung*, 20.1.46.

77 SStA Chemnitz, BPA Karl-Marx-Stadt, I-4/39, Bl. 13.

78 SStA Leipzig, BPA Leipzig, I/3/23, 'Tätigkeitsbericht vom Arbeitsgebiet Markranstädt für den Zeitraum 25.2.46 bis 25.3.46'. For further examples, see Pritchard (n. 14 above), p. 223, n. 95.

79 SStA Chemnitz, BPA Karl-Marx-Stadt, II-3/05, Bl. 22–24.

80 SStA Chemnitz, BPA Karl-Marx-Stadt, II-3/05, Bl. 8.

81 A. Malycha, *Partei von Stalins Gnaden?*, Berlin, 1996, pp. 47–49.

82 SStA Chemnitz, BPA Karl-Marx-Stadt, II-3/09, 'Bericht, Crimmitschau', 23.3.46.

83   SStA Chemnitz, BPA Karl-Marx-Stadt, I-4/39, 'KPD-Ortsgruppe Leubnitz, Stimmungsbericht', 9.1.46.
84   SStA Chemnitz, BPA Karl-Marx-Stadt, I-4/17, Bl. 133–37.
85   Bouvier & Schulz (n. 15 above), pp. 196–97. For further examples, see Pritchard (n. 14 above), p. 223, n. 100.
86   See, e.g., SStA Leipzig, BPA Leipzig: I/3/29, 'Nachrichtenamt Waldheim, Bericht', 27.12.45; I/4/34, 'Betriebsgruppensitzung (Wurzen)', 26.2.46.
87   Bouvier & Schulz (n. 15 above), p. 275.
88   Ibid., pp. 218–19.
89   SStA Chemnitz, BPA Karl-Marx-Stadt, I-4/33, Bl. 46.
90   See Leonhard (n. 63 above), pp. 345–48.
91   SStA Leipzig, BPA Leipzig, I/3/16, 'Bericht von den mit der SPD gemeinsam durchgeführten Schulungsabenden und Massenversammlungen am 7. und 9. November', Bl. 3.
92   SStA Leipzig, BPA Leipzig, III-4/03, Bl. 19.
93   SStA Leipzig, BPA Leipzig, I/3/23, 'Generalversammlung am 14. März 1946 im Kino'.
94   SStA Leipzig, BPA Leipzig, II/2/02, 'Bezirksparteitag der SPD am 30.3.46 im Felsenkeller'.
95   See, e.g.: U. Schröder, 'Der Ausschuß für Wiederaufbau und die antifaschistische Bewegung in Hannover', in L. Niethammer et al., *Arbeiterinitiative 1945*, Wuppertal, 1976; B. Marshall, 'The Democratisation of Local Politics in the British Zone of Germany: Hanover 1945–47' in *Journal of Contemporary History*, vol. 21, no. 3, 1986, pp. 413–51.
96   See, e.g.: P. Brandt, 'Die Kampfgemeinschaft gegen den Faschismus (KGF) in Bremen', in Niethammer (n. 95 above); *Gemeinsam begann es 1945*, Frankfurt/ M, 1978.
97   SStA Chemnitz, BPA Karl-Marx-Stadt, V/5/049, Bl. 14.
98   G. Schaffer, *Russian Zone*, London, 1947, p. 104.
99   PRO/FO/945/28.
100   Marshall (n. 95 above), p. 419.
101   L. Edinger, *Kurt Schumacher*, Stanford, CA, 1965, p. 100.
102   PRO/FO/371/55360, Weekly political summary no. 2, Part 2: The Social Democratic Party (marginal note).
103   See: E. Carlebach, 'Frankfurts Antifaschisten 1945', in U. Schneider et al. (eds.), *Als der Krieg zu Ende war*, Frankfurt/M, 1980, pp. 10–24; E. Carlebach, *Zensur ohne Schere*, Frankfurt/M, 1985, pp. 35–55.
104   R. Ebsworth, *Restoring Democracy in Germany*, London, 1960, p. 27.
105   Bouvier & Schulz (n. 15 above), pp. 256–57.
106   Ibid., pp. 197–98.
107   Loth (n. 1 above), pp. 50–51.

6

Between popular politics and Communist dictatorship

The creation of the SED in April 1946 marked the beginning of a new phase in the history of the East German labour movement. During the previous year, the political scene in the Soviet zone had been dominated by organisations which had been 'popular', not in the sense that they enjoyed the support of the majority of the population, but in the sense that they had been created on the initiative of rank-and-file anti-Nazi activists and workers. At Zero Hour, the *antifas*, workplace councils, the SPD and even the KPD, were not mere tools of the Russians, for the activists of whom they were comprised spoke in their own words, set their own agendas and were animated by their own ideas and aspirations.

Between Zero Hour and April 1946, however, these manifestations of popular working-class politics were either brought under firm Soviet and Communist control or suppressed in favour of alternative, more amenable organisations, such as the FDGB and the SED. After April 1946, none of the organisations of the East German labour movement can be said to have been truly autonomous. However, neither had the labour movement been entirely subordinated to bureaucratic control from above, though that would come later. It was still possible, within limits, for activists and functionaries inside the East German labour movement to act on their own initiative, to express their own ideas and to represent the interests of the working class as a whole.

In short, after April 1946 the labour movement entered a transitional phase, half way between the popular politics of Zero Hour and the naked Communist dictatorship which would be erected in the later 1940s. This in turn seems to have reflected the fact that Soviet occupation and foreign policy were also going through something of a transitional period. Between the last wartime meeting of the 'Big Three' at Potsdam and the outbreak of the Cold War in 1948, Stalin seems to have been unsure what to do with his allotted share of Germany. It is clear from the Soviets' actions that they were not prepared to tolerate any challenge to their authority over the eastern zone. On the other hand, as Wilfried Loth has convincingly demonstrated, Stalin shied away from taking any decisive steps to incorporate East Germany into the Soviet Bloc. No systematic efforts were made during this period to establish a Stalinist, centrally planned economy. No consistent measures were taken to Stalinise the political system. Perhaps most importantly, there was still open political competition between the SED and the two 'bourgeois' political parties. Elections were still held and, though these were by no means entirely fair, the very fact that the SED often did badly in them proves that they were at least relatively free.

What Stalin was hoping to achieve by such delaying tactics is open to speculation. Possibly, he was just biding his time in order to consolidate his grip on the Soviet zone, and for the moment was unwilling to provoke a premature clash with the western allies by imposing his political system on East Germany too rapidly. Alternatively, as Loth argues, Stalin was chary of taking any decisive steps in the Soviet zone because he was intent upon creating a united but neutral and demilitarised Germany: a giant Finland at the heart of Europe. West Germany, after all, was a far more valuable asset to the British and Americans than the Soviet zone was to Stalin, so if both pieces could be taken off the board through the creation of a united and neutral Germany, the Soviets would gain a relative advantage from the exchange.[1]

However, whatever Stalin's long-term intentions may have been, in the short term the vacillations of Soviet occupation and foreign policy were reflected in a distinctive, intermediate phase in the development of the East German labour movement, during which organisations such as the FDGB and the SED functioned both as 'transmission belts' – conveying the policies of the regime to the masses – and also as representative organs, taking the preoccupations of the working population to the civilian and military authorities.

In the factories

At Zero Hour, the workplace councils had given unprecedented powers to workers on the shop-floor in East Germany. The Soviets and the KPD leadership had initially regarded this as a threat and, during the first few months of occupation, had toyed with the idea of suppressing the workplace councils in favour of the eighteen component trade unions which made up the FDGB. Eventually, however, the Soviets came to the reluctant conclusion that they were not yet in a position to disband the workplace councils, and, from September 1945 onwards, a concerted effort was made to discipline the councils and bring them under Soviet and Communist control. At the same time, the authorities continued to develop the more disciplined and centralised FDGB as a means by which their reliance on the workplace councils might be diminished.

Such methods enabled the Soviets and the KPD leadership successfully to increase the degree of influence they could wield on the shop-floor. Yet it would be entirely misleading to characterise the workplace council movement and the official trade unions at this time as 'Stalinist' organisations. Both were acknowledged by the authorities as being the legitimate voice of the workers in their factories and workplaces. Both were recognised as having an important and pro-active role in the organisation of production. In July 1946, for example, the *Leipziger Volkszeitung* proclaimed: 'As the workplace council is, so is the atmosphere in the workplace. If the workplace council is weary, then so is the whole workplace. The workplace council should be the brain and the strong motor of the whole workforce.'[2] As the chairman of the FDGB, Hans Jendretsky, wrote in June 1946: 'In the construction of the new economy, the participation of the workplace councils is of the greatest significance.'[3]

In particular, the principle of *Mitbestimmung*, which was enormously popular amongst the workers, was assiduously supported by the authorities, both in word and in law. Before the local elections of July 1946, for example, the SED, worried about its waning popularity amongst the industrial workers, made much of its support for the 'full right of co-determination of the blue- and white-collar workers in all the affairs of the workplace', as well as for other traditional working-class demands such as paid holidays and guaranteed sick leave.[4] Before the *Land* elections in October 1946, the secretariat of the SED *Bezirksvorstand* in Leipzig noted with concern that in recent months the party had 'concerned itself too little with the interests of the workers', and, in order to make up for this, the SED in its electoral propaganda would have to endorse emphatically the 'right of the workplace councils to co-determination, even in Soviet-run enterprises...'.[5] On occasion, for instance at the Holzbetrieb Kenzler in Leipzig, the authorities even went so far as to permit strikes in private companies in order to compel recalcitrant employers to grant the workplace councils and trade unions the right of 'co-determination' in the management of their companies.[6] As late as January 1948, the SED was complaining that some workplace councils in private enterprises were not making sufficient use of the right of co-determination, as a result of which: 'The capitalist remains the uncontrolled and absolute ruler in his workplace.'[7]

It would, of course, be foolish to judge the status and role of workplace councils and trade unions purely in terms of the regime's own propaganda and legislation, for it has always been a characteristic feature of Communist dictatorships that they rarely practise what they preach. However, the evidence suggests that, at least during the two years between the end of 1945 and the end of 1947, Communist theories about the role and function of workplace councils and trade unions did reflect the reality of workers' experiences. At this stage, shop stewards and delegates to the workplace councils were still elected officials, whose position was dependent on retaining the support and confidence of workers on the shop-floor. In many cases, the individuals who represented the workers were veterans of the labour movement, who had been functionaries before 1933, often in the very same factories, and who had re-emerged as leaders in 1945.[8] Between such veteran functionaries and the rank-and-file workers whom they represented, there was often a strong relationship based on the trust and affection built up over many years of shared struggles and suffering.[9]

Through their elected officials, it was possible for ordinary workers to exert considerably more leverage over their own factories and workplaces than had ever been the case during the Wilhelmine or Weimar periods, even if their influence had declined somewhat since the heady days of Zero Hour. According to a contemporary report from the Holzbetrieb Karl Weinart in Chemnitz:

> The workplace council, the workplace trade union committee as well as the relevant planning commission participate, within the framework of full co-determination, in all planning, including the reconstruction of destroyed plant and the acquisition of machines, raw materials and so on. In simple workplace matters, the involvement of the chairman of the workplace council suffices, in important [matters] that of the whole workplace council. The workplace council is to be kept up-to-date with all financial and other transactions, in order to safeguard the legitimate interests of the workforce and the public at large.[10]

Gordon Schaffer, meanwhile, on his 1947 visit to the Soviet zone, was very impressed by the powerful role played by shop stewards in the running of many workplaces:

> In several factories I was told quite bluntly by the shop stewards' committees 'nothing happens here without our consent'. I saw plenty to prove that this was no empty claim. Questions of employment and dismissal were always decided in conjunction with the shop stewards. Copies of documents relating to supply of raw materials, and to the destination of output were going in duplicate to the shop stewards and the managements. The books were open to shop stewards' inspection, and they were using their right to protest to the government department concerned if profits were too high or if there were evidence of improper methods.[11]

Most importantly, the workplace councils and trade unions in the period before 1948 still had a very important representative function. In the surviving archival records, there are vast numbers of examples of workplace council delegates or shop stewards raising demands on behalf of their members, often in direct opposition to the policies being pursued by the Soviets and the SED regime. Frequently, these demands concerned the traditional 'bread and butter' issues such as wages and conditions. In

Weimar, for example, the local FDGB wrote to the Thuringian government, complaining that the Soviet decision to cut off coal supplies to the town would lead to 'catastrophe', and begging the civilian authorities 'to do everything release once again the supply of coal'.[12] At the St Georg hospital in Leipzig, the workplace council successfully persuaded the hospital management to reduce the nurses' working week to forty-eight hours and to agree to a settlement of the wages issue.[13]

It was, above all, in the so-called 'Soviet Joint-Stock Companies' (SAGs) that the trade unions and workplace councils demonstrated their dogged adherence to the very un-Stalinist view that the primary function of the labour movement was to represent the workers. The Soviet managers in the SAGs, who were often ruthless and exploitative employers, had a very different view of the proper role of shop stewards and workplace council delegates. These considerable differences of culture and practice frequently led to very severe tensions. In Halle, for example, Soviet managers in a number of SAGs paid the workers according to the wage scales at that time pertaining in the USSR, which were considerably below German levels, and failed to make any social security contributions. In response, the workplace councils in the affected factories made such strenuous efforts on behalf of the workers that the Soviets threatened to have them arrested.[14] Similar threats were made against many other workplace councils in years to come.[15] At a meeting in Berlin in March 1946, one frustrated workplace council delegate complained that he and his colleagues had been told by the Russians that unless the workplace council could achieve an increase in productivity it was worthless and would have to resign. According to the delegate: 'The treatment of our colleagues [by Soviet managers] is beneath contempt... I ask myself, are these really politically educated people, or are they just military types?' At the same meeting, a veteran Communist observed that: 'Everywhere it is the same story – friction with the Russian soldiers: ten-hour working days and Sunday shifts, women being used for excavation work, juveniles under sixteen being used for digging.'[16]

Vigorous efforts to defend German workers from ruthless exploitation at the hands of the Soviets were made, not just by rank-and-file workplace council delegates, but also by middle-ranking trade union and SED functionaries. In April 1947, for instance, the secretary of the FDGB in Sömmerda resigned in protest at the behaviour of Soviet managers.[17] In January 1947, the SED leadership in Thuringia begged the central authorities in Berlin to do something to improve the treatment of workers in the SAGs. Not only were the Soviet employers ignoring the legal rights of their employees and in some cases even physically mishandling them, but there was also a considerable problem with non-payment of wages. Some 1.5 million Reichmarks were now owing, which was leading to severe cases of hardship. All attempts by the trade unions, the party and the Thuringian government had failed to resolve the situation.[18]

One aspect of Soviet occupation policy which was of particular concern to workplace council delegates and shop stewards was, of course, reparations, and on very many occasions they attempted to limit the large-scale seizure of equipment and even of whole factories by the Soviets. In the surviving archives, there are literally thousands of letters from workplace councils and trade union functionaries, pleading with the Soviets to reconsider their demands or begging the central party leadership to intervene on their behalf.[19] In April 1946, for example, the FDGB in Gotha approached the Soviet authorities in Weimar and persuaded them to instruct the reparations squads to leave enough machines in the factories to allow work to continue. When the reparations teams, which were not, in fact, accountable to the Weimar SMAD, refused to obey this instruction, the Gotha trade unionists complained both to the Thuringian government in Weimar, and also directly to General I.S. Kolesnichenko, the commandant of SMAD in Thuringia. In its letter to Kolesnichenko, the Gotha FDGB pointed out that the workforce in the firms listed for dismantling were all good trade unionists whose unstinting efforts and self-sacrifice since the end of the war had made possible a remarkably swift revival of production. Rather than see all this hard work wasted, the Gotha FDGB begged Kolesnichenko to spare some 20 per cent of the firms scheduled for seizure.[20]

On the surface, the trade unions and workplace councils thus seemed to be performing the traditional functions of such organisations. Deep inside the body of the labour movement, however, a number of degenerative tendencies were quietly at work, eating away at the vitals of the trade unions and workplace councils. First, the toleration being displayed by the Soviets and the KPD leadership was based, not on any commitment to the principle of workers' representation, but on sheer pragmatism. During the first months of occupation, there had been simply no alternative to allowing the workers a degree of genuine autonomy on the shop-floor, for the old owners and managers had either absconded or were uninterested in fostering an economic revival. The KPD leadership, meanwhile, did not at that time have at its disposal any more reliable instruments through which to influence and control production. Nor did the Soviets have either the personnel or the specialist knowledge to run the factories. Only the workers, through their own rank-and-file organisations, could accomplish the essential task of bringing the factories back into working order. From late 1945 onwards, however, alternative and more reliable levers of control became available to the authorities, a fact which tended to undermine the position of workplace councils and trade unions. In thousands of sequestered or 'masterless' factories, for example, trustees had been appointed by the local authorities or the Soviets to oversee and manage production. Though many of these trustees had been chosen from the ranks of the workforce, and still dressed and talked like ordinary workers, their elevated status and privileged position soon caused them to develop a rather different perspective on life to that of their former workmates. According to Benno Sarel:

> The workers who had won leading functions wanted to remain true to their origins. But their life was now quite transformed. They were thrown into a whirl of meetings, trips and conferences. Their material privileges alienated them from the consciousness that prevailed on the shop floor. And still more so the fact that they had become 'chiefs', that they had to justify the measures of the regime, that they had to drive their former colleagues to greater efforts.[21]

Even more important than the trustees as instruments of Soviet and Communist control in the factories were the workplace cells (*Betriebsgruppen*) of the KPD and, thereafter, the SED. It took time and patience for the authorities to forge the *Betriebsgruppen* into reliable instruments of official policy, for rank-and-file Communists and SED members in the factories did not always agree with the industrial policies they were being expected to implement. Before 1933, for example, the KPD had been resolutely opposed to piecework and payment-by-results. In 1945, however, the KPD leadership soon abandoned its opposition to 'tariffs' and 'accords',[22] arguing that the economic situation was so desperate that incentives needed to be provided to spur on production. Yet many rank-and-file Communists remained unconvinced by their leaders' arguments and continued to cleave to the pre-1933 position that the accord system was exploitative.[23] In May 1946, an SED functionary in Leipzig bemoaned the fact that so many members of the *Betriebsgruppen* were hostile to any system of payment-by-results. 'It is difficult', the functionary complained, 'to argue with these people... One is simply banging here against a brick wall and we have our work cut to explain to the comrades what it's all about.'[24]

Nonetheless, in spite of numerous difficulties, the KPD and SED apparatus eventually succeeded, through intensive schooling and a selective personnel policy, in bringing the *Betriebsgruppen* under tighter control. This was of enormous significance, for in most of the larger enterprises, both management and the workers' own representative bodies tended to be dominated by Communists and later by SED members. In every workplace 'the party must be everywhere', and all other organisations and bodies would have to acknowledge its leading role.[25]

Any individual KPD or SED member who happened to occupy such a post of responsibility was thus continually reminded that his or her primary and paramount loyalty was to the party, and that the party must decide how he or she should exercise his or her duties. Accordingly, before any important meeting of management, the trade union or the workplace council, it was standard practice for the Communists or SED members involved to meet beforehand, in order to discuss, or be told, what positions they would take. Similarly, a KPD or SED manager could expect to get into trouble if he or she took any important decision without first consulting the *Betriebsgruppen*. It followed from this that, in many workplaces, the most important and influential single individual was not the trustee or managing director, for he or she was only responsible for running the business affairs of the enterprise. The chair of the SED *Betriebsgruppe*, by contrast, could effectively intervene in any aspect of the firm's operation, from the grandest decision of management strategy down to the smallest detail of personnel policy.[26]

Thus, the first factor in the erosion of genuine workers' control on the shop-floor was the gradual emergence of bureaucratic levers through which the authorities were able to accomplish what hitherto only the workers themselves had been able to do, namely, the organisation of production. A second factor in the gradual diminution of workers' power was the transfer of a large chunk of East German industry into the hands either of the state or of the Soviets. Despite the fact that Stalin at this point does not seem to have been intent on creating a Socialist, centrally planned economy in the Soviet zone, many thousands of enterprises were taken over by the civilian authorities, either as part of the commitment of the KPD and SED to nationalising the commanding heights of the economy, or because the previous owners had been leading Nazis or war criminals, or simply because they had become 'masterless'. In addition, many hundreds of enterprises were taken over by the Russians, who wanted to extract reparations from current production. By 1948, some 39 per cent of industrial production in the Soviet zone was accounted for by 'People's Own Enterprises' (VEBs), whilst the SAGs manufactured 22 per cent of all goods produced in the Soviet zone of occupation.[27]

As a result of this development, the SED and the Soviets became the direct employers of an increasing proportion of the working class, with the same interest as any employer in maximising production whilst holding down wages and costs. Consequently, the authorities increasingly came to see the workplace councils and trade unions, not as an instrument of workers' control, but as an additional means of imposing labour discipline. They were quite open about this, arguing that the status of workers in VEBs and SAGs was qualitatively different from that of workers under the old Nazi or Weimar dispensations. Under the old system, the argument ran, the primary function of trade unions and workplace councils had been to defend the interests of workers against their capitalist employers. In VEBs and SAGs, however, the employers were the civilian and military authorities, who in turn represented the interests of all working people. According to the authorities, employees in VEBs and SAGs were hence no longer labouring to make profits for the capitalists; now they were working for the interests of the population as a whole.

It followed from this that the tasks of workers' organisations in state-run industries were fundamentally different to those of the trade unions and workplace councils in factories which were still in private ownership. In the words of Willi Stoph, who at that time was in charge of primary industry in the Soviet zone: 'One must make more of a distinction between the tasks of the people's own and private capitalist enterprise. In a private capitalist enterprise, the question of class struggle stands in the foreground; in the people's own enterprise [VEB], the support of management and of all those organs which we have in the enterprise.'[28] As early as March 1946, the KPD was arguing that in companies under state control, the workplace council 'should not presume to set itself above the management'.[29] By 1947, the authorities were stressing the need for 'productivity' and 'efficiency' in terms which would not have sounded out of place on the lips of a capitalist entre-preneur. In October 1947, for example, Walter Ulbricht told a conference in Erfurt:

> It must be made clear to the workforce that, in a People's Own Enterprise [VEB], their relationship to the working class as a whole is quite different to what it would be in a capitalist enterprise. In a capitalist enterprise, the workers make demands of the capitalists without concerning themselves with profitability. In a People's Own Enterprise, wages can only be improved if there is also an increase in production; i.e. that the increase in total wages be brought into line with increased production.
>
> Whilst we fought against piece-work in the capitalist enterprise, in the People's Own Enterprise or SAG, trade unions now have the task of bringing wages into line with the performance of the workers.[30]

This, at least, was the theory. In practice, the sequestration of so many enterprises led to a direct and fundamental clash of interests between the workers and the authorities. In August 1945, for example, the KPD leader-ship in Weimar bitterly criticised the miners of Altenburg for demanding a forty-hour week whilst there was such a desperate shortage of coal.[31] In May 1946, the FDGB leadership in Leipzig complained that trade union cells and workplace councils were inundating it with 'impossible' wage demands.[32] In October 1946, the workplace council for white-collar workers in Leipzig raised the demand that all their members should be paid equal wages, a proposal which the authorities angrily dismissed as 'levelling down' (*Gleichmacherei*).[33] By July 1947, the SED was instructing its *Betriebgruppen* to monitor with special attention the behaviour of the workplace councils, 'because a good many are working against the line of the party and trade unions'.[34] Shortly thereafter, General Kolesnichenko in Thuringia bluntly warned the workplace councils not to meddle in matters which did not concern them.[35]

Aggravating this basic clash of interests between the working class and the regime even further was the fact that many of the new managers appointed by the civilian or military authorities turned out to be corrupt and dictatorial. This is hardly surprising, for, in the prevailing confusion, it was easy for adventurers and fraudsters to inveigle themselves into the confidence of the authorities. This was particularly true of individuals who had been imprisoned by the Nazis on criminal convictions, and who, after 1945, were hence able to pass themselves off as 'victims of Nazism'. Having wormed their way into positions of responsibility, their behaviour often enraged both the workers and elected officials in the FDGB and workplace councils.

A good example of this is furnished by the firm of Moritz-Lindner, a small printing enterprise in the Saxon town of Markranstädt. Before 1945, the managers of the firm had been staunch Nazis, and in addition had been the printers of a Nazi newspaper. For this reason, the firm was sequestered by the local authorities, who installed T.H., a self-professed 'victim of Nazism', as temporary manager. Unfortunately for the workers, T.H. proved to be an unscrupulous and ruthless employer, which in turn led to an open confrontation with L.S., the chairman of the firm's workplace council. L.S., with the complete support of the company's thirty-five employees, began to complain vociferously to the authorities about T.H.'s dictatorial manner, the appalling working conditions and the fact that T.H. was summarily dismissing workers without having consulted the workplace council. T.H., for his part, with the support of the local SED leadership, accused the workplace council of standing in the way of increased production. The story would probably have ended badly for L.S. and the firm's workers, had not the authorities received a letter denouncing T.H. and raising doubts about his status as a victim of Nazism. In the subsequent investigation, it was revealed that T.H. was in fact a fraudster who had been purloining the firm's property for his own personal gain and who had failed to pay any insurance contributions on behalf of the workers for over a year.[36]

The third degenerative process corroding the workplace councils and trade unions from within arose out of the second. As clashes of interest between the workers and the authorities became more and more common, so the authorities became increasingly eager to ensure that, where disputes occurred, trade union and workplace council functionaries should act as agents of discipline rather than as inciters of unrest. To this end, the authorities employed a whole barrage of techniques designed to render shop stewards and workplace council delegates less responsive to pressures from below, and more amenable to manipulation from above. One favoured method of achieving this goal was intensive political schooling, the effectiveness of which will be discussed shortly. The authorities also resorted to chicaneries, such as the rigging of workplace council elections, to ensure that reliable Communists or SED members were elected as delegates.[37] Between April 1946 and July 1947, a concerted effort was made to subordinate the workplace councils to the local authorities, although, at least according to Benno Sarel, this particular tactic was not very successful.[38] On occasion, shop stewards or workplace council delegates who proved too troublesome were simply ejected by the civilian and military authorities and replaced by more tractable individuals.[39]

Another important tool employed by the Soviets and SED authorities, which had already proved its effectiveness during the unification campaign, was corruption. Many trade union or workplace council delegates, like their SPD counterparts before them, were plied with packages of scarce consumer goods (payoks) and other perks. This naturally tended to drive a wedge between functionaries and their less privileged former workmates, which is precisely what the authorities intended. When some shop stewards and workplace council delegates responded by trying to distribute the luxury goods they were receiving amongst their members, the authorities intervened to prohibit this.[40] Even if functionaries proved ungrateful for the favours they were receiving, their privileged status tended to undermine their ability to resist the wishes of the civilian or military authorities. Wolfgang Leonhard, for example, tells of one veteran functionary, who, on account of the long years he had spent in a concentration camp, enjoyed the trust and confidence of the workers. When a Soviet reparations team arrived to remove a large part of the factory's equipment, they asked the functionary to justify this to the workforce. The functionary agreed, for the Soviets promised him that, once they had taken what they had wanted, the factory would be left in peace. Several months later, however, the functionary was summoned by the Soviets, who informed him that his workplace was to suffer a second round of seizures. When the functionary refused to justify this new wave of reparations to the workers, the Soviets produced a detailed list of all the perks and payoks he had received, and threatened to reveal the contents of the list to the factory workers. In the words of Leonhard: 'Only then did the comrade understand the significance of payoks. On the following day he duly justified the second round of reparations before the workers. But he is no longer what he was. He is a broken man.'[41]

As a result of this campaign to discipline the workplace council and trade union movement, the tide of representation did begin gradually to turn in the authorities' favour. Slowly, workplace council and more especially trade union functionaries became more reliable in terms of imposing decisions from above. As functionaries became more disciplined and more privileged, however, so they became increasingly distanced from ordinary workers. Here we see one of the inherent contradictions of Soviet policy. These veteran functionaries in the trade unions and workplace councils had been of value to the authorities precisely because they enjoyed the trust of the workers and had influence on them. The more disciplined and 'reliable' functionaries became, the more they lost this trust, and the less conviction they carried with the workers. As the regime, in direct consequence of its own policies, gradually lost this powerful implement of persuasion, so it necessarily become more and more reliant on coercion.

Overall, in the period between the autumn of 1945 and the autumn of

1947, one can clearly see the emergence of degenerative processes which eventually, in the later 1940s and early 1950s, would destroy the workplace councils and turn the official trade unions from instruments of representation into implements of oppression. The transition, however, was neither immediate nor smooth. Nor, at this stage, do the Soviets or the SED leadership appear to have had any conscious or deliberate plan to undermine the autonomy of workers' organisations on the shop-floor. The gradual bureaucratisation of the trade unions and workplace councils during the period arose, not out of any preconceived strategy, but out of the basic conflict of interests which increasingly began to divide the SED regime from the people who worked in its factories. Consequently, for a period of about two years, the trade unions and workplace councils tended to function both as 'transmission belts' for official policy, but also as representative institutions. In short, for a space of time between 1945 and 1948, the workplace organisations of the East German working class functioned in a fashion not dissimilar to the traditional role of such organisations; that is, they acted as mediators between workers and employers, sometimes defending the interests of the former against the latter, but sometimes acting as instruments of discipline and restraint on the shop-floor.

The SED between foundation and Stalinisation

The unification of the SPD and KPD had brought the Social Democrats safely into the fold, but the SED itself was still far from being a pliant and abject tool of military government. At least during its earliest months, the SED bore very little resemblance to the narrow, conspiratorial cadre party which Lenin had advocated. On the contrary, the SED was in the initial stages of its development a 'broad church', embracing divers strands of political opinion. Many thousands of former Social Democrats who had entered the SED only with reluctance remained suspicious of their new party, but, for the moment, bided their time to see whether their suspicions would be confirmed. On the left of the party, many former Communists and members of the splinter parties had still not lost the habits of independent thought acquired during the Nazi period, and continued to trouble the authorities with their occasional ultra-left activities. By far the largest section of the newly founded SED, however, consisted of former Social Democrats and Communists who believed, or at least hoped, that the SED would eventually bring the German working class to the promised land of Socialism.

Furthermore, the political atmosphere within the SED was still relatively relaxed and tolerant, not only compared with what was to come later, but also compared with the intensity of the unification campaign. During the first eighteen months or so of the SED's existence, the Soviets apparently felt that, having brought the Social Democrats securely under their control, they could afford to relax their grip somewhat. Even opponents of the SED regime, who subsequently fled to West Germany, testify that it was only in the later 1940s and 1950s that the party became a thoroughly authoritarian tool of Communist dictatorship. According to one anti-Communist former Social Democrat from Saalfeld:

> The decisive turning point only came with the proclamation of the 'party of a new type' [in September 1947]. Up to this point in time it was still possible, for example in speeches, to put forward our own ideas; in meetings and conferences we could still operate more or less discretely.[42]

Fritz Schenk, who at that time was a bitterly anti-Communist member of the SED, admits in his autobiography that his fears and reservations about the unification did not seem to be confirmed by his first experiences of party life in the SED:

> After the merger I perceived at first no striking difference in the life of the party. Admittedly propaganda work and schooling was considerably strengthened, and one heard ever more Communist vocabulary; but nobody minced their words and free rein was given to discussion and party meetings were if anything even more interesting than before. One said what one thought...[43]

The relative openness of the party during the first eighteen months of its existence was not just a characteristic of the base of the SED, but was also evident at higher levels of the party apparatus. There were often real and sometimes heated arguments in which the lines of division by no means always corresponded to previous party allegiances.[44] Furthermore, organs of the SED at local, area, district and, even, regional level were no mere rubber stamps for decisions made at the top, but often were openly defiant of their party superiors or even of the Soviets. Two examples should suffice to demonstrate the point.

The first example, which comes from Gera in August 1946, clearly illustrates the unease with which many SED functionaries regarded the authoritarian methods often employed by the Soviets and the attachment of such functionaries to the more democratic traditions of the German labour movement. On 7 August, a certain B.W., a long-standing Communist from Berlin who had spent many years in the Soviet Union, turned up in Gera claiming to be the new *Oberbürgermeister*. When the local SED leaders displayed some doubts about his credentials, B.W. produced documentation showing that 'General Kolesnichenko... had appointed him and installed him in this post', and declared that the local SED leaders must 'pull out all the stops' in their efforts to support him. The SED leaders in Gera were surprised and angered by the unexpected imposition of a total stranger as *Oberbürgermeister*, but, since B.W. was obviously a favoured son of the Soviets, they had little option but to accept him. The incumbent *Oberbürgermeister* was duly ejected and B.W. took over his office, from where he rapidly began to alienate the local SED even further through his bullying and authoritarian behaviour.

To anyone familiar with the political system of the Soviet Union, the sudden imposition of a new leader from outside, who had obviously been given the task of shaking up and disciplining the local party organisation, would have seemed perfectly normal. Had someone like B.W. appeared in a provincial town in the USSR, his credentials and authority would immediately have been accepted, and local party officials would have known that, unless they put all their energies at the newcomer's disposal, they could soon expect to get into difficulties, either with the party or, worse still, with the Soviet People's Commissariat of Internal Affairs (the NKVD). In Thuringia, however, even those SED functionaries who had formerly been members of the KPD were as yet unfamiliar with such methods. Accordingly, the local SED protested bitterly and vociferously about what it perceived as a gross violation of democratic procedures which, it argued, would undermine the party's credibility with the population. In a letter sent to the Thuringian government, the Gera SED area executive committee (*Kreisvorstand*) complained that:

> These methods, so soon before the elections, have placed our party in a completely untenable situation, and unless this measure is immediately reconsidered we shall incur the mistrust of all honest democrats.
>
> Since the case of B.W. concerns a member of the SED, it is certain that nobody will believe that we as a party had nothing, absolutely nothing, to do with his appointment. Moreover, our election propaganda, which contains the demand that the local council alone should have the sole right to appoint and dismiss its leading officials, would publicly be given the lie.[45]

The second example comes from April 1947, and concerns no less a body than the secretariat of the Thuringian SED. At that time, Stalin seems to have been flirting with the idea of re-legalising the SPD in the Soviet zone of occupation as a concession to the western powers, with the aim of clearing the road to an eventual unification of Germany. Certainly, in April 1947, the chief political officer in the SMAD, Sergei Tulpanov, told Erich Gniffke, a member of the SED central secretariat in Berlin, to prepare for the re-emergence of the SPD in East Germany.[46] Shortly thereafter, Heinrich Hoffmann and Werner Eggerath, the two joint chairmen of the Thuringian SED, were summoned to Berlin at short notice for discussions with the SED leadership about the possible legalisation of the SPD.

During the course of this meeting, Otto Grotewohl informed Hoffmann and Eggerath that the Soviets had decided that, in preparation for the legalisation of the SPD, the Thuringian SED would have to make various organisational changes. In particular, in order to try and make the Thuringian SED more attractive to potential SPD voters, the Communist minister for building, Walter Wolf, would have to resign in favour of a former

Social Democrat. Grotewohl also told Hoffmann and Eggerath that the Soviets were concerned because the moderate president of Thuringia, Dr. Paul, who had joined the SED just one year previously, was threatening to resign on account of the extremely bad relationship he had with his colleagues in the Thuringian government. The resignation of Dr. Paul, the Soviets felt, would make the SED in Thuringia even less able to compete with a refounded SPD, and, in order to placate him, the Communist interior minister, Ernst Busse, was going to be transferred to a job in Berlin.

When, upon their return to Weimar, Hoffmann and Eggerath informed their colleagues on the Thuringian secretariat about the changes being demanded by the Soviets and the SED leadership, the news was met with surprise and anger. In particular, the members of the secretariat, regardless of former party allegiance, were outraged by the appeasement of Dr. Paul, whom they regarded as dictatorial, ambitious and quite possibly corrupt. There followed a lengthy debate in which a number of former Social Democrats and Communists suggested that the secretariat refuse to implement the proposed changes. In the end, however, the secretariat agreed with Werner Eggerath that, whilst Dr. Paul was 'a major problem', and whilst the transfer of Busse to Berlin would cause much astonishment and dismay in the ranks of the party veterans, there was no alternative but to comply with a direct instruction from the Soviets. However, the Thuringian secretariat also demanded that Busse and Wolf be found positions in Berlin at least equal in responsibility and status to those which they currently held.[47] Five months later, in September 1947, Dr. Paul repaid the misplaced confidence of the Soviets, and justified the reservations of his SED colleagues, by fleeing to the western zones: a public humiliation for the SED which caused far more damage than his resignation could ever have done.[48]

However, the most important sign that the SED was still by no means a Stalinist organisation was that the party apparatus during this period functioned not just as a 'transmission belt' passing orders down from above, but also as a conduit through which the concerns of the party membership and, to some extent, of the population as a whole could be passed up the SED hierarchy. On numerous occasions, for example, lower SED organs tried to intervene on behalf of the workers on the issue of reparations.[49] In Chemnitz, the local SED leaders repeatedly complained to the Soviet commandant about the lack of discipline amongst Red Army troops.[50] In the small Thuringian town of Ilfeld, the local SED begged the *Land* government to provide more facilities to help alleviate the problems caused by the influx of refugees.[51] Elsewhere, there were numerous instances of SED groups intervening on behalf of individuals who had either been arrested by the Soviets, or who faced being sacked or having their property sequestered as a result of unfair or untrue allegations.[52] On a number of separate occasions, the Thuringian secretariat of the SED complained to the party leadership in Berlin or directly to the Soviets about the activities of the NKVD, and other 'unpleasant events in connection with the occupying forces', and about Soviet interference in economic, political and administrative affairs.[53] In one typical *Stimmungsbericht*, sent to the Thuringian interior ministry during the harsh winter of 1946 to 1947, an SED official called upon the Soviets to provide material help to the hungry and desperate population or else face the consequences:

> It must at this point be openly and urgently pointed out that the moment is approaching when the occupying authorities must show, through effective assistance, that they will not leave the constructive and democratic forces in the country in the lurch... Otherwise it is inevitable that all our work will be in vain and that the endemic crisis of democracy of the Weimar Republic will tragically be repeated.[54]

In many of their activities, SED functionaries displayed a deep and genuine sense of responsibility to the workers whose interests they represented, coupled with an acute awareness that, should they fail in that responsibility, the masses would lose faith in the party. In November 1946, for instance, SED officials in Rothenburg warned the Soviet military government that the scale of reparations in the town would have severe political consequences. 'The mood of our workers', they claimed, 'sinks into deepest despair when what they have created with their own hands is taken away from them again.' Unless the SED could do something to improve the situation, the prestige of the party would suffer a crippling blow. In the small town of Tangermünde, meanwhile, local SED functionaries campaigned vigorously against a decision by the authorities not to rebuild a sugar refinery which had been badly hit by the reparation squads. The sugar refinery, they pointed out, was the only major employer in the town. Its loss would therefore have devastating economic consequences and would also severely undermine the popularity of the SED. According to the local functionaries:

> The SED, as the chosen representative of the broad masses, and in particular of the trade union and Socialist orientated workers, can under no circumstances approve of the closure of the sugar factory, for this is a matter which concerns the very existence of the town of Tangermünde, in which the SED is dominant... The SED therefore stands as the spokesperson of the population and seeks a reconsideration of the decision which has been made.[55]

The fact that lower party organs were so willing to represent the interests of ordinary workers means that the SED at this point cannot be called a Stalinist party, for it lacked the most essential characteristic of such a party, namely, the subordination of all party structures to the interests of the party leadership so that power and representation flow in one direction only, that is, from top to bottom. On the other hand, it would be equally misleading to depict the infant SED as a paragon of democracy. As in the case of the trade unions and workplace councils, beneath the surface there were a number of degenerative tendencies which were corroding the democratic and representational functions of the SED and gradually transforming the party into the Stalinist instrument it was later to become. Though the process was still far from complete by the end of 1947, the outward signs of this degeneration were growing all too visible.

One of the most important of these degenerative tendencies was the creeping 'Communisation' of the SED. In the first eighteen months or so after unification, there were numerous localities where relations between former Communists and Social Democrats inside the SED appear to have been fairly harmonious.[56] In some places, however, particularly where the Social Democrats had put up stiff resistance to the unity campaign, SPD functionaries found themselves coming under increasing pressure both from their Communist colleagues and from the Soviet military authorities.[57] In Erfurt, for example, the Communists and the Soviets made life in the SED so unpleasant for former SPD functionaries that they sought refuge in relatively apolitical jobs in industry or the administration.[58] According to Stanislaw Trabalski, the Social Democrats, as a result of this tendency, 'lost more and more influence, precisely because our comrades no longer wanted to work in the party. It was above all the pressure from SMAD and the Communists which worked in this direction, and indeed there lay herein a concealed tactic of the Communists.'[59] Gradually, the trend towards the domination of the SED by former Communists became more and more pronounced, and by April 1947 even Heinrich Hoffmann, who had always been a staunch advocate of unity, was complaining that the SED party apparatus in Thuringia was falling too much under the control of former Communists. The *Kreisvorstand* in Hildburghausen, Hoffmann noted, consisted of fifteen former KPD members and only six former Social Democrats; a state of affairs which openly breached party agreements about 'parity' and which, in Hoffmann's view, necessitated the dissolution of the current executive and the election of a new one according to party statutes.[60] Even worse, in Hoffmann's view, was the fact that 'leading functionaries of our party who belonged to the SPD are being dragged before the security organs of the occupying power and grilled'.[61]

A further tactic used to undermine the position of former SPD members was the admission to the SED of many tens of thousands of new members, who, it was hoped, would dilute the influence of Social Democratic ideas and traditions. By the middle of 1948 the SED had about two million members, some 600,000 of whom were former Communists, 680,000 of whom were former Social Democrats, but over 700,000 of whom had joined only since unification.[62] Amongst these new members were huge numbers of individuals who were either relatively apolitical or who had become politically active out of purely careerist or criminal motives. According to Herbert Prauss, at that time a fanatical young SED member: 'Many joined on the basis of promises and had only the haziest idea of the party and its true goals. A good many wanted only to find a good position and were therefore prepared in part to swim along in the party.'[63]

On account of their political naivety, their lack of experience of the anti-Nazi struggles of the past and, in many cases, their youth, such individuals often proved to be putty in the hands of the Communist ideologues. A very important role was played here by the party schools of the SED, which, from the very beginning, were largely under the control of former Communists.[64] Party schools were usually situated in isolated rural areas or, in towns, were cut off from the outside world by high fences and walls and by very strict rules making it difficult for students to leave the building. Inside the walls, the teachers used tactics which would not be out of place in a religious cult to reshape people's political ideas and world view. Students, for example, would be allowed very little time to themselves and would be strongly pressured to conform to the group. Anyone who spent too much time by himself or herself, or who remained aloof from the social activities of his or her fellow students, would be accused of being a 'bourgeois individualist' who was lacking in party spirit. Any individual who expressed deviant opinions would be publicly humiliated in rituals of 'criticism and self-criticism', during the course of which the other students would be encouraged to talk in minute detail about the past and present failings of the miscreant. These sessions of criticism and self-criticism might last for hours, and be repeated on a daily basis, until the wrongdoer had been thoroughly humiliated, and was prepared to make extravagant public or written confessions of his or her political errors. It is difficult, perhaps, for people who have not been subjected to such methods of thought control to understand how great an impact they can have. However, SED functionaries who subsequently escaped to the west often comment on how effective the party schools were at altering the human personality in order to produce fanatical Stalinists who gave their unconditional loyalty to the SED leadership, and who were prepared to follow the party line without hesitation.[65]

At this stage, the party schools were still relatively lenient compared with what was to come later. It was still possible, within limits, to express one's own ideas in seminars and meetings. Nonetheless, throughout 1946 and 1947, the schools began to churn out an increasing number of young, ambitious apparatchiks who were more disciplined and better educated, but far less independent, than the veterans of the anti-Nazi resistance. Above all, this new generation of functionaries had no real basis in the traditions of the German labour movement, nor any significant roots in the working class. The regime, however, was interested only in their greater reliability and superior technical abilities, and great efforts were made to promote them in the party and state apparatus. Accordingly, in July 1947 the SED leadership instituted a unified card index or 'nomenklatura' of all party members, ostensibly in order to ensure that 'the appropriate comrades will be installed in the right place',[66] but in reality as a means of changing the character and composition of the SED in favour of the neophyte Stalinists.

It is perhaps worth mentioning in this context the significant role which was also played by POWs who had been captured by the Soviets and who, during their period of incarceration, had attended NKFD or 'antifascist' schools. These men were usually regarded as being particularly reliable, partly because their political indoctrination had been carried out under immediate Soviet tutelage and partly because they normally lacked any background in left-wing politics. They were, hence, unlike veteran Communists or Social Democrats, free from any ideological baggage from the past. Between 1945 and 1948 such individuals returned in considerable numbers from the USSR, and, upon their arrival in East Germany, they normally joined the SED and were given responsible posts in the party and state apparatus.[67] From the point of view of the regime, the influx of these former prisoners of war helped to water down the influence of elements who were regarded as unreliable, such as ultra-left Communist sectarians and right-wing Social Democrats. By the veterans of the labour movement, how-ever, the newcomers were often regarded with resentment and contempt. One Social Democrat from the Dresden area, for example, records that, at the time, he regarded the invasion of the SED by former POWs, most of whom were 'dreadfully radical', as an extremely threatening development.[68] Fritz Schenk, meanwhile, recalls in his autobiography the contempt he felt for one of his superiors, who was

> the prototype of a Stalinist: conceited, arrogant, unscrupulous and perfidious to a degree that I have seldom encountered in a person. He could prove no proletarian origins, and had been a zealous Hitler Youth leader and officer cadet. As a POW in the Soviet Union he had been sent to one of the many antifascist schools and repainted from brown to red.[69]

Of all the degenerative processes at work inside the SED, however, none was more destructive than the widening gulf between the party and the population. Upon its foundation in 1946, the SED had enjoyed the support of a large section of the East German working class, which saw the party as a step forward on the road to Socialism. In a referendum in Saxony on 30 June 1946 on the issue of expropriating the enterprises of Nazis and war criminals, 77.7 per cent of those who voted endorsed the regime's policy, thereby demonstrating that the political programme of the SED still pos-sessed a measure of genuine mass working-class support.[70] By the time of the *Land* elections in October 1946 the popularity of the SED had waned somewhat, for even in the traditional labour stronghold of Saxony the SED could only win 49.1 per cent of the vote. Though this was perceived at the time, and subsequently, as a defeat for the SED, the fact that nearly half the population was prepared to vote for it nonetheless demonstrates, in Herman Weber's words, that the party 'still found support in the population'.[71]

Beneath the surface, however, working-class support for the SED was being inexorably eroded as a direct result of the regime's own policies. As working-class members were promoted to positions of responsibility in the party, state and industry, and as the new generation of apparatchiks emerged from the party schools, so the class composition of the SED was gradually but fundamentally altered. From being a party of the industrial proletariat, it was increasingly becoming a party of managers, bureaucrats and officials, who enjoyed all kinds of perks and privileges which were unavailable to the people they were supposed to represent. The party, in opening its doors to all and sundry, had also made it possible for numerous corrupt elements to rise to positions of power, which in turn had a detrimental impact on the SED's popularity. In the Saxon town of Bucha, for example, only 55 per cent of the population voted for the regime's policy of expropriation in the referendum of 30 June 1946. Upon investigation, it appeared that the reason for this was the disgust of the population at the criminal activities of one high-ranking SED functionary.[72] In 1947, police reports from Thuringia repeatedly complained that 'there are still many unclean elements in the administration, whose backs are protected by the Russians, and whose misdemeanours are scarcely punished or not punished at all'.[73]

Even more damaging than the changing composition of the SED was the serious economic situation. In 1946, the workers had been told that the creation of the SED, and the sequestration of large-scale industry, was the best guarantee of a rapid return to prosperity. Many workers seem to have believed this promise.[74] In March 1946, for example, a report from Weimar noted that: 'Morale in the workplaces had been repeatedly described as good, for the workers have recognised that in the sequestered enterprises they are working for themselves.'[75] Through 1946 and 1947, however, not only did the promised economic recovery fail to materialise, but in some respects the situation actually worsened. In Leipzig, for example, industrial production in the first half of 1947 was a full 10 per cent lower than it was during the first half of 1946.[76] In Thuringia, 86.7 per cent of ration coupons for meat were honoured during the first quarter of 1946. By the first quarter of 1947 this figure had fallen to 58 per cent, and in the second quarter of 1947 it fell again to just 45 per cent.[77]

These economic difficulties were not, in fact, entirely the fault of the Soviets and the SED leadership. The whole of Europe was still struggling to recover from the devastation of war, and two exceptionally bad winters in 1947 and 1948 caused massive disruption in the East German economy and led to severe hardship for the population. Another factor in the poor performance of the economy was, of course, reparations, which the Soviets continued to extract and which the SED continued, in public, to justify. Gradually, the working class began to lose patience with the regime which had promised them so much but which had delivered so pitifully little. In

January 1947, for example, a report to the Thuringian interior ministry noted that 'in the circles of the working population considerable ill feeling prevails about the insufficient supply of food', and that many workers were angry because, in their view, the SED had betrayed its electoral promise to improve the lot of the working man.[78] According to another report sent to the same body later on in 1948, the general mood amongst the workers was bad, the attendance at SED meetings was very poor, and the main reason for this was the shortage of food which only really affected the working population.[79] A contemporary report from Halle noted that: 'The question of food is intensively discussed in the workplaces. The workers regard even the recent increases in rations as insufficient in view of this year's record harvest.'[80] When functionaries in Thuringia visited factories to talk about the government's plan for economic reconstruction, the workers were only interested in the immediate question of food and repeatedly interrupted the speakers with cries of 'How does fulfilling the plan benefit us, if it doesn't bring us a better supply of food?'[81] According to the report of an SED informant, sent to the Thuringian interior ministry in 1947:

> I often use the trams, which gives me the opportunity to hear the opinions of all classes of people. I scarcely need to mention that the food situation is discussed at every opportunity. The SED is always and without exception held responsible and, again and again, references are made to the next elections [i.e. as an opportunity to exact revenge].[82]

If, with the passing of time, the bulk of the working class began to lose its faith in the SED, the 'passive majority' of the population, who had disliked the party from the beginning, grew to hate it. For most Germans, the SED was simply the KPD by another name, and, like the KPD before it, the SED was held responsible for all the numerous unpleasantnesses of life under Soviet occupation and, above all, for the behaviour of Red Army troops. As one political report from Gera commented: 'Huge difficulties in all our work are caused again and again by the attitude of the people towards the occupying power, for people throw us and the occupying power into the same pot.'[83] According to a political report from Weimar in January 1947:

> We must point out quite clearly and unambiguously that through the attacks, the disregard of law and justice, the rejection of old Marxist demands and the support of active fascists, an antipathy towards the Russian occupying power is taking hold of wide circles of the Thuringian working class. Since all the petitions of the German authorities, the FDGB and the SED have produced no, or no perceptible, reduction in reported complaints, the FDGB and above all the SED is blamed for these things. Especially the party is ever more closely identified with the measures of the Russian authorities, in no instance attempting to defend against them.[84]

Here again we see an inherent contradiction in the occupation policies of the Soviets. The military government had forced the merger of the Social Democrats and Communists in order to remove the SPD as a vehicle for popular anger against the occupation regime. For the same reason, the SED was subordinated ever more closely to Soviet control and supervision. But destroying the vehicle did not destroy the anger, it merely made it more difficult to channel.

Notes

1 W. Loth, *Stalins ungeliebtes Kind*, Berlin, 1994, chapters 2 & 3.
2 *Leipziger Volkszeitung*, 18.7.46, p. 1.
3 H. Jendretzky, *Neue deutsche Gewerkschaftspolitik*, [East] Berlin, 1948, p. 122.
4 *Leipziger Volkszeitung*, 5.7.46, p. 3.
5 SStA Leipzig, BPA Leipzig, IV/BV/04, Bl. 135.
6 D. Staritz, *Sozialismus in einem halben Land*, [West] Berlin, 1976, p. 97.
7 SAPMO-BArch, DY/30 IV 2/6.02, Nr. 15, Bl. 150.
8 S. Suckut, *Die Betriebsrätebewegung in der sowjetisch besetzten Zone Deutschlands* (doctoral thesis, University of Hanover, 1978), pp. 135–36.
9 See, e.g., W. Leonhard, *Die Revolution entläßt ihre Kinder*, Frankfurt/M, 1962, pp. 408–09.
10 Quoted in Staritz (n. 6 above), pp. 97–98.
11 G. Schaffer, *Russian Zone*, London, 1947, p. 84.
12 ThHStA Weimar, BdM, Bl. 239.
13 *Leipziger Volkszeitung*, 18.7.46, p. 1.
14 Stadtarchiv Halle, BAdSt Halle, 10, Bl. 029/R22.
15 SAPMO-BArch, DY/30 IV 2/6.02, Nr. 18, Bl. 189.
16 SAPMO-BArch, DY/30 IV 2/6.02, Nr. 52, Bl. 171–71.
17 SAPMO-BArch, DY/30 IV 2/6.02, Nr. 18, Bl. 189.
18 Ibid., Bl.185-86 & letter from Landesvorstand to the Zentralsekretariat, 15.1.47.
19 See, e.g., SAPMO-BArch, DY/30 IV 2/6.02, Nr. 52.
20 ThHStA Weimar, MdI, 307, Bl.51-53. For similar examples, see G. Pritchard, *German Workers under Soviet Occupation* (doctoral thesis, University of Wales, 1997), p. 266, n. 83.
21 B. Sarel, *Arbeiter gegen den 'Kommunismus'*, Munich, 1975, pp. 21–22.
22 The 'accord system' involved the setting of targets for both individual workers or groups of workers and for whole enterprises. The pay which workers received would vary according to whether or not their targets had been fulfilled.
23 SStA Leipzig, BPA Leipzig, I/3/28, Bl. 3.
24 SStA Leipzig, BPA Leipzig, IV/BV/01, 'Bezirksvorstandssitzung der SED Leipzig', 29.5.46, Bl. 83.
25 SAPMO-BArch, DY/30 IV 2/6.02, Nr. 4, Bl. 288.
26 See, e.g., SStA Leipzig, BPA Leipzig, I/3/13, Bl. 305–25.
27 W. Ulbricht, *Gewerkschaften und Zweijahresplan*, [East] Berlin, 1948, pp. 67–68.
28 SAPMO-BArch, DY/30 IV 2/6.02, Nr. 4, Bl. 288.

29   SStA Leipzig, BPA Leipzig, I/3/13, 'Protokoll zur Sitzung in Böhlen', 25.3.46, Bl. 322.

30   ThHStA Weimar, BPA Erfurt, IV/L/2/1-008/1, 'Referat des Genossen Ulbricht am 8.10.47', Bl. 3.

31   ThHStA Weimar, BPA Erfurt, I/1-002, 'Protokoll der erweiterten Bezirksleitungs-Sitzung', 18.8.45, Bl. 3.

32   SStA Leipzig, BPA Leipzig, IV/BV/01, 'Bezirksvorstandssitzung der SED Leipzig', 29.5.46, Bl. 67.

33   SStA Leipzig, BPA Leipzig, IV/BV/04, 'Protokoll zur Sekretariatssitzung', 7.10.46.

34   SStA Leipzig, KV Leipzig, 382, Bl. 4.

35   Sarel (n. 21 above), pp. 34–35.

36   SStA Leipzig, KV Leipzig, 370, Bl. 3, 6, 12–14, 22–23.

37   G. Sandford, *From Hitler to Ulbricht*, Princeton, N.J., 1983, pp. 163–64.

38   Sarel (n. 21 above), pp. 33–34.

39   See, e.g., ThHStA Weimar, MdI, 270, Bl. 110.

40   Sarel (n. 21 above), p. 23.

41   Leonhard (n. 9 above), pp. 408–09.

42   B. Bouvier & H. Schulz, '*...die SPD aber aufgehört hat zu existieren*', Bonn, 1991, p. 284.

43   F. Schenk, *Im Vorzimmer der Diktatur*, Cologne & [West] Berlin, 1962, pp. 16–17.

44   For examples, see Pritchard (n. 20 above), p. 267, n. 110.

45   ThHStA Weimar, BdM, Bl. 146–52.

46   Loth (n. 1 above), pp. 79–81.

47   ThHStA Weimar, BPA Erfurt, IV/L/2/3-031, 'Sekretariatssitzungen' of 15.4.47, 30.4.47 and 12.5.47.

48   ThHStA Weimar, BPA Erfurt, IV/L/2/3-031, 'Sekretariatssitzung', 4.9.47.

49   For examples, see Pritchard (n. 20 above), p. 267, n. 115.

50   N. Naimark, *The Russians in Germany*, Cambridge, MA., 1995, pp. 88–89.

51   ThHStA Weimar, BdM, 265, Bl. 15.

52   For examples, see Pritchard (n. 20 above), p. 268, n. 118.

53   See, e.g.: ThHStA Weimar, BPA Erfurt, 'Sekretariatssitzungen' of 16.2.47, 1.4.47, 15.4.47, 30.4.47, 5.6.47, 23.7.47, 5.8.47 and 17.11.47; SAPMO-BArch, DY/30 IV 2/6.02, Nr. 4, Bl. 266–69; SAPMO-BArch, DY/30 IV 2/6.02, Nr. 15, Bl. 29.

54   ThHStA Weimar, MdI, 955, Bl. 36.

55   SAPMO-BArch, DY/30 IV 2/6.02, Nr. 52, Bl. 1, 9–10, 15, 17–19 & 22–25..

56   For examples, see Pritchard (n. 20 above), p. 268, n. 121.

57   A. Malycha, *Partei von Stalins Gnaden?*, Berlin, 1996, pp. 165–72.

58   SAPMO-BArch, NY4076/157, Bl. 5.

59   Bouvier & Schulz (n. 42 above), pp. 218, 222 & 247.

60   ThHStA Weimar, BPA Erfurt, IV/L/2/3-031, 'Sekretariatssitzung', 15.4.47.

61   ThHStA Weimar, BPA Erfurt, IV/L/2/3-031, 'Sekretariatssitzung', 30.4.47.

62   H. Weber, *Geschichte der DDR*, 3rd edition, Munich, 1989, p. 133.

63   H. Prauss, *Doch es war nicht die Wahrheit*, [West] Berlin, 1960, p. 219.

64   Bouvier & Schulz (n. 42 above), p. 219.

65 See, e.g.: Prauss (n. 63 above), pp. 37–46; Schenk (n. 43 above), pp. 55–60; Leonhard (n. 9 above), pp. 181–89.
66 ThHStA Weimar, BPA Erfurt, AIV/2/5-141, Bl. 31.
67 For examples, see Pritchard (n. 20 above), p. 269, n. 132.
68 Bouvier & Schulz (n. 42 above), p. 267.
69 Schenk (n. 43 above), p. 36.
70 Sandford (n. 37 above), pp. 20–17.
71 Weber (n. 62 above), p. 142.
72 SStA Leipzig, BPA Leipzig, IV/BV/04, Bl. 63.
73 ThHStA Weimar, MdI, 141, Bl. 18.
74 See, e.g.: SStA Leipzig, BPA Leipzig, II/2/02, report from the SPD in Leipzig to the Soviet military commander, 24.1.46; ThHStA Weimar, MdI, 954, Bl. 17.
75 SAPMO-BArch, DY/30 IV 2/6.02, Nr. 18, Bl. 33–35.
76 G. Krüger, 'Auf dem Wege zur sozialistischen Großstadt', in K. Czok et al., *Leipzig: Geschichte der Stadt in Wort und Bild*, [East] Berlin, 1978, p. 99.
77 ThHStA Weimar, BPA Erfurt, IV/L/2/3-031, 'Sekretariatssitzung', 23.7.47.
78 ThHStA Weimar, MdI, 955, Bl. 9.
79 ThHStA Weimar, MdI, 142, Bl. 64.
80 SAPMO-BArch, DY/30 IV 2/6.02, Nr. 4, Bl. 263.
81 Ibid., Bl. 264.
82 ThHStA Weimar, MdI, 141, Bl. 31.
83 Ibid., Bl. 40.
84 SAPMO-BArch, DY/30 IV 2/6.02, Nr. 18, Bl. 189.

7

The Stalinisation
of the SED

Soviet occupation policy in East Germany was always determined primarily, though by no means entirely, by the foreign policy interests of the USSR. It followed, therefore, that when Soviet foreign policy entered a dramatic new phase of development in the period 1947 to 1948, this had an enormous influence on occupation policy and hence on Soviet policy towards the German labour movement. Underlying these changes were two major developments in international relations, namely, the quarrel between Tito and Stalin and the outbreak of the Cold War.

Before these two developments, the official line emanating from Moscow was that every country must follow its own, national road to Socialism, and that no attempt would be made to impose the Soviet political system on the nations which had fallen into the Soviet sphere of influence. On the basis of this moderate ideological orientation, a measure of genuine political diversity had been tolerated in Poland, Hungary, Czechoslovakia and East Germany. After the events of 1947 and 1948, however, Stalin evidently decided that the time had come to haul the line back in and to lock the countries of Eastern Europe more firmly into orbit around the USSR. From Stalin's point of view, there were, in fact, a number of very good reasons why he should have wanted to do this, for, from 1948 onwards, the vigorous economic revival in western Europe led to much envy amongst the more impoverished nations of the East. In particular, the populations of Eastern Europe coveted the American money which, from the beginning of 1948, was becoming available to their western neighbours. In East Germany, there were numerous reports of discussions amongst the population along the lines of: 'The Americans ensure that the population in West Germany has enough to eat, which is not the case in our [zone].'[1] In August 1947, the leadership of the SED appealed in vain to Stalin for some material assistance with which to counter the impact which the Marshall

Plan was having on public opinion in East Germany, for, according to the SED leaders: 'The promised dollar aid has a very strong impact on the working masses, connected with the hope that it will bring an end to the daily misery of the masses.'[2]

Just as Marshall Aid exerted a powerful influence on the attitudes of the populations of the countries of Eastern Europe, so there were many Communists and Socialists in Eastern Europe who felt a great deal of sympathy for the Yugoslav experiment. When, towards the end of 1947, Tito had visited Bulgaria, Hungary and Romania, he had been given an ecstatic reception in all three countries.[3] Even in distant East Germany, many SED members looked favourably on Yugoslavia as an alternative model of Socialist development, which, in their eyes, still possessed the vigour, the freshness and the idealism which were so sadly lacking in orthodox Stalinism. Fritz Schenk, a leading SED apparatchik who subsequently fled to West Germany, reports that within the party apparatus there were numerous self-conscious anti-Stalinists whose primary goal was the 'liberation of the satellite states from Soviet tutelage' and 'the ordering of internal relations along the lines of what has happened in Yugoslavia since 1948'.[4] According to Wolfgang Leonhard, who himself eventually defected to Belgrade, such pro-Yugoslav tendencies were to be found even amongst the leading ranks of the SED.[5]

In order to ensure that the satellite states of Eastern Europe were led astray neither by the lure of American gold nor by the siren voice of Yugoslav idealism, Stalin initiated a policy of ruthless Sovietisation. Thenceforth, all talk of national roads to Socialism would be regarded as aberrant, and the Soviet Union was to be held up as the sole legitimate model of Socialist development. Accordingly, all the satellite states were expected to introduce Soviet economic and political practices, regardless of the national peculiarities which had hitherto served as a pretext for not imposing a Soviet system. Stalin himself was thenceforth to be presented as the great leader and hero, the father and teacher of all the working peoples of the world. Soviet-style terror was also introduced, and between 1948 and 1953 a wave of purges in Eastern Europe led to the imprisonment, torture or execution of many thousands of people, the vast majority of whom were entirely innocent of the charges of which they stood accused.[6]

East Germany, no less than the other satellite countries of Eastern Europe, underwent this process, though there is some debate about whether the Stalinisation of the Soviet zone was driven by Stalin himself, or by hard-line fanatics such as Ulbricht and Tulpanov in the SED and in SMAD respectively, who, it has been suggested, seized the opportunity created by the general political climate to push forward their own political agenda. Whoever the main architect of the Stalinisation of East Germany actually was, by the time of Stalin's death in March 1953 the metamorphosis was largely completed.

Towards a party of a new type

The most obvious manifestation of the Stalinisation of the SED was the official abandonment of the doctrine of the 'German road to Socialism' in September 1948. In the place of slogans about parliamentary democracy and the creation in Germany of a *Rechtsstaat* (a state in which the behaviour of the authorities is governed by established rules and laws), ever-increasing stress was placed on the inevitability of the class struggle, and on the need for vigilance and ruthless counter-measures against the class enemies, spies and saboteurs who, the authorities claimed, were to be found on every side. During the first two years or so of occupation, both SMAD and the civilian authorities had continually sought to justify their policies in terms of the struggle against Nazism, its roots and its legacy. After 1948, however, more and more of the rhetoric of the regime focused on a new set of enemies: the 'reactionary' Adenauer, the 'traitor' Schumacher, the 'renegade' Tito and, behind them all, pulling all the strings, the 'American imperialists', whose cruelty 'throws the cruelty of the German fascists deep into the shade'. In order to resist the machinations of these new enemies, the SED – the party leadership argued – would have to be ruthless, united and insulated from contact with the West.[7]

As official party policy became increasingly hostile to the West, so more and more stress was laid on the necessity of learning from the 'greatest ally and friend' of the German working class, the Soviet Union. As one party slogan put it: 'Learning from the Soviet Union means learning victory!'[8] Already by 1947 the party leadership was making it clear that henceforth a positive attitude to the USSR was a prerequisite of party membership.[9] In June 1947, the authorities founded the so-called 'Society for the study of the culture of the Soviet Union' (renamed 'Society for German–Soviet Friendship' or DSF in 1949), the purpose of which was to promote knowledge of the USSR and friendship towards its peoples. Membership of the DSF soon became a badge of loyalty to the USSR, and SED members who refused to join were likely to find themselves in hot water.

One year later, in June 1948, the SED made a further lurch in the direction of Stalinisation when the party leadership officially introduced the policy of transforming the SED into a 'party of a new type'. According to Ulbricht, the primary distinguishing feature of such a party was its frank recognition that the Communist Party of the Soviet Union (CPSU) provided a model for the working class in every country of the world, including Germany.[10] In order to press home this message, SED functionaries were put under even greater pressure to attend courses at party schools,[11] at which the standard and obligatory fare would be Stalin's 'classic' works such as the *Foundations of Leninism* and the *History of the CPSU (Short Course)*.[12] The rank-and-file members of the SED, meanwhile, were continually reminded 'what a huge contribution Stalin's work has made to the enrichment of Marxist–Leninist theory', and Stalin's writings were systematically promoted amongst the membership.[13]

As part and parcel of the drive to turn the SED into a 'party of a new type', a whole series of changes were made to the internal structure and constitution of the party to bring it more into line with its Soviet counterpart. At the first party congress of the SED in January 1949, the principle of parity, according to which responsible positions in the SED were divided equally amongst former Communists and Social Democrats, was abolished. As in the Soviet Union, a one-year period of candidacy was introduced, during which the political reliability of potential recruits could be monitored and verified. A Soviet-style politburo was established, and, above all, the SED officially introduced the doctrine of 'democratic centralism'.[14] In June 1950, even more of the procedures and trappings of the CPSU were introduced into the SED after the return of an official delegation which had travelled to Moscow to study how the 'party of Lenin exercised its leading role in the Soviet Union'.[15]

There was considerable discontent inside the SED at the blanket imposition of Soviet practices and political culture, for the older traditions which were being displaced had deep roots in the history of the German labour movement. Moreover, many of the veterans who still cleaved to those traditions were men and women of conviction who had been hardened by long years of struggle and sacrifice. However, the Soviets and the SED leadership had at their disposal a whole armoury of weapons with which to break any real or potential resistance, not the least amongst which was terror. Thus, as in the other satellite states, a whole number of leading party functionaries were arrested and imprisoned as part of the so-called Slansky–Rajk conspiracy, an alleged American plot which supposedly involved thousands of veteran Communists throughout Eastern Europe.[16] In East Germany, the most notable victim was Paul Merker, a member of the SED politburo who had allegedly been recruited by the American secret services during his wartime exile in Mexico.[17]

After Merker had been tried and convicted of treason in the autumn of 1950, the SED leadership, in true Stalinist style, decreed that all party members should attend special meetings to discuss the 'lessons' of the Merker affair. Merker, it was claimed, had been seduced by the American secret service because he had possessed insufficient trust in the party, because he had underestimated the threat posed by American imperialism and, above all, because he had been lacking in faith in the Soviet Union and its great leader, Joseph Stalin. The 'lessons' to be drawn from the Merker case were therefore that all SED members must place their trust in the party, must be ceaselessly on the look-out for the traitors, agents and saboteurs in their midst and must give their unconditional loyalty to the USSR. According to notes sent out by the party leadership for the benefit of functionaries speaking on the Merker affair at special meetings: 'The touchstone for every member and functionary is their attitude to the Soviet Union. Unshakeable faith in the Soviet Union and unconditional loyalty to Stalin are the best protection against falling victim to the imperialists.'[18]

An important aspect of this process of Stalinisation was the greater degree to which the authorities began to spy on people and gather 'intelligence' about them. Perhaps rather surprisingly, nobody was kept under closer scrutiny than members of the SED itself. In the East German archives, for example, one can find vast numbers of private letters, written by party members, which were either intercepted by the authorities, or handed over to the authorities by their recipients. The authorities also encouraged people to inform on their friends and relations, arguing that a willingness to supply incriminating information on one's associates was a sign of 'ideological consciousness' and 'vigilance'.[19] On all too many occasions, SED members succumbed to the blandishments of the party leadership, and colleague informed upon colleague, brother upon brother, friend upon friend. What is striking about many of these letters of denunciation, particularly when the person being informed upon was a workmate or neighbour of the informant, is the petty and spiteful nature of the denunciations. The drive to root out the enemies of the SED, like all witch hunts, tended to bring out the worst in people. It gave ambitious people an incentive to inform on their superiors. Individuals prone to exaggerated suspicions were given license to see treason and plot all around them. Above all, petty, spiteful and malicious people were able to indulge their vendettas and wreak vengeance on those who had crossed them.

It is here, perhaps, that we see the most telling and tragic difference between the early years of occupation and the period of Stalinisation which began in 1947. In 1945, the Soviets and the KPD leadership had tried to mobilise people by appealing to their repugnance against Nazism and their desire to build a better and fairer world. To some degree, the authorities were indeed able to harness the genuine idealism and enthusiasm of the anti-Nazi section of the population. After 1947, by contrast, it was not so much people's idealism that the authorities manipulated, but their petty ambitions, their jealousies and their narrow prejudices.

This, in turn, had a devastating effect on party life, for the solidarity of comrades was gradually eroded, to be replaced by what Fritz Schenk has referred to as 'the icy silence, the mistrust of everybody'.[20] Equally, the initiative of rank-and-file members and functionaries was steadily undermined by the debilitating fear of saying or doing anything which might incur the wrath of the authorities. As one SED functionary in Erfurt complained, 'many comrades are of the opinion that one should hold one's tongue, otherwise one gets hits on the head. For this reason, although they do have something to say, they prefer to say nothing.'[21] As a result, there was a very strong tendency throughout the later 1940s and early 1950s for SED members to become more and more passive, and for the local groups and factory cells of the SED to become increasingly inert and lifeless. Indeed, so powerful was this trend that even the SED leaders had to acknowledge its existence, though they invariably blamed it not on their own policies but on the insufficient schooling of the membership, and on the 'bureaucratic methods' of lower-ranking functionaries and officials.[22]

Examples of this phenomenon are to be found in great abundance. In November 1948, for instance, the SED *Kreisvorstand* in Leipzig complained that the typical member 'too often waits for instructions and circulars, without reacting speedily when it is necessary'.[23] It apparently never occurred to the bigwigs in the Leipzig leadership that if one punishes or humiliates rank-and-file members and functionaries for the slightest deviation from the party line, it is only to be expected that they will become hesitant and cautious. A report from the Abus-Maschinenbau factory in Nordhausen asserted that the factory cell was very inactive, and that many SED members 'have recently become much less active, perform no party work, and do not concern themselves with their political duties'.[24] At the 'Metall- und Federnfabrik' in St. Egidien, a report of February 1953 noted that, whilst the political activity of the SED factory cell had been relatively good until 1950, it had in the meantime virtually ground to a halt. According to the report, political schooling was 'regarded by the majority of comrades as a "necessary evil", and is accordingly pursued superficially and almost without interest'.[25] At the Martin-Hoop coal mine, it was reported in 1953 that party decisions were now only being implemented by a handful of full-time functionaries, that attendance at party meetings was low and unenthusiastic, and that, in general, the life of the factory cell was withering on the vine.[26]

The party control commissions

Eventually, the scrutiny of the membership of the SED for any sign of ideological weakness or deviance was given organised and formal expression with the creation, in September 1948, of the 'Party Control Commissions' (PKKs), the purpose of which was to root out the heretics and doubting Thomases. Organised hierarchically, at the apex of the hierarchy of control commissions was the so-called 'Central Party Control Commission (ZPKK) in Berlin, which, under the chairmanship of Hermann Matern, oversaw and guided the work of the five '*Land* Party Control Commissions' (LPKKs). At the base of the structure were the various '*Kreis* (Area) Party Control Commissions' (KPKKs) which were responsible for the donkey-work of sifting through the tens of thousands of rank-and-file members and low-ranking functionaries. Staffing the PKKs were 30,000 trained inquisitors, most of whom were veteran Communists or younger apparatchiks who had recently emerged from the party schools.[27]

Often, SED members were brought to the attention of the PKKs either because they had been reported for making 'anti-party' comments or because they had allegedly been engaged in activities which were in some way damaging to the party. Most commonly, however, individuals fell under suspicion, not so much because of anything they had said or done, but because they belonged to a category which was considered to be particularly susceptible to heresy and treason. SED members who had spent time in the West, either as POWs or as refugees from Hitler, were especially suspect, for one of the most important 'lessons' of the Slansky–Rajk affair was that all such comrades had been exposed to negative political influences during their time in the West, and many had been recruited by the British or American secret services.[28] Accordingly, the ZPKK compiled long lists of names of SED members who had been in the West, which were duly sent out to the party commissions so that the named individuals could be brought before tribunals.[29] Even more suspect were SED members who had been POWs in Yugoslavia, for a number of these had been converted to Communism during their stay with the partisans, and had subsequently maintained the link with Yugoslavia by making return visits to the country or subscribing to Yugoslav party newspapers and journals.[30] After the break with Belgrade in June 1948, the authorities strongly suspected, probably correctly, that many of the SED members who had links with Yugoslavia were far from convinced by the regime's hysterical anti-Yugoslav propaganda.

In accordance with the claim of the SED leadership 'that Anglo-American imperialism leaves no stone unturned in its efforts to penetrate the party of the working class in order to subvert it and deflect it from its path',[31] the PKKs soon began to harbour suspicions against anybody who had any contact whatsoever with the West which had not been officially sanctioned by the party.[32] Given the fact that many thousands of SED members had friends or relatives living in the western zones of occupation, this widened the scope of the PKKs' activities considerably. Particularly suspect were people such as Esperantists, who frequently came into contact with foreigners, and were hence considered to be likely candidates for recruitment by the American or British secret services.[33] Jewish members, meanwhile, were seen as potential Zionists, and were also subjected to particularly intense scrutiny.[34] Even former inmates of concentration camps were not above suspicion, for many of these, during their incarceration, had struck up friendships with fellow inmates from western European countries. The fact that these links were frequently maintained once the war was over again aroused the attention of the PKKs, for anybody who received private mail from the West was, in their ever suspicious eyes, a potential weak link through which foreign influences could penetrate and infect the SED.[35]

The PKKs compiled substantial dossiers, which often catalogued in painstaking detail the political and personal histories of those they suspected. Colleagues and party comrades were asked to provide detailed reports on the activities and views of the individuals under investigation. The individuals themselves were required to fill out lengthy questionnaires, in which they had to answer vast numbers of questions, not just about themselves, but also about their parents, siblings, spouses and children. Most importantly, members were summoned to appear before PKK tribunals, where they would be interrogated about their past, their political knowledge, their views and their activities. Did they, for example, have any contact with foreigners? What did they think about the Marshall Plan? What was their attitude to the drive to increase production? Did they regularly attend party meetings and pay their subscriptions? Were they members of the DSF? Most importantly of all – a question to which the inquisitors returned time and time again – what was their attitude towards the USSR and towards Stalin?

The archives of the PKKs, bulging with confiscated correspondence, letters of denunciation and painstaking reports, bear witness to the increasing authoritarianism of the East German regime in the later 1940s and early 1950s, but they also furnish the historian with an extremely rich source of evidence. With the aid of this mass of previously inaccessible information, it is possible for the historian to take a fresh look at the whole process of the Stalinisation of East Germany. Before 1989, the story of how and why the Soviets and the SED leadership went about Stalinising the SED was reasonably well known in the West, even if many of the finer details remained obscure. What western scholars did not know, however, was how these developments were regarded by ordinary members and lower-ranking functionaries of the SED. This lacuna, however, tended to cause distortions in the way in which the process of Stalinisation was perceived. Knowing little about what had gone on at the base of the East German labour movement, western historians tended to describe the process of Stalinisation in East Germany purely in terms of Soviet foreign policy. Though it would of course be foolhardy to deny that Soviet foreign policy was indeed the primary determinant of Soviet occupation policy, it would be equally wrong to overlook the significance of developments at the base of the East German labour movement.

For, at the very heart of the process of Stalinisation in East Germany, there was an interaction between the policies being imposed from above, and the response to those policies on the part of ordinary trade unionists, SED members and functionaries. For example, there had from the outset been numerous deviant opinions and festering grievances amongst the SED membership, but before 1947 these had not attracted much attention, for the simple reason that nobody had been looking for them. As the regime became more vigilant, however, so the members were subjected to ever closer scrutiny, which in turn revealed all the aberrant attitudes and grievances which until then had remained hidden beneath the surface. Similarly, as the regime became more dogmatic and intolerant, so the boundaries of what was permissible became ever more narrow, which in turn meant that many SED members suddenly found themselves being denounced for expressing ideas which had previously been tolerated. Thus, the more intolerant and vigilant the regime became, the more heresy it discovered, which in turn pushed the authorities into becoming yet more narrow-minded and suspicious. Eventually, in October 1950, this degenerative process culminated in the decision that every single member of the SED, regardless of his or her background, would have to appear before the PKKs in order to be interrogated.[36]

Moreover, the very methods by which the authorities sought to address the problem of ideological deviance tended to make things even worse. Many SED members understandably resented being spied on, bullied and intimidated, and, as a result, their oppositional sentiments were intensified. By attempting to stamp out heresy, the regime only succeeded in creating the bitterness and resentment of official policy in which heretical ideas and opinions could thrive. The more tightly the leadership sought to control its members, the wider the gulf became between the rank-and-file of the party and the party elite. This vicious cycle reached its violent denouement in the summer and autumn of 1953, when many thousands of SED members and functionaries either participated in the workers' uprising of 17 June or, in the aftermath of the bloody suppression of the Uprising, were expelled from the party or left it in disgust.

To understand these processes fully, it is not enough to view them purely 'from above', that is, in terms of the grand strategies and purposes of the Soviets and the SED leadership. We must also lift off the lid of the SED, in order to examine the thoughts, feelings and political behaviour of ordinary party members and functionaries. What such an exercise reveals is that, at the base of the SED in the late 1940s and early 1950s, there were very large numbers of discontented or deviant individuals, whose assorted crimes, misdemeanours and heresies spurred the regime to become ever more inflexible and intolerant.

Rogues, renegades and heretics

The most common reason why people fell foul of the PKKs was not that they had deep-seated political disagreements with the regime and its policies, but that they were deemed to be apathetic, corrupt or immoral. Since 1946, thousands of people had joined the SED for purely careerist reasons, or had joined out of genuine conviction but had subsequently become disillusioned and had dropped out of political activity. Moreover, many of the people who had streamed into the SED in the first two years of its existence had a very low level of political knowledge and understanding. As the party apparatus had mushroomed, so many of these relatively apolitical people had found themselves being promoted to positions of considerable responsibility. At the Blechwalzwerk in Olbernhau, which employed 600 people and had a

'Workplace Party Organisation' (BPO) of 172 people, one of the members of the BPO leadership, despite her highly responsible position, was nonetheless a committed Christian. Indeed, so religious was she that, when her child fell suddenly ill, she interpreted this as a punishment from God for having recently sung the Internationale at an SED conference in Leipzig! At the next conference, she had apparently remained silent.[37] The fact that the SED, even at the higher levels of the party organisation, was riddled with such people was, in a self-styled 'party of a new type', clearly anomalous. The SED leadership recognised this, and internal party bulletins and circulars continually noted that the biggest single obstacle to the SED becoming a party of a new type was 'the inadequate ideological clarity in the ranks of the membership'.[38]

One of the most important functions of the PKKs was thus to identify and attempt to remedy these weaknesses. Often, if the individuals identified as being ideologically weak were nonetheless deemed to be 'true to the party' and 'class conscious', no disciplinary action would be taken against them; they would simply be packed off to a party school or given Marxist literature to read, and their party cells or BPOs would be instructed to monitor and report on their future progress. In many instances, however, the PKKs came to the conclusion that the individuals concerned had joined the party for entirely cynical reasons, and they were expelled.

The majority of the people who had flooded into the SED were simply politically ignorant. Numerous corrupt elements, however, had also penetrated the party, seeking to exploit the opportunities for graft which party membership presented. In the coal industry, for example, there were numerous instances of SED officials using cars and petrol for their own private purposes, filing bogus expense claims, making illegal trips to the West to stock up on black-market goods, and selling the property of their enterprises for their own profit.[39] Such flagrant corruption tended to cause political complications in terms of the relationship between the party and the general population, for the nefarious activities of SED officials only served to increase people's alienation from the party still further. The PKKs tried hard to weed out such individuals, and many thousands were indeed expelled on account of their corrupt or illegal activities. In the last six months of 1947 alone, some 2,500 SED members were expelled from the party because of their involvement in crime.[40]

There was also a considerable problem inside the SED with loose moral standards which, in a 'party of a new type', were considered to be inappropriate, particularly as the 'immoral' behaviour of SED officials often had an even more damaging impact on public opinion than corruption. In the Martin-Hoop coal mine near Zwickau, for example, an SED member who was also a leading functionary of the FDGB was a notorious drunkard and womaniser who, on account of his nocturnal activities, was very often absent from work. This, according to one report, caused much head-shaking amongst the miners and 'does not contribute to strengthening [the workers'] faith in the trade union]'.[41] In the small village of Großdalzig near Leipzig, the local SED group complained in August 1948 that J.R., the SED *Bürgermeister*, had started an affair with a female comrade whose husband had until recently been incarcerated in a POW camp. Even after the return of the husband, the affair was 'continued despite all our admonitions. This circumstance has gradually become an object of village gossip and the population finds it most amusing. The children of the woman comrade talk about it at school etc. In our opinion, Comrade J.R. is undermining the reputation of the party and can no longer be tolerated.'[42]

The PKKs took the opportunity to relieve many such individuals of their responsibilities and either issued them with a reprimand or expelled them from the party. Others were expelled for sins such as incest, wife-beating and child abuse.[43] Whilst one feels little sympathy for such individuals, who incurred the wrath of the PKKs because they had been involved in genuinely immoral activities, there were also many cases where people were victimised simply because they offended against the narrow prejudices of the PKK inquisitors. In 1952, for example, the KPKK in Chemnitz expelled one S.P., even though, by the KPKK's own admission, S.P. 'had developed since 1945 in a very positive fashion'. Yet, in spite of his excellent political development, S.P. was revealed to be a homosexual, which not only was considered to be a violation of party discipline, but was also deemed to be damaging to the reputation and 'cleanliness' of the party.[44]

If one major category in the demonology of the PKKs was made up of individuals who were deemed to be culpable of the relatively apolitical sins of indifference, corruption or sexual immorality, a second major category consisted of party members who were guilty of the undeniably political crime of being hostile to the Soviet Union. In many cases, the grievances which members harboured against the USSR dated back to 1945 or even before, but only after 1947, when the authorities began to search for such deviant attitudes, did the anti-Soviet views of many SED members become a significant problem. For the most part, particularly amongst the newer and less politically developed members, the grievances aired about the Soviet Union were not so different to those of the population as a whole. The behaviour of Red Army troops, for instance, was often cited by SED members as a reason for refusing to join the DSF. Amongst the SED members at a large textiles factory in Plauen, only 6.5 per cent had joined the DSF by August 1949, for the factory was situated next door to a Red Army barracks, and the mainly female workforce was consequently subjected to a good deal of harassment as they walked to and from work.[45] Reparations and the economic exploitation of the Soviet zone continued to be a festering sore for many individuals, such as the SED member from Plauen who was brought before the KPKK for having described the SAGs as an 'an instrument with the help of which we are exploited by the Soviet Union'.[46] Similarly, the border changes imposed by the Soviet Union continued to cause anger amongst many SED members. At a meeting in Erfurt, for example, a party member condemned the Oder–Neisse border, and 'declared that on this question we should not abide by the Potsdam agreements'.[47]

Often, it was the process of Sovietisation itself, and the endless trumpeting of the superiority of Soviet politics, culture and industry, which caused the hackles of SED members to rise. One veteran Communist from Altenburg, when hauled before a PKK tribunal and questioned about his attitude to the USSR, declared that Karl Marx had called upon proletarians of all nations to unite, and that it was therefore un-Marxist to place one particular nation on a pedestal.[48] In Schönfeld, F.N., who was a veteran Social Democrat and a victim of Nazism, and who had consequently been appointed as the manager of a VEB, found himself in difficulties after having argued at a party meeting against the introduction of Soviet-style economic practices such as the Hennecke movement and work norms. Moreover, F.N. had argued at the meeting 'that there is no need to imitate the Russians in everything, for the German worker has always been the best'. Significantly, when F.N. was subsequently brought before a PKK tribunal, he refused to retract his comments, but instead reminded his inquisitors of the persecution he had suffered under the Nazis. With regard to the introduction of Soviet-style economic practices, F.N. maintained his assertion that it was ridiculous to try and introduce work norms into his factory, since the machines were too old and kept breaking down.[49]

Amongst veteran Social Democrats and former members of the various splinter parties, meanwhile, there were often deeply rooted reservations about the whole political system and historical development of the USSR. In Freiberg, a seventy-seven-year-old veteran Social Democrat refused to become a member of the DSF on the grounds that he could not, in all conscience, subscribe to the argument that the Soviet Union was a 'peace-loving' and 'anti-imperialist' power, for had not the USSR been guilty of 'red imperialism' by invading Georgia in 1922 and Poland and Finland in 1939?[50] In Erfurt, a veteran syndicalist found himself in hot water after a schooling session at which the Stalinist tract the *History of the CPSU (Short Course)* had been discussed. During the course of the session, the syndicalist had expressed doubts as to whether 'the development of the Soviet Union is moving forwards', and had advised his fellow students not to believe everything they read about the marvellous achievements of the Soviet Union.[51]

The pervasive nature of such anti-Soviet views amongst SED members can be judged by the large numbers who refused to join the DSF. Since party members were placed under great pressure to join the DSF, it must be concluded that those who failed to do so were not merely lazy or indifferent, but had made the conscious decision not to join, even though this might well result in unpleasant consequences. At the VEB Abus-Maschinenbau in Nordhausen, for example, only 140 out of 511 SED members (27 per cent) had joined the DSF by November 1950.[52] In Grimma, only 48 per cent of SED members had enrolled in the DSF by December 1952, and the story was broadly similar in neighbouring areas.[53] Even as late as August 1953, only 40 per cent of the SED members at the Martin-Hoop coal mine had enrolled in the DSF.[54]

Closely related to this hostility towards the Soviet Union was another form of ideological deviance which was frequently identified by the control commissions, namely, 'reconciliationism' (*Versöhnlertum*). This catch-all label was applied by the PKKs to the many party members who, whilst they might or might not be antagonistic towards the Soviet Union itself, were certainly opposed to the Sovietisation of their party and their country. The significance of the word 'reconciliationism' was that, in the eyes of the authorities, such elements in the SED did not recognise or understand that enemies were all around, and that only through the greatest possible discipline, watchfulness and unity could the party defend itself against its numerous foes. There was thus much discontent in the ranks of the SED at the rigid and stifling ideological conformity now being demanded of party members, and at the use of spies and informants to enforce conformity. In Olbernhau, a member of the *Kreisleitung* complained to the local KPKK 'that one can no longer speak one's mind when one has a different opinion'.[55] In a letter to the regional leadership (*Landesleitung*) of the SED in Leipzig, a veteran of the labour movement complained that, at the party schools, men and women who had given their lives to Socialism often found themselves 'accused of just about every criminal tendency', such as Trotskyism, Bukharinism and opportunism. Such severe and unwarranted criticisms, far from helping comrades, threw them into 'deepest mental shock'.[56] At the Konsumgenossenschaft in Arnstadt, there were stormy scenes at a meeting of the SED factory cell when an elderly comrade began to threaten and abuse a younger SED member who had been passing information on deviant opinions in the group to the local *Kreisleitung*.[57] At the VEB 'Lowa' in Altenburg, a veteran Communist and leading trade union functionary was expelled from the SED in 1953 for having opposed the use of informants in his factory. According to the KPKK judgement on the case: 'His hostility to the party further manifests itself in the fact that he threatened and denounced as informers those comrades who had contributed to the unmasking of enemy elements in the workplace.'[58]

A particularly revealing insight into the thinking of many SED members at this time is furnished by the KPKK dossier on L.M., a young paediatrician from Freiberg who had found himself in difficulties, amongst other things for having criticised the shortage of western medicines for sick children. When he was brought before a tribunal of the Freiberg KPKK, L.M. assured his inquisitors that, in general, he saw the GDR as a positive and progressive state, and that he was in agreement with the basic thrust of the SED party line. However, there were also various matters on which he had grave reservations, above all, the pressure being put on individual members to conform to every tiny detail of official policy, which, in L.M.'s opinion, was smothering the life out of the party. At discussion meetings, for example, only the leader spoke, whilst everybody else stayed mute for fear of saying something wrong and landing themselves in trouble.[59]

One especially common form of 'reconciliationism' was hostility to the commissions themselves. Veterans of the labour movement and of the anti-Nazi resistance found it deeply humiliating to be summoned before a PKK tribunal to be interrogated and harangued by apparatchiks and careerists, many of whom had only recently emerged from the party schools and who had never had to suffer for the faith.[60] In Heiligenstadt, for example, a veteran Communist complained bitterly about being hauled over the coals by the 'young upstarts' of the PKKs.[61] At a party meeting in Pöhl, two SED members argued that they would have supported the PKKs had they started their work with the party bigwigs. Instead, the PKKs had started from the bottom and only the 'ordinary member' had to endure their attentions. In Plauen, meanwhile, a certain P.L. was summoned before the KPKK, where he managed to convince the inquisitors that he was true to the party line. In the train on the way home, however, P.L. 'described the members of the commission as "stupid pigs" and "layabouts" '. Unfortunately for P.L., his remarks were overheard by an informant and he was consequently expelled from the party.[62]

Often, SED members were so hostile to the PKKs that they preferred to leave the party rather than appear before a tribunal. Elsewhere, they failed to co-operate by refusing to hand in the three photographs of themselves which the PKKs demanded.[63] On many occasions, members of SED party cells refused to ratify the decision of the PKK to expel a comrade. At the Tewa factory in Altenburg, for example, a veteran Communist, who had fought in the Red Army during the Russian civil war, was expelled by the KPKK for having claimed that Leon Trotsky had made a huge contribution to the victory of the Bolsheviks. When the matter came up before a meeting of the BPO, however, twenty-three members voted in favour of expulsion, but twenty voted against and there were eighteen abstentions.[64] Similarly, at the 'RAW 7. Oktober' plant in Zwickau, an SED functionary was expelled for having made anti-Soviet comments. At a subsequent meeting of the BPO, there was a lengthy debate about the affair, at the end of which eighteen members voted for expulsion, thirteen against, whilst fourteen abstained.[65] In one SED meeting in Aue, the members voted by ninety-four votes to sixty-two against the decision of the KPKK to expel one of their comrades for having refused to call Schumacher a traitor, though, in the event, the individual concerned was expelled anyway.[66]

Closely linked to the deviation of 'reconciliationism' was the treason of 'Social Democracy'. As the authorities in the Soviet zone lapsed ever further into 'spy fever', so they became increasingly insistent that the West German

SPD had built up 'an extensive network of agents across the whole of the Soviet zone', whose mission was the 'systematic dissemination of lies and provocative false reports'.[67] These agents, asserted the SED leadership, were for the most part former Social Democrats who had concealed their opposition to unification in April 1946 in order to be able to infiltrate the SED, and who were now being controlled by the so-called *Ostbüro*, which Schumacher had established in West Berlin in April 1946. Fortunately, however, it was possible to identify Schumacher agents by the sort of statements they made. According to one SED functionary, speaking to the *Bezirksleitung* of the SED in Leipzig in March 1953:

> Social Democracy manifests itself here in the most varied forms. It manifests itself in the underestimation of theory, in the underestimation of the significance of Lenin and Stalin. It manifests itself in the underestimation of the Soviet Union as the leading force in the camp of peace and socialism. It finds expression in the denial of the necessity to organise the armed defence of our homeland... It manifests itself in particular in reactions to criticism and self-criticism, in the fear of a scientifically bold debate with old, mistaken and harmful ideas.[68]

Since anybody who expressed one or more of the above sentiments was, in the view of the authorities, a potential Schumacher agent, the field of suspicion embraced a large chunk of the party. Indeed, judging by the frequency with which references to the apprehension of '*Ostbüro* agents' crop up in the archival sources, one might assume that Schumacher's agents had penetrated to every corner of life in East Germany.[69] Though there do seem to have been a few die-hard Social Democrats who continued a forlorn struggle against Communist dictatorship, usually by sending anonymous letters to former party comrades or by distributing oppositional leaflets,[70] they never had much of an impact. The overwhelming majority of former Social Democrats seem to have abstained from organised resistance, either because they still felt some degree of loyalty to the SED, or because they regarded any such organised resistance as futile. In the words of one Social Democrat from Dresden: 'The creation of any kind of illegal cadre organisation was not planned by us. It was quite clear to me that the more the Russians and the SED dug themselves in, the more senseless it was to offer up endless victims.'[71]

On the other hand, what is beyond question is that very many former SPD members were, as individuals, still committed to their own, Social Democratic traditions and were becoming increasingly – and in many cases openly – disenchanted with the inexorable progress of the SED towards orthodox Stalinism. Many found themelves in trouble for having publicly criticised Leninist concepts such as 'democratic centralism',[72] or for denying that a consistent Marxist must also be a Leninist,[73] or for clinging to the doctrine of the 'German road to Socialism',[74] or for speaking of the merits of old SPD heroes such as Lassalle, Bernstein and Kautsky.[75] Others refused to participate in schooling, usually on the grounds that the SED had become the KPD by another name, and they saw no reason why they should be packed off to party schools in order to be harangued and bullied by dogmatists and fanatics.[76] Still others refused to submit to the demand that they stand up at party meetings and beat their breasts in remorse at having been members of the SPD during the Weimar period. At one such meeting in Altenburg, for example, a veteran SPD and German General Trade Union Federation (ADGB) functionary soon found himself in difficulties when he tried to defend the party to which he used to belong against the slanders of the Stalinists: 'As Social Democratic leaders and trade union functionaries... we made no mistakes. We always fought as hard as we could in the best interests of the workers.'[77]

Though such discontented Social Democrats only rarely grouped together in self-conscious resistance cells, they did often belong to loose oppositional networks of former SPD members, amongst whom grievances were shared and political issues discussed. This is hardly to be wondered at, for many veteran Social Democrats had worked, lived and struggled alongside one another for decades and were bound together by enduring bonds of friend-ship and memory.[78] It was only natural that they should meet together and confer about the political problems they faced; indeed, it would have been very strange had they not done so. Particularly amongst former SPD functionaries, these loose unofficial networks extended across the whole of the Soviet zone, and sometimes former functionaries even remained in contact with friends and former colleagues in the western zones of occupation.[79] In some cases, former Social Democrats in positions of respon-sibility inside the SED, inside the state apparatus or in industry used their powers to provide jobs for their political friends and acquaintances, hence building up concentrations of former Social Democrats in particular towns or factories.[80] Moreover, long-standing functionaries of SPD provenance often enjoyed a very close relationship of trust and affection with the workers they had represented, and in this sense, too, one can speak of oppositional SPD networks.[81] In short, whilst there was no grand conspiracy as alleged by the SED leadership, one can speak of an SPD 'resistance' in the sense that an oppositional SPD 'milieu' inside the SED existed.

Former Social Democrats were by no means the only ones in the SED to suffer for their erstwhile party allegiances. Also targeted were members of the left-wing 'splinter parties' such as the Communist Party Opposition (KPO) and the Socialist Workers' Party (SAP), both of which had been strong in the region before 1933. Most of these people had joined either the KPD or SPD in 1945, had subsequently gone over to the SED in 1946 and had often risen to considerable heights in the party and state apparatus. From 1948 onwards, however, they found themselves being scrutinised with unfriendly eyes by the PKKs, for, it was claimed, individuals who had proved to be politically unreliable in the past were likely to attract the special attention of enemy agents on the look-out for weak links inside the SED.[82]

Accordingly, there was an intensive press campaign, the purpose of which was to demonstrate how damaging and traitorous the activities of the splinter parties had been during the Weimar period and how the danger of 'sectarianism' was still very much present in the SED. Former members of splinter groups were repeatedly required to stand up in party meetings and 'self-critically' acknowledge the political treachery which they had committed twenty years previously. They were obliged to send long, self-abasing letters to the PKKs, in which they were supposed to demonstrate their genuine contrition for their past errors and 'objective crimes' against the working class.

The suspicion with which the authorities regarded members of the former splinter parties was not entirely groundless, for many such individuals did indeed harbour ideas which could not be tolerated in any Stalinist organisation. In particular, when the PKKs began, in the later 1940s, to investigate the opinions and political behaviour of former members of the splinter parties, they discovered to their horror a strong current of Trotskyism. At a party school in Neuhausen, for example, one such individual – in a discussion based upon the Stalinist tome, the *History of the CPSU* – portrayed the book as a falsification of history, 'since it does not take account of Trotsky's contribution to the construction of the Soviet Union, and in particular of the Red Army'. The individual refused, when put under pressure by the teachers at the party school, to retract his comments, and subsequent investigations revealed that for some time he had been spreading such ideas in his home town of Colmnitz.[83] In a similar case in Plauen, a member of a former splinter party appeared one evening at a meeting of a local discussion group ('Stalin circle'). When the subject of Trotsky came up, the man accused the group leader of putting forward false and misleading arguments, particularly with regard to the leading role played by Trotsky in the creation of the Red Army.[84] Clearly, anybody who still held a brief for the heresiarch Trotsky was not going to be tolerated in a 'party of a new type'; indeed, it is rather surprising that such people were ever admitted even to the SPD or KPD. The fact that they were allowed into these parties, and were even able to gain positions of responsibility, bears witness to the relative openness of political life in the Soviet zone during the first two years of occupation.

Given the fact that the former members of the splinter parties were often people of a high level of political knowledge and commitment, the campaign against them was always likely to meet with opposition and resistance. Often, either in private or in public, members of the former splinter parties denounced the 'lies' and 'distortions' which were now being printed in the newspapers about the KPO, SAP and other groups, defended the politics of the splinter parties as having been correct under the circumstances or praised the 'outstanding role' of individual leaders of former splinter parties such as the KPO chieftain Heinrich Brandler.[85] On numerous occasions, they complained bitterly about the fact that the party was pushing old comrades against a wall.[86] In Weimar, for example, a former KPO member, who himself at one time had been a candidate member of the local KPKK, 'regards the debate with anti-party groupings as mistaken and sees therein a campaign of persecution against old, good comrades'.[87] In Erfurt, a former splinter party member was denounced during an SED meeting for having failed to make a self-critical public announcement concerning his erstwhile political activities. In response, the individual pointedly failed to make the declaration demanded from him, but instead he 'attempted to trivialise the mistakes of the anti-party groupings and declared that one must draw a line under the past'.[88] Twelve former KPO members in Altenburg, meanwhile, steadfastly refused to make any self-critical declarations, as a result of which they were hauled before the PKK, where they continued to refuse to submit. As one of the twelve remarked defiantly to his inquisitors: 'I regard this as harassment that I am sitting here before a tribunal. We really are being treated worse than the Nazis. What have you done with the Nazis and the Social Democrats? Have you demanded a declaration from them?'[89]

A final political tendency inside the SED which came under increasing pressure in the period after 1947 was made up of 'old believers': veteran Communists who had never been quite at ease with the course of developments since 1945, and who often became increasingly disenchanted once the Stalinisation drive had begun in earnest. Many such individuals had long-standing grievances going back to Zero Hour or even before, which now began to come out into the open. In Plauen, for example, one veteran Communist was brought before the party commission for having criticised the leaders of the KPD for having fled the country with such alacrity in 1933, thereby, in his view, abandoning the rank-and-file members and functionaries to the Nazis.[90] There were continuing complaints amongst ultra-left Communists that the land reform had been too mild, that collectivisation and nationalisation were not proceeding with sufficient vigour, and that the KPD should never have compromised itself by merging with the reformist SPD.[91] In the Saxon village of Unterheinsdorf, a group of ultra-left Communists in the local leadership even argued that the SED was still too soft, and that the party should deal as ruthlessly with its opponents as the Nazis had dealt with theirs.[92]

Many veteran Communists who, in their youth, had become addicted to the subversive activities and radical slogans of the Weimar KPD, found that the essentially bureaucratic character of the SED dictatorship left them feeling out of place and unsatisfied. In the words of one veteran Communist from Altenburg: 'I would prefer it if the old KPD still existed, or if I were in the KPD in West Germany. At least I could do some fighting there.'[93] What made KPD veterans particularly uneasy was that many aspects of the new state they saw emerging around them did not correspond with their expectations and was not what they felt they had struggled and suffered for. They despised the corruption which they saw in many party and state officials.[94] After the creation of the GDR in 1949, and above all during the campaign to reunify Germany during the early 1950s, they objected to the nationalistic rhetoric, the red-black-gold flags and the disappearance from political life of traditional Communist symbols such as the red flag and the singing of the Internationale.[95] They detested the more lenient approach to former Nazis that accompanied the introduction of Stalinist economic practices in the later 1940s.[96] Above all, Communist veterans deeply resented being elbowed aside in the party hierarchy by the ambitious young apparatchiks who were being systematically fostered by the regime and appointed to responsible positions. In Chemnitz, for example, SED members who had joined the party only since April 1946 accounted for 21.6 per cent of the membership but 30 per cent of the functionary corps.[97] From the point of view of the SED leadership, the new generation of bureaucrats now being hatched out in the party schools were more reliable, more competent and better educated than the old KPD veterans, who were often still stuck in the politics and political mind-set of the Weimar period.[98] Many KPD veterans, by contrast, viewed the young apparatchiks who were displacing them as 'conformists, subservient grovellers, crawlers, obsequious yes-men'.[99]

Ironically, discontented old Communists were far better organised than either their SPD counterparts or the former members of the various splinter parties. More ironically still, the organisation through which many veteran Communists sought to express their grievances was entirely legal. In February 1947 the authorities had established the so-called 'Union of the Persecuted of the Nazi Regime' (VVN) for former anti-Nazi resisters.[100] By 1948, the organisation, which was always dominated by Communists, had some 28,000 members in the Soviet zone, amongst whom were seventeen ministers, fifty *Oberbürgermeister* and 230 SED and FDGB chairpeople.[101] In the later 1940s, as many veteran Communists became more and more disenchanted with the SED and its policies, they increasingly began to look to the VVN as an alternative. In 1950, for example, one party veteran in Plauen wrote to the local VVN, complaining bitterly about the degeneration of political life in the GDR. According to the letter writer: 'As individuals we can unfortunately do nothing in this matter, but your VVN could intervene here in order to bring about a change.'[102] In Altenburg, a number of leading members of the local VVN argued openly that 'the leading role belongs by right to the VVN and not to the party'.[103] In Waltershausen, local VVN members were condemned by the SED for pursuing 'their own politics, detached from the party' and for asserting that the VVN 'is the avant-garde of the proletariat and not the messenger boy for any other organisation [i.e. the SED]'.[104]

It would be going too far to present the VVN as a self-conscious oppositional organisation, for the VVN leadership in Berlin was always firmly under the control of the regime. For much of the time, the VVN loyally fulfilled its function as a mouthpiece of the authorities.[105] Nonetheless, the fact that the VVN was showing any signs of independent life at all was, from the point of view of the SED regime, unacceptable. Hence, from 1950 onwards, the PKKs began to keep a watchful and suspicious eye on the VVN. Members of the PKKs, for example, were sent to VVN conferences and instructed to report back in detail on what they found there.[106] Eventually, in February 1953, the VVN was abolished altogether and replaced by a new organisation for victims of Nazism which was entirely under the control of the authorities. Perhaps rather surprisingly, there does not seem to have been any resistance to the dissolution of the VVN on the part of the Communist veterans who had hitherto placed so much faith in it.[107]

Resistance and resignation

With the demise of the VVN, the Stalinisation of the East German labour movement can be regarded as having been completed, for henceforth none of its organs possessed any real life or volition of its own. There were still, of course, many discontented individuals within the SED and the FDGB, but their oppositional sentiments had no organisational focus. In organisational terms, all power and authority in the labour movement had by 1953 been caused to flow in one direction only: from top to bottom. The bodies which ostensibly represented the interests of the workers had in reality been turned into instruments of their oppression. The labour movement, in short, had become a living corpse, the flesh and lifeless sinews of which were enslaved to the will of the moustachioed zombie-master of the Kremlin.

Yet, there are still two highly significant questions about the Stalinisation of the labour movement which remain to be answered. First, we have still to explain why the process of Stalinisation in East Germany was not quite as brutal as it was elsewhere in Soviet Eastern Europe. The purge of the party membership, for example, cut far less deep in East Germany than in the other Communist states. Between 1949 and 1954, the membership of the SED shrank by approximately 20 per cent.[108] In Hungary, by contrast, the party decreased by 30 per cent between 1948 and 1951. In Bulgaria, the party lost about 40 per cent of its membership during the same period. In Czechoslovakia, where the purges started later and lasted longer, the party had, by 1954, expelled some 30 per cent of its membership.[109]

The process of Stalinisation in East Germany was also mild in the sense that, on the whole, the authorities did not resort to terror. Individuals who had been expelled from the party could certainly expect to be demoted at work, to lose any privileges they had hitherto enjoyed and to be spied on. However, they were not normally subjected to arrest, torture, imprisonment or execution. In the other countries of the Soviet stable in Eastern Europe, by contrast, and above all in Hungary and Czechoslovakia, the purges achieved a level of intensity reminiscent of the Great Terror in the Soviet Union in the period 1934 to 1939. Between 1948 and 1954, some 150,000 Czechoslovaks were arrested by the security forces. In Budapest, 'the vans set out at 2 a.m. on Mondays, Wednesdays and Fridays to bring in the latest batch of victims, who by 1953 numbered somewhere in the region of 700,000, of whom 98,000 were branded as spies and saboteurs; 5,000 of them were executed.'[110]

The relative mildness of the purges in East Germany is perhaps most revealingly demonstrated, not by raw statistics, but by the numerous examples one can find in the archives of how even openly oppositional elements were often treated with surprising leniency. In Freiberg, a seventy-seven-year-old Social Democrat who had openly denounced the Soviet invasions of Georgia in 1922, and Poland and Finland in 1939, was not even issued with a reprimand, but, in recognition of his age and his long-standing membership of the labour movement, was simply instructed to read some pamphlets and party literature.[111] In the Vogtland town of Jähnstadt, an SED official denounced the Czech army for having driven so many Germans out of their homes on the Czech side of the nearby border and said that he would like to shoot the 'criminal' Czech border guards down from their watch towers. Despite the fact that the individual concerned refused to retract his comments, a five-hour meeting of the local party leadership decided not to expel him, but merely to issue him with a reprimand.[112] Particularly interesting is the saga of A.K., who was expelled from the party for 'behaviour damaging to the party' in September 1950. A.K. promptly appealed against this decision and, as a gesture of defiance, he refused to hand in his party membership book. In January 1951, he was summoned before a KPKK tribunal which informed him that his expulsion had been confirmed and that his party membership book was the property of the SED which he had no alternative but to return. A.K.'s only response to this demand was to exclaim 'Quite out of the question!' and, turning on his heel, he stormed out of the building. For the next five months, the party made repeated and unsuccessful attempts to prise A.K.'s membership book away from its owner, and, before the affair was finally resolved, the LPKK in Erfurt, the ZPKK in Berlin, the criminal police and the People's Police (*Volkspolizei*) had all been dragged into it. Only in May 1951 was the KPKK in Eisenach able to inform the ZPKK that, some eight months after his expulsion, the criminal police had finally managed to get their hands on A.K.'s membership book. Even now, however, A.K. refused to admit defeat, and he continued to protest that he had been unjustly expelled from the party.[113]

What such incidents demonstrate is that East Germany's road to Stalinism was considerably less traumatic and bloody than those of its southern and eastern neighbours. In Hungary, somebody who openly criticised the foreign policy of the Soviet Union, or who argued that Czech border guards were criminals who should be shot, would face almost certain arrest. In Budapest, a man such as A.K., who was effectively thumbing his nose at the might of the state, would simply have been hauled off in a van at two o'clock in the morning and executed.

The most common explanation put forward by historians to account for the relative mildness of the Stalinisation process in East Germany is that it was constrained by considerations of Soviet foreign policy. Stalin, the argument runs, was extremely anxious to prevent the emergence of a hostile and powerful West German state, and, to this end, he never abandoned the goal of constructing a united but neutral Germany. The GDR should therefore not be regarded as just another Soviet Bloc country. It was a bargaining chip which Stalin hoped to trade with the West. For this reason, Stalin was reluctant to allow the East German Communists to do anything which might make reunification impossible. According to historians such as Monika Kaiser, it is very much in this light that the mildness of the Stalinisation process in East Germany should be seen. Just as the Soviets hesitated to introduce the other characteristic features of a Stalinist society into East Germany, so too did they pull their punches when it came to the introduction of terror, the most characteristic feature of all.[114]

There can be little doubt that the intricacies of Soviet policy on the German question go a long way to explaining why the East German experience of Stalinisation was rather less traumatic than that of Poland, Hungary and Czechoslovakia. There was also another important factor, however, which has not received much attention from historians, but which is strongly suggested by the archival evidence which has now become available. The German labour movement was the oldest in the world, and far older than those in the neighbouring countries of Eastern Europe. The labour movement in East Germany therefore had deeper roots and longer traditions than its Polish, Czech or Hungarian counterparts. As a result, it proved to be more 'resistant' to being subordinated to the alien, Stalinist tradition, not in the sense that the SED apparatus consciously resisted the process of Stalinisation, but in the same sense that a material is said to be 'resistant' to conducting electricity, or a body is 'resistant' to infection.

Thus, one of the most frequent complaints of the SED party leadership during the period under discussion was that a whole range of party organs were not proceeding with sufficient energy and ruthlessness against the enemies of the SED. Within the FDGB, for example, there were still some veteran functionaries who continued to believe that the purpose of a trade union was to represent its members, and who therefore tried to defend individuals who, for political reasons, found themselves in trouble at work. In December 1952, Paul Fröhlich, the first secretary of the SED in the city of Leipzig, denounced a local FDGB group which had opposed the sacking of a female worker at the RFT-Funkwerk merely because she had happened to be on friendly terms with a number of 'Schumacher agents' who had fled to the West.[115] More commonly, it was the VVN which irritated the authorities by trying to intervene on behalf of veteran anti-Nazis who had fallen foul of the regime. Given the important role which VVN members played in the party and state apparatus, their reluctance to abandon their comrades constituted a significant barrier to the Stalinisation of the labour movement. In Limbach, for example, the VVN vigorously protested against the persecution of one of its members, who had been a stalwart of the anti-Nazi resistance and who, it was claimed, deserved better treatment.[116] In Chemnitz, the local VVN appealed to the VVN leadership in Berlin against the demand that one of their members, who had been expelled from the SED, should also be cast out from the VVN. Much to the annoyance of the PKK, the VVN leadership assured the Chemnitz veterans that the expulsion of someone from the SED did not necessarily entail expulsion from the VVN as well.[117]

This 'resistance' to the implementation of Stalinist terror was to be found, not just in the FDGB and VVN, but also in the apparatus of the SED itself. On numerous occasions, local or district leaderships of the SED aroused the wrath of their superiors by failing to prosecute the 'class struggle' with sufficient determination. In Schwarzenberg, the local KPKK complained in 1952 that leading SED functionaries were allowing openly anti-Soviet elements to flourish. A typical example of this, according to the Schwarzenberg KPKK, was the individual who at an SED party meeting had proclaimed that he would leave the party rather than join the DSF, but who had not been disciplined in any way by the local SED leadership.[118] In Grimma, the SED area secretariat (*Kreissekretariat*) was strongly criticised for having 'underestimated' the importance of information supplied to it on the activities of spies and saboteurs. In other words, the members of the secretariat had proved insufficiently willing to accept without question the truth of allegations made by informants and denunciators.[119] The SED secretariat in Schmölln, meanwhile, came under fire for having released P.K., a functionary who had been arrested for sabotage, and installing him as the manager of a local VEB. According to the party leadership, the secretariat had insisted that P.K. was 'a good functionary', thereby wilfully disregarding the 'evidence' against him.[120]

However, the most significant obstacle to the transformation of the organs of the labour movement into instruments of terror was the fact that, even within those organisations at the cutting edge of the Stalinisation process – the security forces and the legal system – such 'reconciliationist' tendencies were rife. Fritz Schenk, for example, claims that many members of the People's Police were unwilling to fabricate evidence against their former comrades.[121] This assertion is supported by a leader of the People's Police in Leipzig, who, at a meeting of the SED *Bezirksleitung*, claimed that a great many members of the security forces did not understand, and perhaps did not want to understand, the tremendously important role which they must play 'in the creation of the foundations of Socialism'. At the same meeting, Paul Fröhlich bemoaned the fact that 'a whole series of party organisations... as well as functionaries in the state apparatus in Leipzig distinguish themselves by their pronounced mildness in the class struggle'. As an example of this reprehensible tendency, Fröhlich mentioned an SED public prosecutor who had wanted to release a prisoner on the grounds that there was insufficient evidence against him. As far as Fröhlich was concerned, the fact that the public prosecutor took account of such things as the amount of evidence against a person was not a sign that he was doing his job properly, but, on the contrary, was an indication that he was lacking in trust in the GDR.[122] In a similar complaint in January 1953, Fröhlich condemned the large number of SED judges and public prosecutors who proceeded far too leniently against the enemies of the party. The reason for this, according to Fröhlich, was that instead of being guided in their work 'in the first instance by the decisions of our party', they were far too obsessed with the 'formal interpretation of the paragraphs of the criminal code'.[123]

Even the PKKs, the most characteristic organs of the Stalinisation process, did not always, in the eyes of the party leadership, demonstrate sufficient ruthlessness in the struggle against the party's enemies. In June 1951, for instance, the Thuringian LPKK in Erfurt sent an observer to the KPKK in Altenburg, who returned with the disquieting news that:

> Reconciliationism in the *Kreis* of Altenburg in connection with the review of party membership is very strong and there is a great lack of ideological clarity. Particularly important, it seems to me, is the underestimation of former members of the splinter groups. In my opinion, the struggle against Social Democracy is carried out inadequately and as a formality.[124]

Exasperated by this resistance to the introduction of naked terror, the authorities began, in the early 1950s, to take measures to try and overcome it. Conferences were convened, for example, at which rank-and-file members were encouraged to criticise the dilatoriness and 'reconciliationism' of their local or district leadership.[125] Local SED leaders who were proving too prone to 'reconciliationist' tendencies, such as the members of the *Kreisleitung* in Oschatz, found themselves the targets of vitriolic campaigns which resulted in their own expulsions and public humiliation.[126] In the Saxon town of Cämmerswalda, the entire local leadership of the SED 'was completely re-built and almost entirely reconstituted out of younger and more forceful people, who, after having undergone self-criticism, accepted the correctness of the instructions of the *Kreissekretariat*'.[127]

All in all, there can be little doubt that the 'resistance' of the party apparatus was a significant impediment to the introduction of Stalinist terror. Though this 'resistance' would almost certainly have been broken in the course of time, the death of Stalin halted the drift to terror before it had reached the same levels as were being experienced in Hungary and

Czechoslovakia. On the other hand, it would be quite misleading and wrong to overemphasise the importance of these impediments to terror. As always, the prime determinant of the course of events was Soviet foreign and occupation policy, albeit modified by conditions on the ground in East Germany. Moreover, the men and women of the party apparatus who 'resisted' the implementation of Stalinist terror should in no way be seen as conscious anti-Stalinists risking life and limb in the name of freedom. For the most part, they were loyal servants of the regime who, for all their political qualms (*politische Bauchschmerzen*), were nonetheless committed to the general principles of the party line. However, steeped as they were in the traditions of the German labour movement, they found it difficult to think and act like the hard-bitten Stalinist fanatics the regime was expecting them to become. It was not so much that they consciously rejected Stalinism; they simply were not very good at it.

If the answer to the first question is that the relative mildness of the Stalinisation process in East Germany was at least partly due to the 'resistance' of those who were expected to implement it, the second question is why was there so little resistance on the part of the victims of Stalinism. For example, the vast majority of veterans who fell foul of the regime on account of their oppositional sentiments did not leave the party voluntarily; they were ejected from it against their will. In many cases, even stubborn trouble-makers fought long and hard to try and get back in. Furthermore, the majority of those who were expelled for political reasons did not continue their oppositional activities, but relapsed into sullen and embittered passivity. A typical example of this is H.W., a former KPO member and FDGB functionary from Arnstadt who was expelled from the SED for having refused to acknowledge that workers in VEBs should be paid at a different rate from those in private firms. According to one report on his subsequent political development: 'Although, during the initial period after his expulsion from the party, he still attempted to justify himself and for this reason remained in contact with various comrades, he later cut himself off more and more.' By July 1950 he was reported as living a retired life, abstaining entirely from any political activity.[128] A similar case is that of B.W., a former KPO member from Reichenbach who was expelled for 'failing to break with anti-party ideas'. In a PKK report on his behaviour subsequent to his expulsion, it was noted that he was 'bitter about his expulsion. His manner is in general passive and reserved.'[129]

The unwillingness of many veterans to be cast out from the ranks of the SED, and their passivity once they had been expelled, is rather surprising. These former members of the SPD, KPD or splinter parties were often men and women of proven courage, who had spent the whole of their adult lives fighting for Socialism. Many of them had genuine and deep-seated objections to the current dispensation in East Germany. Why, then, were they so reluctant to break with the SED and go into illegal opposition?

Perhaps even more surprising than the passivity of those who were expelled from the SED was the abject capitulation of most of those who managed to remain in the party. The price which the authorities demanded of former Social Democrats or splinter party members who wanted to stay in the SED was unconditional surrender and public humiliation. Yet, astonishingly, very large numbers of such individuals were prepared to pay this price. In the surviving archives, for example, one can find huge numbers of letters of 'self-criticism', in which former Social Democrats or splinter party members acknowledged their former political errors and 'crimes' in the most extravagant and abject of terms. W.K. from Erfurt, for example, was a veteran of the labour movement who had joined the SPD in 1920, and the SAP in 1926. After 1933 he had been active in the anti-Nazi resistance, as a result of which he was arrested in 1936 and spent the next nine years in various prisons and concentration camps. Clearly, W.K. was neither a political greenhorn nor a coward, and yet, in 1950, he was prepared to admit that 'seen objectively' his membership of the SAP had been 'class treachery'.[130] A similar case is that of B.E., who joined the KPO in 1929 and also participated in the anti-Nazi resistance. Yet, in 1950, this man who had defied the Nazis was prepared to write a cringing letter of recantation, in which he stated that having read the *History of the CPSU (Short Course)*, he now realised 'that in those years I travelled down a false path, a path which, as we know today, led always to the camp of the enemies of the working class, the enemies of Socialism, into the camp of imperialism'.[131]

Explaining why veterans of the labour movement who had withstood the Nazis were broken by the lesser tyranny of the SED dictatorship is no easy matter. The men and women concerned were driven by a complex mixture of sentiments of which they themselves were not necessarily conscious. Moreover, the motives which impelled these veterans to behave as they did varied considerably from individual to individual. Nonetheless, there do appear to have been two general factors which, in conjunction, seem to provide at least a partial explanation.

First, it should be remembered that the majority of these veterans felt a tremendous emotional attachment to the movement into which they had been born, and for the sake of which they had striven so long and suffered so much. Most of them took an intense pride in their tradition, their struggles during the Weimar and Nazi periods, and their achievements since 1945. Herbert Prauss, who in 1948 spent some time at an SED sanatorium in the company of anti-Nazi veterans whose health had been broken by their persecution by the Nazis, relates that, despite their physical ailments, they were 'ardently enthusiastic Communists. Their eyes lit up when they talked of the struggles of the past.'[132]

At a deeper level still, the labour movement had given these veterans an almost spiritual sense of purpose to their lives. According to a Communist from Chemnitz: 'I simply cannot imagine life without active political work, since from childhood on I fought actively for the goals of the working class in the Young Spartakus, in the KJVD [Young Communists] and in the party.'[133] In the words of a veteran Social Democrat, also from Chemnitz: 'I am glad that in my long life I have served the great goals of the labour movement. The purpose of life is life itself. What gives meaning to life was something I found in my work for Socialism.'[134] Herbert Prauss, commenting on the psychology and world-view of such veterans, reports:

> They did not believe in God, but they were filled with the inspirational feeling that they had devoted their whole lives to the service of the party and to the alleged liberation of humanity. They were filled with the unshakeable belief that their lives had possessed a deep purpose, and that they would receive an honourable place in party history.[135]

The second factor one must bear in mind when trying to comprehend the failure of the veterans of the German labour movement to resist the imposition of Stalinism is that, for all their pride in the past, they had also been left deeply scarred by their experiences. In purely physical terms, they were usually of advancing years and indifferent health. More importantly, the many defeats and disappointments which they had suffered had undermined their self-confidence. They were acutely conscious of the fact that they had failed to stop the slide to imperialist war in 1914, and that they had failed again in 1918 to vanquish German reaction once and for all. Above all, they had failed to stop the rise to power of Hitler in 1933, and, thereafter, all their attempts to overthrow the Nazi regime had been in vain. Liberation, when it finally came, had been delivered to them by the allied armies of occupation. Since 1945, they had failed to win over the 'passive majority' of the population to their cause, and any power which they had enjoyed had been granted to them, not by the people, but by the Russians.

Taken together, these two factors go a long way to explaining why the great majority of veterans offered so little resistance to the Stalinisation of the East German labour movement. To break with the regime would mean acknowledging that all their struggles and sufferings had achieved nothing, and that the German working class was no nearer emancipation than it had been when the SPD was founded at Gotha some eight decades previously. Breaking with the SED dictatorship would also mean placing themselves in opposition to their former comrades still inside the party, and to the movement to which they had devoted their entire lives. To take such a step would necessarily require enormous moral strength. Weakened by their physical sufferings, their age and, above all, by the lack of confidence engendered by decades of failure and defeat, they simply did not possess the strength to go back to the beginning and to start the struggle for Socialism from scratch.

Thus, the possibility of being thrown into the political outer darkness, even for veterans who had significant doubts about the new dispensation, was a prospect which filled them with terror. In December 1951, the local

VVN group in Frankenberg appealed to the authorities not to expel one of its members, who had already been thrown out of the SED, from the VVN as well. According to the Frankenberg VVN, to expel him from the VVN 'would amount to his social death. The consequences of such a decision can only be appreciated by somebody who has himself spent decades belonging to and fighting for the labour movement.'[136] In a similar case, a former KPO member from Chemnitz, shortly after his expulsion from the SED, wrote to the inquisitors of the local KPKK, pleading with them to reverse their decision:

> Comrades, naturally it is easy to express my loyalty to the party in words. But I am attached to the party and I love the party... For forty years I have been part of the labour movement, and I have always served the party faithfully. I devoted all my strength to it, apart from the above years when I sided with the opposition and took up the position of an enemy of the party.[137]

There was, in fact, nothing new about the dilemma with which the veterans of the German labour movement found themselves confronted in the early 1950s. Twenty years before in the Soviet Union, the veterans of the October Revolution had found themselves in a similarly tragic situation. They, too, were men and women who had been hardened by long years of imprisonment, exile and revolution. They, no less than their German counterparts in the 1950s, had enormous pride in their tradition. As in the GDR, the Russian revolutionaries who had devoted their lives to the party of Lenin found themselves confronted with a choice of either capitulating to a regime about which they had grave reservations, or breaking with the party and moving into outright opposition. In the vast majority of cases, they, too, capitulated, and for very similar reasons to those of the East German veterans twenty years later. After his arrest, Nikolai Bukharin explained his decision to submit to Stalin in the following words:

> For three months I refused to say anything. Then I began to testify. Why? Because while I was in prison I made a revaluation of my entire past. For when you ask yourself: 'If you must die, what are you dying for?' – an absolutely black vacuity suddenly rises before you with startling vividness. There was nothing to die for, if one wanted to die unrepented... And when you ask yourself, 'Very well, suppose you do not die; suppose by some miracle you remain alive, again what for?' Isolated from everybody, an enemy of the people, an inhuman position, completely isolated from everything that constitutes the essence of life.[138]

The main difference, of course, between the old Bolsheviks in the 1930s and the veterans of the German labour movement in the 1950s was that, in the case of the former, their capitulation proved to be entirely in vain. Having humiliated and broken them, Stalin, in the later 1930s, killed them anyway. The East German veterans, by contrast, were spared the prospect of a similar fate when, in March 1953, Stalin descended to hell to meet his maker. Rather than ending their days in labour camps or prison cells, the veterans of the East German labour movement lived on into the 1960s and 1970s, either as loyal but marginalised servants of the SED dictatorship, or as isolated and disillusioned political outsiders. In either case, however, there was precious little left of the idealism, enthusiasm and spontaneity of Zero Hour, for whilst Stalinism feeds upon these qualities, it also, by its very nature, destroys them.

Notes

1   SStA Chemnitz, BPA Karl-Marx-Stadt, V/5/199, Bl. 19.

2   W. Loth, *Stalins ungeliebtes Kind*, Berlin, 1994, p. 93.

3   G. Swain & N. Swain, *Eastern Europe since 1945*, Basingstoke, 1993, pp. 62–65.

4   F. Schenk, *Im Vorzimmer der Diktatur* , Cologne & [West] Berlin, 1962, pp. 84–85.

5   W. Leonhard, *Die Revolution entläßt ihre Kinder*, Frankfurt/M, 1961, Chapter 9.

6   P. Lewis, *Central Europe since 1945*, London & New York, 1994, pp. 88–92.

7   ThHStA Weimar, BPA Erfurt, AIV/2/4-105, 'Notiz von dem Kursus in Berlin vom 3. bis einschließlich 5.11.49', Bl. 2.

8   C. Stern, *Ulbricht: A Political Biography*, London, 1965, p. 111.

9   ThHStA Weimar, BPA Erfurt, AIV/2/5-141, Bl. 40.

10 N. Naimark, *The Russians in Germany*, Cambridge, MA, pp. 310–11.

11 ThHStA Weimar, MdI, 279, Bl. 3.

12 For examples, see G. Pritchard, *German Workers under Soviet Occupation* (doctoral thesis, University of Wales, 1997), p. 331, n. 102.

13 ThHStA Weimar, BPA Erfurt, AIV/2/3-95, Bl. 144.

14 M. Kaiser, 'Change and Continuity in the Development of the Socialist Unity Party of Germany', in *Journal of Contemporary History*, vol. 30, 1995, pp. 689–91.

15 M. McCauley, *The GDR since 1945*, Basingstoke, 1983, p. 52.

16 See D. Kartun, *Tito's Plot Against Europe*, London, 1949.

17 W. Kießling, 'Im Widerstreit mit Moskau: Paul Merker und die Bewegung Freies Deutschland in Mexiko', in *Beiträge zur Geschichte der deutschen Arbeiterbewegung*, Nr. 3, 1992, p. 33.

18 ThHStA Weimar, BPA Erfurt, AIV/2/4-119, 'Rededisposition'.

19 SStA Chemnitz, BPA Karl-Marx-Stadt, IV/2/4/14, Bl. 265.

20 Schenk (n. 4 above), p. 26.

21 SAPMO-BArch, NY4076/157, Bl. 2.

22 See, e.g., SStA Leipzig, BPA Leipzig: IV/2/1/25, Bl. 26; IV/2/3/40, Bl. 148–49.

23 SStA Leipzig, KV Leipzig, 382, Bl. 18.

24 ThHStA Weimar, BPA Erfurt, AIV/2/3-95, Bl. 164–65.

25 SStA Chemnitz, BPA Karl-Marx-Stadt, IV/2/4/82, Bl. 42–45.

26 SStA Chemnitz, BPA Karl-Marx-Stadt, IV/2/4/71, Bl. 115–19. For further examples, see Pritchard (n. 12 above), p. 333, n. 123.

27   H. Weber, *Geschichte der DDR*, 3rd edition, Munich, 1989, pp. 176–80.

28   See, e.g., ThHStA Weimar, BPA Erfurt: AIV/2/4-105, 'Bericht von der Sitzung der ZPKK mit den Überprüfungskomissionen', 31.1.50; AIV/2/4-105, 'Niederschrift über die Besprechung der Mitglieder der Kommissionen, November 1949'; AIV/2/4-105, 'Plan zur Überprüfung der Genossen aus der westlichen Emigration und Kriegsgefangenschaft', 7.11.49.

29   See, e.g., ThHStA Weimar, BPA Erfurt: AIV/2/4-105.

30   See, e.g., ThHStA Weimar, BPA Erfurt: AIV/2/4-140, 'Aktennotiz, Erfurt', 22.4.50.

31   ThHStA Weimar, BPA Erfurt, AIV/2/4-105, 'Plan zur Überprüfung der Genossen aus der westlichen Emigration und Kriegsgefangenschaft', 7.11.49.

32   ThHStA Weimar, BPA Erfurt, AIV/2/4-105, 'Abschlußbericht zum Beschluß des Polit-Büros zur Überprüfung der Genossen in westlicher Kriegsgefangenschaft und Emigration', 9.3.50.

33   See, e.g., SStA Chemnitz, BPA Karl-Marx-Stadt, IV/2/4/4 (Bd. 1), Bl. 69 & IV/2/4/61, Bl. 276–77.

34   See, e.g., SStA Chemnitz, BPA Karl-Marx-Stadt, VVN, 43.

35   See, e.g., ThHStA Weimar, BPA Erfurt, AIV/2/4-104.

36   A. Klein, 'Die Überprüfung der Mitglieder und Kandidaten der SED in Sachsen-Anhalt, 1951', in *Beiträge zur Geschichte der deutschen Arbeiterbewegung*, Nr.1, 1992, pp. 14–15.

37   SStA Chemnitz, BPA Karl-Marx-Stadt, IV/2/4/70, Bl. 2.

38   See, e.g., ThHStA Weimar, BPA Erfurt, AIV/2/3-95, Bl. 144.

39   SAPMO-BArch, DY/30 IV 2/6.02, Nr. 96, Bl. 104.

40   Naimark (n. 10), p. 297.

41   SStA Chemnitz, BPA Karl-Marx-Stadt, IV/2/4/71, Bl. 138.

42   SStA Leipzig, KV Leipzig, 383, Bl. 17.

43   See, e.g., SStA Chemnitz, BPA Karl-Marx-Stadt, IV/2/4/10, Bl. 249.

44   SStA Chemnitz, BPA Karl-Marx-Stadt, IV/2/4/20, Bl. 122.

45   SStA Chemnitz, BPA Karl-Marx-Stadt, IV/2/4/10, Bl. 344.

46   SStA Chemnitz, BPA Karl-Marx-Stadt, IV/2/4/14, Bl. 265.

47   ThHStA Weimar, BPA Erfurt, AIV/2/4-139, 'LPKK Erfurt', 31.3.52.

48   SStA Leipzig, BPA Leipzig, IV/2/3/148, Bl. 88.

49   SStA Chemnitz, BPA Karl-Marx-Stadt, IV/2/4/10, Bl. 184–85.

50   Ibid., Bl. 51 & 255–56.

51   ThHStA Weimar, BPA Erfurt, IV/2/4-139, 'LPKK Erfurt', 31.3.52.

52   ThHStA Weimar, BPA Erfurt, IV/2/4-95, Bl. 164–65.

53   SStA Leipzig, BPA Leipzig, IV/2/1/24, Bl. 64.

54   SStA Chemnitz, BPA Karl-Marx-Stadt, IV/2/4/71, Bl. 116.

55   SStA Chemnitz, BPA Karl-Marx-Stadt, IV/2/4/70, Bl. 3.

56   SAPMO-BArch, DY/30 IV 2/6/02, Nr. 96, Bl. 176.

57   ThHStA Weimar, BPA Erfurt, IV/2/4-140, 'Aktennotiz, Erfurt', 22.3.50.

58   SStA Leipzig, BPA Leipzig, IV/2/3/148, Bl. 87.

59   SStA Chemnitz, BPA Karl-Marx-Stadt, IV/2/4/10, Bl. 270–71. For further examples, see Pritchard (n. 12 above), p. 335, n. 161.

60   SStA Chemnitz, BPA Karl-Marx-Stadt, IV/2/4/14, Bl. 265.

61 ThHStA Weimar, BPA Erfurt, IV/2/4-119, letter from the SED Kreisleitung Worbis to the LPKK, 9.2.51.

62 SStA Chemnitz, BPA Karl-Marx-Stadt, IV/2/4/14, Bl. 266.

63 See, e.g., SStA Chemnitz, BPA Karl-Marx-Stadt: IV/2/4/10, Bl. 126–35; IV/2/4/20, Bl. 7–50; IV/2/4/61, Bl. 271–73 & 278–80.

64 ThHStA Weimar, BPA Erfurt, AIV/2/4-139, 'Trotzkistische und nationalistische Tendenzen in der Partei'.

65 SStA Chemnitz, BPA Karl-Marx-Stadt, IV/2/4/46, Bl. 279.

66 SStA Chemnitz, BPA Karl-Marx-Stadt, V/5/333, Bl. 3.

67 From a speech delivered by Otto Grotewohl in January 1949, quoted in K.W. Fricke, *Selbstbehauptung und Widerstand in der Sowjetischen Besatzungszone Deutschlands*, Bonn & [West] Berlin, 1964, p. 35.

68 SStA Leipzig, BPA Leipzig, IV/2/1/26, Bl. 4.

69 For examples, see Pritchard (n. 12 above), p. 335, n. 172.

70 SAPMO-BArch, NY4076/158, Bl. 1–4.

71 B. Bouvier & H. Schulz, '...*die SPD aber aufgehört hat zu existieren*', Bonn, 1991, 242.

72 See, e.g., SStA Chemnitz, BPA Karl-Marx-Stadt, IV/2/4/10, Bl. 55.

73 See, e.g., SStA Chemnitz, BPA Karl-Marx-Stadt, IV/2/4/14, Bl. 176.

74 See, e.g., ibid., Bl. 265.

75 See, e.g., ibid., Bl. 315 & SStA Leipzig, BPA Leipzig, IV/2/1/27, Bl. 37.

76 See, e.g.: SStA Chemnitz, BPA Karl-Marx-Stadt, IV/2/4/61, Bl. 163 & 256; ThHStA Weimar, BPA Erfurt, AIV/2/3-195, Bl. 152; SStA Leipzig, BPA Leipzig, IV/2/1/30, Bl. 71.

77 ThHStA Weimar, BPA Erfurt, AIV/2/4-119, letter from the SED Kreissekretariat to the LPKK, 14.2.51.

78 See, e.g., SStA Chemnitz, BPA Karl-Marx-Stadt, IV/2/4/10, Bl. 79.

79 See, e.g., SStA Chemnitz, BPA Karl-Marx-Stadt, IV/2/4/62, Bl. 311.

80 See, e.g.: SStA Chemnitz, BPA Karl-Marx-Stadt, IV/2/4/61, Bl. 256 & V/5/333, Bl.1-2; ThHStA Weimar, BPA Erfurt, AIV/2/4-119, 'Berichterstattung über parteifeindliche Zentren innerhalb unserer Partei'.

81 See, e.g., SStA Chemnitz, BPA Karl-Marx-Stadt, IV/2/4/62, Bl. 284.

82 ThHStA Weimar, BPA Erfurt, AIV/2/4-105, 'Notiz von dem Kursus in Berlin vom 3. bis einschließlich 5. November 1949', 7.11.49.

83 SStA Chemnitz, BPA Karl-Marx-Stadt, IV/2/4/20, Bl. 81.

84 SStA Chemnitz, BPA Karl-Marx-Stadt, IV/2/4/14, Bl. 96. For further examples, see Pritchard (n. 12 above), p. 337, n. 191.

85 For examples, see ibid., p. 337, n. 192.

86 SStA Chemnitz, BPA Karl-Marx-Stadt, IV/2/4/61, Bl. 243.

87 ThHStA Weimar, BPA Erfurt, AIV/2/4-119, letter from the SED Kreisleitung Weimar to the LPKK, 7.2.51.

88 Ibid., letter from the LPKK Erfurt to the ZPKK, 9.2.51.

89 ThHStA Weimar, BPA Erfurt, AIV/2/4-139, 'KPO Altenburg'.

90 SStA Chemnitz, BPA Karl-Marx-Stadt, IV/2/4/14, Bl. 7.

91 See, e.g., SStA Chemnitz, BPA Karl-Marx-Stadt: IV/2/4/4 (Bd. 1), Bl. 446; IV/2/4/10, Bl. 155; IV/2/4/14, Bl. 267.

92 SStA Chemnitz, BPA Karl-Marx-Stadt, IV/2/4/14, Bl. 334.

93   ThHStA Weimar, BPA Erfurt, AIV/2/4-119, 'Niederschrift über die Sitzung des VVN-Sekretariats Altenburg', 30.12.50.

94   See, e.g., SStA Chemnitz, BPA Karl-Marx-Stadt, V/5/198, Bl. 64–82 & ThHStA Weimar, BdM, 660, Bl. 86.

95   See, e.g., SStA Leipzig, BPA Leipzig, IV/2/3/150, Bl. 239 & ThHStA Weimar, BPA Erfurt, AIV/2/4-139, 'Trotzkistische und nationalistische Tendenzen in der Partei'.

96   See, e.g., ThHStA Weimar, MdI, 142, Bl. 17–19.

97   SStA Chemnitz, BPA Karl-Marx-Stadt, IV/2/4/4 (Bd. 1), Bl. 446.

98   See, e.g., ThHStA Weimar, BPA Erfurt, AIV/2/4-119, letter from the LPKK Erfurt to the KPKK, 9.2.51, Bl. 3.

99   A. Herbst et al. (eds.), *So funktionierte die DDR*, Band 2, Rinbeck bei Hamburg, 1994, p. 1129.

100   For a detailed history of the VVN, see E. Reuter & D. Hansel, *Das kurze Leben der VVN von 1947 bis 1953*, Berlin, 1997.

101   Herbst et al. (n. 99 above), pp. 1126–28.

102   SStA Chemnitz, VVN, 47, letter from the VVN Kreisvorstand Plauen to the SED Kreisvorstand Plauen, 15.9.50.

103   ThHStA Weimar, BPA Erfurt, AIV/2/4-119, 'Niederschrift über die Sitzung des VVN-Sekretariats Altenburg', 30.12.50.

104   Ibid., letter from the KPKK Gotha to the LPKK, 12.2.51.

105   See, e.g., SStA Chemnitz, VVN, 47, 'Arbeitsplan der VVN Kreis Plauen vom 1. bis 14.9.52'.

106   See, e.g., SStA Chemnitz, BPA Karl-Marx-Stadt, IV/2/4/4 (Bd. 1) Bl. 159 & IV/2/4/14, Bl. 108.

107   Herbst et al. (n. 99 above), p. 1130.

108   Lewis (n. 6 above), p. 83.

109   R.J. Crampton, *Eastern Europe in the Twentieth Century*, London & New York, 1994, pp. 262–63.

110   Ibid., pp. 266–68.

111   SStA Chemnitz, BPA Karl-Marx-Stadt, IV/2/4/10, Bl. 265.

112   SStA Chemnitz, BPA Karl-Marx-Stadt, IV/2/4/46, Bl. 280.

113   ThHStA Weimar, BPA Erfurt, AIV/2/4-111. For further examples, see Pritchard (n. 12 above), p. 339, n. 226.

114   Kaiser (n. 14 above), pp. 689-91.

115   SStA Leipzig, BPA Leipzig, IV/2/1/34, Bl. 71.

116   SStA Chemnitz, VVN, 43, letter from the VVN Ortsgruppe Limbach-Oberfroha to the Bezirksprüfungsausschuß, 29.1.53.

117   SStA Chemnitz, BPA Karl-Marx-Stadt, IV/2/4/4 (Bd. 1), Bl. 284.

118   SStA Chemnitz, BPA Karl-Marx-Stadt, IV/2/4/82, Bl. 7.

119   SStA Leipzig, BPA Leipzig, IV/2/1/24, Bl. 27–28.

120   SStA Leipzig, BPA Leipzig, IV/2/1/27, Bl. 34–35.

121   Schenk (n. 4 above), p. 21.

122   SStA Leipzig, BPA Leipzig, IV/2/1/24, Bl. 68–73 & 89.

123   Ibid., Bl. 60–68.

124   ThHStA Weimar, BdM, 674, Bl. 280.

125   See, e.g., SStA Leipzig, BPA Leipzig, IV/2/1/24, Bl. 60–68.

126   See SStA Leipzig, BPA Leipzig, IV/2/1/24 and IV/2/1/25.

127   SStA Chemnitz, BPA Karl-Marx-Stadt, IV/2/4/10, Bl. 140.
128   ThHStA Weimar, BPA Erfurt, AIV/2/4-139, letter from the LPKK to the SED Kreisvorstand Arnstadt, 18.7.50.
129   SStA Chemnitz, BPA Karl-Marx-Stadt, IV/2/4/61, Bl. 187.
130   ThHStA Weimar, BPA Erfurt, AIV/2/4-139, letter from W.K. to the SED secretariat Erfurt, 30.12.45.
131   Ibid., letter from B.E. For scores of similar letters see ThHStA Weimar, BPA Erfurt, AIV/2/4-119 and AIV/2/4-139.
132   H. Prauss, *Doch es war nicht die Wahrheit*, [West] Berlin, 1960, pp. 48–49.
133   SStA Chemnitz, BPA Karl-Marx-Stadt, V/5/041.
134   SStA Chemnitz, BPA Karl-Marx-Stadt, V/5/069, Bl. 4.
135   Prauss (n. 132 above), p. 49.
136   SStA Chemnitz, VVN, 45, letter from the VVN Ortsgruppe Frankenberg to the VVN Landessekretariat, 13.12.51.
137   SStA Chemnitz, BPA Karl-Marx-Stadt, IV/2/4/61, Bl. 33–38.
138   Quoted in R. Conquest, *The Great Terror: A Reassessment*, London, 1990, p. 118.

8

Workers' party
versus working class

The Stalinisation of the Soviet zone after 1947 affected not just those workers organised in the SED, but the whole of the East German working class. Above all, the introduction of Soviet economic practices led to material privation, ruthless exploitation and a determined campaign to subordinate the workplace councils and trade unions entirely to the economic and political goals of the SED leadership. However, the harder the regime squeezed the working class, the more the workers lost faith in the labour movement which once had represented their interests, but which was now becoming the primary instrument of their oppression.

The culmination of this process arrived on 17 June 1953, when tens of thousands of workers throughout the GDR went on strike and marched into the streets to vent their anger against the party leadership. Only the timely intervention of the Red Army saved the SED regime from the workers in whose name it purported to govern. Nothing could illustrate more clearly the gulf that now divided the 'workers' party' from the working class.

Yet, even as late as June 1953, the break between the party and the working class was not entirely complete. The party and the proletariat still, to an extent, overlapped. Many veteran SED and FDGB functionaries still had roots in the class from whose ranks they had come and were still under the influence of the native German traditions of Socialism. Many older workers, for all their grievances, had not yet broken completely with the state they had helped to create, nor had they entirely abandoned the dream of Socialism in Germany. These ambiguities were to have a very significant impact on the behaviour of both groups and, in part, determined the whole course and character of the June Uprising.

Turning the screw on the workers

On 4 June 1947, the Soviet military authorities issued an order (*Befehl Nr. 138*) establishing the so-called 'German Economic Commission' (DWK), the purpose of which was to oversee and co-ordinate the economic development of the five *Länder* of the Soviet zone of occupation. Over the next six years, most of the major features of a Soviet-style command economy fell into place. In February 1948, a new SMAD order (*Befehl Nr. 32*) was issued, which gave greater powers to the DWK at the expense of the various *Land* authorities,[1] and, between 1948 and the foundation of the GDR in 1949, the DWK effectively functioned as an incipient East German government.[2] On 1 January 1949, a 'two-year plan', modelled closely on Soviet economic practices, came into effect. This in turn was succeeded in January 1951 by a full five-year plan. After Ulbricht had announced in July 1952 that the GDR was ready to make the transition to Socialism, the Sovietisation of the economy was extended to the agricultural sector, with 128,000 farmers being persuaded or compelled to join collective farms.[3] Although by the time of Stalin's death in 1953 the collectivisation of agriculture was still far from complete, in most other respects the East German economy had been effectively Sovietised.

For ordinary workers in the factories and workplaces, the transition to Soviet-style economics brought with it inequality, hardship and exploitation. In order to boost production and fulfil the plan, individuals who were deemed to be of particular importance to the economy were given material incentives at the expense of their more expendable colleagues. The main beneficiaries of this policy were the members of the so-called 'technical intelligentsia' (engineers, technicians, scientists, specialists, etc.) whose services were considered invaluable, but who had been departing in large numbers to the West. Consequently, from the late spring of 1947, the authorities made a concerted effort to conciliate highly skilled and professional people, even those of compromised or reactionary provenance. In the words of the main SED speaker at an economic conference in Leipzig in April 1947: 'We have the absolute duty of enlisting the co-operation of scientists, engineers, technicians, doctors, indeed all those men who are so urgently needed in economic life, above all when they were nominal Pgs [*Parteigenossen*, i.e. members of the NSDAP].'[4]

In accordance with this new policy of appeasing the technical intelligentsia, many of the Nazi specialists, engineers and managers who had been ejected from their posts in 1945 and compelled to perform menial physical labour were reinstated in their former positions. As one SED functionary put it: 'We must take these specialists away from the shovel and reinstate them where they are needed.'[5] Special and superior canteens and wash-rooms were set up for their benefit, whilst the ordinary workers had to continue using whatever dirty and dilapidated facilities had not been destroyed during the war.[6] A network of special shops (*Handelsorganisation* or HO) was established, in which the technical intelligentsia, and the equally privileged party bigwigs, had access to commodities which were either of far higher quality than those available in the normal shops or which could otherwise only be purchased on the black market.[7] Most importantly, the relatively egalitarian wage policies of the immediate post-war period were forgotten, and managers and specialists began to leave the shop-floor workers far behind in terms of wages and bonuses. At one plant in Hennigsdorf, for example, the firm's directors took one half of all the money which had been allocated as bonuses for themselves, leaving the other half to be shared amongst the entire workforce.[8] At a typical factory in the Thuringian town of Straußfurt, the firm's book-keeper received a monthly salary of 1,000 marks, whilst the ordinary workers were paid an hourly wage of just 75 pfennigs. If the firm fulfilled the plan, the book-keeper was rewarded with a 100 percent bonus, whilst the ordinary workers received not one pfennig extra.[9]

Amongst the workers on the shop-floor, and also amongst many rank-and-file members and low-ranking functionaries of the SED, all this was a cause of bitter resentment, particularly in the many instances where individuals being thus favoured were former Nazis. Indeed, judging by the frequency with which SED members complained about this matter, the existence of the HO, the ever more visible differentiation within the workplace and, above all, the favouritism shown towards former Nazis were amongst their primary grievances at this time. A typical report from the Thuringian town of Hermsdorf noted that the workers were grumbling 'that many old Nazis are doing better than the workers in terms of food'.[10] A visitation of SED dignitaries in 1950 to the Abus-Maschinenbau near Nordhausen in Thuringia noted with concern 'that within the workforce there is a great aversion to the [technical] intelligentsia... above all amongst former KPD comrades'.[11] Heinrich Fomferra, an SED functionary and veteran Communist, complained about having to work with ex-Nazi 'slime people' who, with the explicit support of the Soviets and the SED leadership, were once again oozing their way up the social ladder.[12] According to a report from Zschopau in 1953, many SED members were arguing: 'The intelligentsia must be brought to account once and for all. The preferential treatment of the intelligentsia is bullshit. The stores where the intelligentsia have the right to go shopping must be smashed.'[13]

On numerous occasions, ordinary workers, and SED and FDGB functionaries, did more than simply complain about what was happening in their workplaces, and attempted to modify, hinder or prevent the introduction of what they saw as capitalist working practices. Often, workers tried to intimidate their more privileged colleagues by sending them threatening letters.[14] Elsewhere, SED or FDGB functionaries flatly refused to co-operate with former Nazis, or dragged their feet about promoting them, no matter how necessary their skills were deemed to be by the authorities.[15] In many instances, both ordinary workers and functionaries resisted the introduction of 'achievement' bonuses, which were intended mainly for the pockets of managers, engineers and specialists. At the Kombinat Friedländer, for example, there was such a strong feeling that the annual bonus should be divided equally amongst the workers, rather than creamed off by managers and technicians, that the police had to be called in so that the money could be distributed without incident.[16] In November 1948, the authorities abolished the traditional Christmas bonus, which had been paid equally to every worker, and created in its place a 'productivity bonus', which was supposed to be distributed only amongst those members of staff who were deemed to have made a special contribution in the previous year. In many factories, however, SED and FDGB functionaries ensured that the bonus money was shared out equally amongst the entire workforce in what the leadership of the SED in Leipzig referred to contemptuously as 'Christmas alms'.[17] In Thuringia, a number of SED factory cells sent delegations to Berlin to complain about the withdrawal of the workers' traditional Christmas bonuses.[18] All such efforts, however, were in vain, and functionaries who squealed too hard in protest at the increasing differentiation inside the workplace were either dismissed, expelled from the party or schooled into submission.[19]

What made the privileges of the new elite particularly galling for most workers was the fact that, whilst former Nazis were apparently being allowed to flourish, they themselves were being expected to make ever greater sacrifices in the name of fulfilling the plan. At meetings in their factories, in their newspapers and on the radio, workers were constantly admonished 'that the construction of the foundations of Socialism in the GDR cannot proceed without the great efforts of the party – that is self-evident – but also on the part of the working class', and that it was entirely erroneous to believe, as many workers and SED members did, that the 'basic law' of Socialism was the satisfaction of human need.[20] Accordingly, the workers were expected to put up with low wages, high prices, poor conditions and ever harsher discipline.

Though it rarely admitted this in public, the SED was well aware that its economic policies were causing hardship on the shop-floor. Internal party or trade union reports from the period are full of accounts of the miserable conditions under which workers were being compelled to labour. In August 1948, for example, an official inspection of the Moritz Lindner printing works in Markranstädt found that the thirty-five employees were having to work in a badly lit, dirty workroom in which neither the heating, the water supply nor the sanitation facilities were functioning properly.[21] At the Vereinigte Trikotagewerke in Crimmitschau, a report from 1953 noted that 600 female workers had access to just six toilets and two showers.[22] In many larger factories, meanwhile, security guards (*Betriebsschutz*) or even policemen were employed both to patrol the shop-floor during working hours and to search workers on their way home at the end of their shifts in order to prevent 'sabotage' and petty pilfering. Though theft does indeed seem to have been a serious problem at many workplaces, the workers bitterly resented the indignity of having to work under guard, and the humiliation of being treated as potential criminals and saboteurs.[23]

However, the most important instruments through which the authorities attempted to squeeze the workers were the so-called 'Technical Work Norms' (TANs). As was seen in Chapter 6, as early as the summer of 1945 the KPD had dropped its traditional opposition to any form of piece-work, arguing that, given the desperate material circumstances, it was in the interests of the working population to raise production by any means possible. However, in the first two years of occupation progress on this front was slow, for the hostility of the labour movement to such practices was too great, and the grip of the regime on the shop-floor was still too tenuous. By the autumn of 1947, the authorities were more firmly in the saddle, the organs of the labour movement had been cowed and disciplined, and this, coupled with the overall political climate, made possible the more widespread introduction of piece-work and production norms. Accordingly, on 9 October 1947, the Soviet military government issued an order (*Befehl Nr. 234*) entitled 'Measures for the Raising of Labour Productivity', which demanded the blanket introduction of Soviet-style working practices.[24] In the ensuing months and years, workers, particularly in VEBs and SAGs, were pressured and bullied into 'voluntarily' accepting the new work norms.

At the same time, the regime also created a movement of highly paid and privileged 'shock workers', named after the Saxon coal miner Adolf Hennecke, who, on 12 October 1948, overfulfilled his daily norm by 287 percent. As in the Soviet Union, the Stakhanovite activities of these 'norm busters' were supposed to provide an example to their fellow workers,[25] but in reality they were used as a ratchet, providing the authorities with an excuse continually to raise the norms expected of the rest of the workforce. Unsurprisingly, shock workers tended to be extremely unpopular with their less privileged colleagues. When Hennecke stood in the trade union elections of November 1948, he got a derisory vote, even amongst the miners at his own pit. In the face of this open snub, the authorities were reluctantly compelled to admit 'that our colleague Hennecke does not possess the full trust of all those organised in the trade union in the coal-field. That means, therefore, that the Hennecke movement is rejected by a not inconsiderable section of the miners in your coalfield.'[26]

As in the Soviet Union during the 1930s, the ruthless and crude economic policies employed in East Germany after 1947 often proved counter-productive. Driving men and machines to their limit might boost production in the short term, but, in the long term, the constant pressure to fulfil the plan at all costs led to mechanical break-downs, escalating sick rates and more frequent accidents. This became particularly evident after 1952, when, in association with the decision to 'build Socialism', even greater pressure was put on industry to increase production. By the first half of 1953, the economy was becoming so overstrained and overheated that, like a rusty and badly tuned engine being run at far too rapid a speed, it was beginning to shake itself to pieces.

For example, at the VEB Kombinat 'Otto Grotewohl', a producer of lignite briquettes, a report of March 1953 was forced to concede that, although the individual workers at the plant were fulfilling their norms, they were only able to do so by taking short cuts which were both dangerous and damaging. The workers, the report noted, had removed protective devices from machines in order to speed up their output, and the finished briquettes were being taken out of the presses before the machines had come to a stand-still. Moreover, the slipshod work practices being employed at the plant were damaging the equipment and leading to a final product of inferior quality. As a result of these factors, the productivity of the plant, which had been increasing at a monthly rate of 7 percent in April and May 1952, had by December 1952 fallen by 0.2 percent. Whilst individual workers were fulfilling their norms by an average of 108.5 percent, the factory as a whole was only producing 96.6 percent of its target. In other words, more than 10 percent of the work done at the plant was of such poor quality that it contributed nothing to the overall production figures.[27]

In the Zwickau-Oelsnitz coal-field, meanwhile, the relentless drive to in-crease the output of this key commodity was similarly proving counter-pro-ductive. At the Karl-Marx-Werk, there had been an average of one serious fire a year throughout the period 1946 to 1950. In 1951, however, as a direct result of unsafe working practices, there were no fewer than eight serious fires, and in the first three quarters of 1952 there were a further nine serious fires. At the Martin-Hoop coal mine near Zwickau, the percentage of workers reporting sick at any one time increased from 12.1 percent in the first quarter of 1951 to 16.7 percent during the first quarter of 1952.[28] In January 1952, the Martin-Hoop coal mine produced 95.9 percent of its monthly target, but this fell to 86 percent in March 1952.[29] By October 1952, production in the entire coal-field had dropped by 5.1 percent in the preceding twelve months, and the coal-field's managers were predicting a further drop of 12 percent for the following year.[30]

As the regime applied increasing pressure to the economy throughout the later 1940s and early 1950s, it thus found itself confronted by a problem entirely of its own making. The harder it pushed on the economic levers, the more wastage and inefficiency there were in the economy. It is a characteris-tic feature of Stalinist dictatorships, however, that they are extraordinarily reluctant to acknowledge their own mistakes, for to do so necessarily tends to undermine the party's claim to be the infallible teacher and guide of the working masses. The whole logic and dynamic of Stalinism thus drives the party to respond to economic failure by increasing the level of political oppression, for, if the party's own policies are not responsible for the economic difficulties being experienced, then somebody else must be found to shoulder the blame.

Thus, if managers and officials displayed their scepticism about the realism of the party's economic plans, as they often did, they were accused of lacking faith in the working class and of holding back production through their defeatism and dilatoriness.[31] If, however, managers strove to meet the plan by driving their workers relentlessly, they were often accused of using brutish and dictatorial behaviour which was impeding the creative participation of the workers in the production process.[32] With increasing frequency, the authorities blamed the workplace councils, trade unions and SED workplace cells for not explaining to the workers the necessity of pushing themselves to the limit in the interests of fulfilling the plan.[33] Above all, the regime blamed the economic crisis on 'enemy agents' and 'saboteurs', who, it was claimed, had systematically infiltrated the entire industrial apparatus of East Germany with the sole intention of wrecking it from within. The SED *Bezirksleitung* in Leipzig, for example, when considering the alarming rise in the number of industrial accidents in the period 1952 to 1953, came to the conclusion: 'For the most part these are organised acts of sabotage.'[34] In the Zwickau-Oelsnitz coal-field, the spate of serious fires was eventually blamed on a group of 'treacherous' officials and managers, who were duly brought before a show trial and imprisoned on the grounds that they had deliberately introduced unsafe working practices in the hope of causing fires. As so often in the crazy, twisted world of Stalinist demonology, there was in fact some truth in the allegation, for the officials do indeed appear to have cut so many corners that they were at least partly responsible for the crisis in the coal industry.[35] The devil in whose name they had perpetrated their crimes, however, was not 'American imperialism', as was alleged at the trial, but the Stalinist cult of production, upon the altar of which they were now to be offered up as scapegoats.

Inevitably, the merciless economic vice in which the East German working class was being squeezed also produced a mounting wave of discontent and resistance. Though neither the Soviets nor the SED government acknowledged this in public, internal police, interior ministry and SED reports documented in vivid detail the final and decisive break between the regime and the working class in whose name it governed. When, in October 1947, the Soviet authorities issued their *Befehl Nr. 234* on improving industrial productivity, it was hailed in the press and at SED public meetings as a great step forward, which corresponded to the will of the overwhelming majority of the working population. However, as internal reports compiled by the Thuringian Ministry of the Interior bluntly noted: 'The opinions which have been published in the press with regard to the Sokolovsky order in no way correspond to the mood and the opinion in the workplaces themselves.'[36] Shortly thereafter, the Thuringian Interior Ministry was deluged with reports that many workers were complaining that they were worse off than under the Nazis,[37] that workers who made illegal border crossings were returning with tales of the vigorous economic upturn in the western zones and that the SED slogan 'Produce More, Live Better' was regarded with contempt by the majority of workers, because it 'stands in contradiction to experience, since production has indeed been increased, yet life has not become better'.[38]

Over the following years, as the teeth of the economic vice gripped ever tighter, so the divisions between the party and the proletariat became more and more apparent. By 1950, the authorities in Nordhausen were reporting that workers on the shop-floor were refusing to talk to SED activists, ostensibly on the grounds that they could not afford to lose time on the job.[39] In 1951, SED activists in Chemnitz were admitting that the only way they could get to talk to workers was by approaching them in their own homes; otherwise, the workers would simply walk away.[40] In the workplace council elections of 1947, more than 50 percent of the vote went to non-SED candidates, despite the party's massive logistical and organisational advantages.[41] In 1949, the SED in Plauen reported that, whilst the highly qualified workers and 'technical intelligentsia' were happy with the course of events, the party no longer enjoyed the trust and the confidence of the 'broad masses'.[42] In the trade union elections held in Thuringia in the spring of 1950, only 33 percent of delegates elected in private firms were SED members, whilst in many VEBs, where the SED had a greater stranglehold, as many as 16 or 18 percent of ballot slips were rendered invalid, often because the workers had scrawled anti-SED slogans across them. Significantly, the number of invalid votes was highest in the larger VEBs, which had been the first to be involved in the new approach to production, and which were hence further down the road to Stalinisation.[43]

On numerous occasions, the bitter opposition of workers to developments in their factories and workplaces spilled over into covert or open resistance. Most commonly, working-class opposition to the regime and its policies did not go beyond the defacement of posters or the writing of graffiti.[44] Often, however, workers resorted to more violent or threatening measures, such as writing threatening letters to SED functionaries or the hated 'technical intelligentsia'.[45] In June 1948, for example, an anonymous letter was sent to the management of the Baumwoll-Spinnerei Mittweida, denouncing the tyranny of Communism for turning the worker into a 'beast of burden for the state' and for reducing the human being to 'a nothing, a slave'. According to the writer of the anonymous letter, oppositional groups were being created which would take bloody vengeance on all the managers and party officials who collaborated with the Russians ('These people should just have their faces smashed in!')[46] Though the oppositional groups referred to in the letter were almost certainly fictitious, now and again, in a more spontaneous manner, groups of workers did take their revenge on those they perceived as either traitors or oppressors. Norm-breakers, for example, were occasionally beaten up by their fellow workers,[47] whilst it was not unknown for SED officials to be set upon in lonely alleys or viciously attacked in bar-room brawls.[48]

However, the most obvious weapon with which discontented workers have traditionally sought to defend their economic interests is, of course, the strike. This, too, was an increasingly prominent feature of industrial life in East Germany in the years after 1947, and in particular after 1952. Normally, such instances of industrial unrest were isolated, local and of short duration. However, by the late spring of 1953, the deteriorating economic situation, coupled with the increasingly tense political climate, led to a positive rash of such incidents. In Leipzig, for example, there was in May 1953 a whole series of strikes which revealed the diverse grievances festering beneath the surface. In one factory, the workers exceeded their target significantly and were therefore due to be paid a sizeable bonus. On pay day, however, the firm only had enough money in its coffers to cover 90 percent of the employees' wages, as a result of which the workers immediately walked out on strike.[49] For similar reasons, there were also short strikes at the VEB 'Eko' in Oschatz, at the Leipzig 'Eisen- und Stahlwerke', and at the VEB 'EGB' in Leisnig.[50] At the Leipziger Bekleidungswerk, meanwhile, there was a short strike in protest at the dictatorial way in which norm increases had been imposed, whilst in the VEB Bodenbearbeitungsgeräte Leipzig the workers struck for one day because they were opposed in principle to the introduction of norms into their factory.[51]

For the workplace councils and trade unions, the polarisation between the party and the working class rang the death knell, for their very existence as real, living organisations of the labour movement depended upon their role as mediators between the employers (the SED state) and employees. However, in the new, Stalinist economy now under construction there was no longer room for mediation of any sort. In the long term, there were only two possibilities for the further evolution of the workplace organisations of the East German working class. Either they would remain true to their constituents, in which case they could expect an open confrontation with the regime and certain prohibition, or they would become abject tools of the authorities, which in turn would lose them the trust and support of the workers they purported to represent.

Of the two types of shop-floor organisation, it was the workplace councils which, on account of their decentralised character and their proximity to the shop-floor workers, proved most resistant to the ongoing ossification of the labour movement. After the disappointing council elections of 1947, the Soviets and the SED authorities began to adopt a much harder line towards the workplace councils, stressing the responsibility of delegates to place the raising of production at the very forefront of all their activities. In Thuringia,

General Kolesnichenko publicly warned council delegates not to interfere in the many aspects of workplace life which were now deemed not to concern them.[52] In November 1947, the Central Administration for Industry in the Soviet zone warned that the workplace councils were not doing enough to raise productivity, and were interfering too much in the work of the technical and managerial personnel, which in turn was having a deleterious impact on production.[53] In Leipzig, an instruction was sent out to SED workplace cells to keep a very close eye on the newly elected delegates, 'because a good many work against the line of the party and the trade union'.[54] Shortly thereafter, in conjunction with the release of *Befehl Nr. 234*, a new 'Order for Work in VEBs, SAGs and other Workplaces' was released, in which numerous duties but no specific rights of workplace councils were mentioned, and which cancelled all previously existing agreements on 'co-determination' where they contradicted the new order.[55]

In the following year, there was a further, dramatic hardening of official attitudes towards the workplace councils. In May 1948, the FDGB leadership announced that the trade unions were going to take over many of the functions hitherto performed by the councils. In July, the 'right of co-determination' of the workplace councils was limited to those matters which directly affected the welfare of workers, and, in the following month, even this tightly circumscribed sphere of activities was taken over by the trade unions.[56] Throughout 1948, meanwhile, workplace council elections were repeatedly postponed, no doubt because the authorities feared a repetition of the previous year's debacle.[57] Finally, in November 1948, an FDGB conference in Bitterfeld decided, 'in order to comply with the wishes of thousands of workplaces', to dissolve the workplace councils in any enterprise where more than 80 percent of the workforce was organised in the trade union. Shortly thereafter, this decision was extended to all workplaces.[58] Officially, the justification for the abolition of the workplace councils was that, whilst they had performed a useful function in an economic environment that had been dominated by capitalist enterprise, in the context of a society moving towards Socialism they were no longer appropriate. Underlying this argument, however, was the assumption that an organ under direct party control (the FDGB) would serve the general interest better than an organ elected by the workers themselves.

The official trade union federation was always a more reliable tool of official policy than the workplace councils, for it was a highly centralised organisation, the leadership of which had always been firmly under Communist control. Even in the FDGB, however, the Soviet tradition of Spencer unionism did not overcome the native German tradition without a struggle. In many localities, particularly in those areas which had originally been captured by the Americans rather than the Soviets, large numbers of moderate Social Democrats and former functionaries of the ADGB had penetrated the re-emerging trade union movement. In Leipzig, the

Americans helped the moderate trade unionist Erich Schilling to establish himself as the dominant figure in the city's trade union movement, much to the annoyance of local Communists.[59] By the time the Soviets marched into Halle in July 1945, the SPD had penetrated the trade unions to such an extent 'that the trade union and the SPD were practically identical'.[60] Although, in the ensuing two years, the Communists expended much effort to bring such local trade union organisations under their control, there were many localities or individual factories where traces of the earlier SPD predominance could still be seen even in the late 1940s and early 1950s. In Heiligenstadt, for example, the *Kreisvorstand* of the FDGB in July 1948 contained six former Social Democrats but only three former Communists. In the various FDGB local executive committees in the *Kreis* of Heiligenstadt, there were three former KPD members but no fewer than sixteen former Social Democrats.[61]

The non-Communist element inside the FDGB was further strengthened after the suppression of the workplace councils in November 1948, for many thousands of former council delegates took over functions in the trade union movement.[62] These former council delegates, steeped as they were in the more democratic traditions of the workplace councils, changed, albeit temporarily, the character and composition of the FDGB. Within a month of the dissolution of the councils, hard-line Stalinists in the FDGB were complaining that their activities were being hindered by the former council delegates, who 'in most cases attempted to solve their allotted tasks in the style of the workplace councils'.[63]

What the former Social Democrats and the former workplace council delegates in the FDGB had in common was the fact that they tended to be deeply attached to the notion, now considered by the authorities to be obsolete, that the primary function of workers' representatives was to represent the workers rather than the employers. This attachment to the traditional function of trade unions, however, was condemned by the authorities as 'only-trade-unionism' (*Nurgewerkschaftlertum*),[64] and individual functionaries who held such views either became extremely disillusioned, or got into serious trouble, or both. In 1949, for example, the *Kreis* secretary of the FDGB in Gera was expelled for having written in a letter that the authorities should 'finally desist from trying out Russian methods here in Germany on our own poor mates'.[65] In 1950, a leading FDGB functionary in Arnstadt was thrown out of the union for having refused to acknowledge that it was in the interests of the working class as a whole for employees in VEBs to be paid less than employees in private firms,[66] whilst another functionary at the Reichenbach printing works got into hot water for leading a campaign against the introduction of work norms.[67] In 1952, the chairman of the FDGB branch at the FEMA plant in Dommitzsch persuaded the workers to send a resolution to Berlin demanding a seven-fold increase in the money they were receiving as bonuses.[68] At the VEB 'Ruma' in Mittweida, there was an incident in May 1953 after there had been a considerable delay in paying the workers their wages. In response, the workers approached a long-standing and popular functionary and pleaded with him to intervene on their behalf, which he agreed to do. When, however, all attempts to prise some money out of the management had failed, there was a thirty-minute strike in which the veteran functionary 'took a decisive part'.[69]

In many localities, *Nurgewerkschaftlertum* was more than just a problem confined to individual functionaries, but was deeply embedded in the whole trade union apparatus. In Crimmitschau, for example, the SED authorities complained in 1950 that in a number of important local VEBs, and in almost all the private factories of the Crimmitschau textile industry, the trade unions were dominated by former Social Democrats who were operating a policy of *Nurgewerkschaftlertum*, and who were hence not performing their duties 'from the standpoint of class'.[70] Similar complaints were made by the SED leaderships in Schmalkalden, Reichenbach and Werdau.[71] In other words, trade unionists in Crimmitschau and elsewhere were guilty of putting the immediate interests of their members above the interests of the working class as a whole, as interpreted, of course, by the SED leadership.

In order to eradicate such troublesome relics of past traditions, the SED launched a vigorous campaign in the late 1940s to bring the trade unions firmly and finally under control from above. FDGB functionaries were hauled off to party schools where they were lectured interminably about the evils of *Nurgewerkschaftlertum*. Trade unionists who proved resistant to such arguments were expelled from the FDGB and SED. In November 1950, for instance, five leading functionaries of the FDGB in Reichenbach, all of whom were former members of the SPD, were dismissed from their posts on account of their alleged *Nurgewerkschaftlertum*.[72] In December 1950, there were sweeping personnel changes at the Karl Marx coal mine near Zwickau in order to loosen the grip of former Social Democrats on the trade union apparatus.[73]

From the point of view of the regime, the campaign to discipline the trade unions was successful, for gradually but systematically the FDGB was transformed from being an intermediary organisation between employees and employers into being a passive and pliant tool of the latter. On the other hand, the Stalinisation of the trade unions was not achieved without a political price having to be paid. As the unions became more and more subservient to the authorities, so the workers lost faith in them and came increasingly to regard them as just another branch of management. At the Martin-Hoop coal mine, for instance, a report from 1952 noted that 533 of the enterprise's 5,292 workers had failed to join the union, that 400 trade union members were behind with their subscriptions, and that: 'According to our information and observations, the miners have no faith in the trade union.'[74] In the Thuringian town of Meiningen, it was reported that the workers at the Reichsbahnausbesserungwerk had lost all interest in the trade union, which now existed only on paper.[75] At the Maschinenfabrik Meuselwitz, the trade union leadership gave up even trying to mobilise the workforce on the grounds that 'they no longer possessed the trust of the workforce'.[76]

The June 1953 Uprising

These mounting discontents were eventually unleashed by a chain of events which began with the death of Stalin in March 1953 and which culminated, between 16 and 20 June 1953, in a series of strikes and violent demonstrations against the SED regime and its policies. At the beginning of June, Grotewohl and Ulbricht had been summoned to Moscow where the new Soviet leadership had instructed them to adopt more moderate policies in the GDR. Upon their return to Berlin, the SED leaders duly, if reluctantly, implemented the so-called 'New Course'. Many measures against the middle classes, farmers and Christians were rescinded. Crucially, however, the government insisted that a 10 percent increase in work norms, announced the previous May, would under no circumstances be cancelled. On 16 June, building workers in Berlin downed tools and marched into the city centre to protest at what they perceived as this unfair treatment of the working class. On 17 June, the protests spread throughout the whole of the GDR, affecting almost every major town and city. With the SED and state apparatus paralysed by the internal conflict between reformers and hard-liners, only the intervention of the Red Army saved the regime from ignominious collapse. Although by the evening of 17 June the main threat to the regime had been neutralised, there were a number of small-scale strikes and disturbances for a few days afterwards.

There is no need at this point to give a blow-by-blow description of the June Uprising, for there are already a number of monographs which give excellent narrative accounts.[77] It would seem more profitable to concentrate on exploring how the various trends and processes outlined in the preceding chapters impacted upon the course and character of the Uprising. In particular, we shall address the fierce historiographical debate which has raged between the various political factions in Germany ever since 17 June 1953.

As so often in questions of post-war German history, one can identify three main schools of thought: the official East German version, the mainstream western interpretation and the analysis provided by radical but anti-Stalinist historians. Each of these three groups, as one would expect, characterised the Uprising in very different ways. By historians working in the GDR, it was always regarded as an 'attempted counter-revolutionary coup' (*konterrevolutionärer Putschversuch*). For mainstream western scholars and politicians, by contrast, it was a 'people's uprising' (*Volksaufstand*), the purpose of which was to end the experiment of Socialism in the GDR and bring about the reunification of Germany. Amongst radical western historians, 17 June was seen first and foremost as a 'workers' uprising' (*Arbeiteraufstand*) against Stalinism, the goal of which was not to destroy Socialism in East Germany, but to free it of its bureaucratic and authoritarian distortions.

17 June 1953 as 'attempted counter-revolutionary putsch'

Historians working in the GDR always attempted to dispose of this most inconvenient of uprisings by filing it away under the label 'attempted counter-revolutionary putsch'. According to this account, the strikes and demonstrations of 17 June were part of an attempted coup organised by reactionary forces in German society, supported by the Western powers, and instigated by provocateurs and secret agents who had been smuggled across the border into the GDR.[78]

This official East German interpretation of the June Uprising was hatched as early as the evening of 17 June itself, when leading SED members met with Russian commanders at Karlshorst in order to discuss how the Uprising could best be explained away.[79] The legend of the 'counter-revolutionary putsch' remained the orthodoxy in the GDR until 1989, and, even today, there are hard-line Party of Democratic Socialism (PDS) members who cling doggedly to this explanation. It should be noted, however, that although the basic lines of this interpretation remained unchanged through thirty-six years of GDR history, there were, over time, considerable shifts of emphasis. In the weeks immediately following the Uprising, the SED apparatus was prepared to acknowledge, at least in private, that the party and the government had made considerable mistakes, which in turn had created 'legitimate grievances' amongst the population. The strikes and demonstrations may have been organised and instigated by provocateurs, but it had been the mistakes of the party which had created such an explosive situation in the first place.

On 7 July 1953, for example, the *Bezirksleitung* of the SED in Leipzig assembled in order to discuss the events of the previous weeks. Though none of the functionaries at the meeting dissented from the official interpretation of the Uprising as a counter-revolutionary putsch, the mood of the meeting was highly self-critical and, indeed, angry. Many of the functionaries complained that they had received no information or instructions from Berlin on 17 June, and that they had only been able to find out what was going on by asking workers who had been listening to RIAS, the anti-Communist radio station based in West Berlin. The SED *Oberbürgermeister* of Leipzig, one Uhlig, complained that he had been sent to talk to the crowds on Karl-Marx-Platz who were demonstrating behind a giant banner proclaiming that 'We declare our solidarity with Berlin!' Since Uhlig had not the faintest idea of what was actually happening in Berlin, he was unable to argue effectively with the protesters.

Other members of the *Bezirksleitung* argued that the Uprising had only been possible because the party and the trade unions had 'ignored people's concerns' and allowed themselves to become separated from the masses. According to one functionary: 'It was thereby demonstrated that we as a party and as a trade union were not at all orientated towards all these questions [i.e. the material problems of the population], that we in practice no longer fulfilled our task, namely the personal care of the people.' In a direct attack on Walter Ulbricht, the first secretary of the Leipzig SED, Paul Fröhlich, even went so far to argue that it was about time the Central Committee 'should also begin to get rid of the exaggerated cult of the personality'.

A particular complaint of the Leipzig leadership was that the party had been taken by surprise on 17 June because of 'white-washing' (*Schönfärberei*), that is, the tendency of official reports to dwell in a fantasy land where every year's grain harvest was better than the year before, where steel production rose inexorably and where the working class, united behind the party, strode ever onwards to the sunlit uplands of socialism where life is better and more cheerful. But now the time had come to face hard realities – 'no more white-washing!' – and to recognise that the SED had lost the trust of the masses and would have to work hard to win it back.[80]

Such trenchant self-criticism gives documents produced in the immediate aftermath of the Uprising a distinctive flavour. As the situation in the GDR gradually stabilised, and as Ulbricht regained control of the apparatus, such self-critical references became more and more infrequent. By the autumn of 1953 they had disappeared altogether. Thereafter, any functionary referring to 'legitimate grievances' or 'mistakes' would soon find himself or herself in difficulties. In the SED leadership in Leipzig, the functionaries who on 7 July had been so self-critical were by the end of the year not only denying that the party had made any mistakes at all, but were also castigating lower-ranking functionaries for making the very same criticisms of the party which they themselves had been making only a few months earlier.[81]

The official GDR notion of the 'counter-revolutionary putsch' has usually been dismissed out of hand by western historians, who have regarded it as a groundless fabrication. In fact, the arguments of East German historians were not entirely without foundation. The June Uprising, it should be remembered, occurred just eight years after the collapse of the Third Reich. We know for a fact that in 1953 large sections of the West German population were still deeply ambivalent about the new democratic order in their country and harboured nostalgic memories of Hitler and the Third Reich.[82] There is no reason to assume that the situation was any different in East Germany. Under these circumstances, it would have been very strange indeed had such Nazi-influenced elements not made their presence felt in some way during the disturbances of 17 June.

There is a certain amount of evidence that they *did* make their presence felt. Walls, bridges and school blackboards were defaced by swastikas and Nazi slogans. Here and there, Nazi songs were sung on demonstrations. There were numerous renditions of the *Deutschlandlied* (the West German national anthem), not a Nazi song in itself of course, but, in the circumstances of the time, a song which was not particularly associated with the ideals of democracy.[83] Former Nazis were often involved in strikes, though rarely as ringleaders.[84] It seems unlikely to say the least that all those who participated in the Uprising were pristine lovers of democracy. Whatever the motives and aspirations of the majority of strikers and demonstrators, amongst a significant minority the ideas of Nazism, and of a Nazi-influenced brand of German nationalism, were still festering.

On the other hand, despite these manifestations of pro-Nazi sentiments, there is no evidence whatsoever that the Uprising was an organised attempted Putsch. The demonstrators, for example, vented their fury on the most visible symbols of the regime, such as prisons and party headquarters. Such buildings were significant in political terms, but were not essential to the functioning of the state and security apparatus. Had the Uprising really been an attempted coup, the demonstrators would certainly have focused their attention on vital centres of communication such as railway stations, telephone exchanges and radio stations. Even more telling is the fact that there was not one single instance anywhere in the GDR of protesters using firearms against the security forces. Had there really been an organised conspiracy to topple the SED regime, the provision of arms to the insurgents would surely have been a basic necessity for the Uprising to stand any chance of success.[85] Whatever else 17 June may have been, it was certainly not an attempted counter-revolutionary coup.

17 June 1953 as a 'people's uprising'

Ever since 1953, there has been a strong tendency in the West and, in particular, in West Germany, to regard 17 June as a 'people's uprising', a rising of the East German people against Communist dictatorship, the purpose of which was to win freedom, western-style democracy and, above all, national unity.[86] According to Terence Prittie, the Uprising was 'an epic of courage, common sense and solidarity in the face of Communist repression'.[87] This was also the view of the June Uprising which was assiduously promoted by the government in Bonn in the 1950s and early 1960s. It was for this reason that 17 June was celebrated in West Germany as the 'Day of German Unity'.

With the coming of *Ostpolitik*[88] in the 1970s, the propaganda value of 17 June to the Bonn government was lessened. But the idea of 17 June as a 'people's uprising' was never entirely abandoned and has even enjoyed something of a revival since the collapse of the GDR in 1989. In their 1993 book, for example, Armin Mitter and Stefan Wolle depicted the Uprising as a kind of unsuccessful forerunner of 1989, a democratic revolution which differed in outcome, but not in character, from the great citizens' demonstrations in Leipzig and elsewhere which brought down the Berlin Wall. According to Mitter and Wolle, the purpose of the Uprising was to overthrow not just the SED state but also socialist property relations in the GDR. The Uprising was, in short, a 'revolutionary uprising' which, had it not been crushed by Russian tanks, 'would inevitably have led to reunification'.[89]

Unlike the official East German view of the Uprising as a counter-revolutionary putsch, the mainstream western view of 17 June 1953 as a 'people's uprising' against Communism would seem to be supported by much of the evidence which has recently become available in the East German archives. It is true, for example, that a common demand made by protesters throughout the GDR was the holding of free elections. It is true that a very common demand of the strikers and demonstrators was the resignation of the East German government and, in particular, of Walter Ulbricht. It is true, as Mitter and Wolle point out at length, that many strikers demanded that their factories be taken out of state ownership and returned to the original employers, or that employers who had been imprisoned be released from gaol.[90] All this, it could be argued, would seem to support the contention that the Uprising constituted a rejection of everything the GDR stood for, in favour of the liberal, democratic and capitalist alternative which was presented by West Germany. The Uprising, according to this reading, was first and foremost a struggle for the values, the ideals and the economic prosperity of the West.

Yet there are also significant problems with this analysis, one of which has already been touched upon. Nazis are not heroes of democracy, and the manifestations of pro-Nazi sentiment on 17 June make it difficult to accept without qualification the proposition that the Uprising was above all about freedom. Nor should one over-emphasise the extent of the Uprising. To establish convincingly that 17 June was indeed a 'people's uprising', it is necessary to demonstrate that the people, or at least a significant section thereof, participated in it. Yet the proportion of the population which took part in the unrest was actually very small. In the whole of the *Bezirk* of Karl-Marx-Stadt, for example, the only major and protracted strike occurred amongst the building workers in Freiberg.[91] Elsewhere in the *Bezirk* there was a rash of short strikes, but in most workplaces 17 June was worked without interruption. In the two *Bezirke* of Leipzig and Karl-Marx-Stadt, only in the city of Leipzig itself was there a violent demonstration against the regime, and this involved no more than 25,000 people at the utmost. In other parts of the GDR, the crowds were not significantly larger: 32,000 in Magdeburg, 43,000 in Dresden and 53,000 in Potsdam. Only in Halle and Berlin did the crowds approach anything close to 100,000. Of the eighteen million inhabitants of the GDR at that time, fewer than 500,000 (3 percent) participated in strikes, and fewer still in the demonstrations.[92] In the spring of 1947, by contrast, there had been strikes and violent demonstrations of hundreds of thousands of people in West German cities such as Hanover and Bottrop against the shortage of food and the lack of progress towards denazification and nationalisation.[93] Yet nobody talks of a West German 'people's uprising' against the British Military Government.

Furthermore, even amongst those East Germans who *did* participate in the Uprising, the demands they raised were often purely local and economic in character. The available evidence simply does not support the contention that most of those who struck or demonstrated on 17 June were motivated by the political goals of freedom, parliamentary democracy, capitalist economics and German reunification. At the Feinspinnerei in Karl-Marx-Stadt, where sixty female workers participated in a short strike, the point at issue was an unpopular Sunday night shift which the strikers wanted to be cancelled.[94] The builders in Hainichen were agitated by a severe shortage of bread in their particular locality.[95] In private companies in the textile industry in the Plauen area, the main demand of the workers on 17 June was that they receive the same wages as workers in state-run factories.[96] The demands of workers sometimes focused on issues as trivial as the number of toilets in the workplace,[97] or the fact that tea was being served in rusty urns.[98] It is of course possible that there were deeper but unspoken political motives behind these economic demands, but we should be careful about making any assumptions which are not supported by evidence.

However, perhaps the most significant problem with the thesis of the 'people's uprising' is that it obscures the central role played on 17 June by the working class. Although, as Mitter and Wolle point out, there was also a degree of unrest in the countryside, there can be no doubt about the fact that it was above all the industrial working class, rather than any other section of the population, which played the leading role in the Uprising and determined its character.

17 June 1953 as 'workers' uprising'

Amongst left-wing but anti-Stalinist historians in the West, an alternative version of the meaning of 17 June has been developed. Scholars such as Lutz Niethammer, Benno Sarel and Torsten Diedrich have presented the June Uprising as first and foremost a struggle between the German tradition of Socialism on the one hand, and Stalinism on the other. From this perspective, the Uprising should be seen as the last, violent spasm of the East German labour movement before finally succumbing to Stalinism.

It was no accident, such historians claim, that the Uprising was at its most intense in precisely those towns and cities, such as Leipzig, Halle, Bitterfeld and Berlin, which had long been the traditional strongholds of the German labour movement. The Uprising, they assert, bore all the hallmarks of organised working-class discontent, such as the formation of factory committees and factory councils, the shouting of traditional Socialist slogans and the singing of Socialist songs.[99] In Bitterfeld, for example, the demonstrators shouted the slogan: 'We don't want to be slaves. Colleagues, join us!' According to Lutz Niethammer: 'That was a slogan imbued with the spirit of the old workers' movement; it was a reaction, not just to Stalinism, but to Fascism and to the oppression of workers everywhere.'[100]

In their eagerness to stress the proletarian and Socialist character of the Uprising, historians of this school of thought have tended to play down the degree to which the desire for German reunification was a powerful factor on 17 June. In the words of Torsten Diedrich, writing in 1991:

> the demand for the abolition of the GDR simply was not raised. The main reason for this is arguably that the majority of workers in the GDR did not regard the political system in the GDR... as the alternative. The thrust of the workers' rising therefore aimed at the democratic transformation of the East German state...[101]

As with the thesis of the 'people's uprising', a scholar who wanted to argue that 17 June was above all a 'workers' uprising' could find plenty of evidence in the archives to support this contention. The working class did, indisputably, play a central role in the Uprising. In Leipzig, for example, some 143 people had by 10 August been arrested in connection with the events of 17 June. Of these, 85 per cent were working class.[102] By 30 June, some 6,171 people had been arrested in the whole of the GDR in connection with the Uprising. Of the 5,296 individuals whose class origin is known, 65.2 per cent were workers.[103] For adherents of the theory of the 'workers' uprising', the conclusion to be drawn from this is clear. The Uprising was not so much a forerunner of 1989 as a re-run of 1919, 1910 and 1898: a struggle of organised labour against ruthless and exploitative employers. The difference was that, in East Germany in 1953, the ruthless and exploitative employer was the East German state itself.

One particularly significant sign that the Uprising was at least in part a confrontation between the native traditions of the German labour movement on the one hand, and the authoritarian traditions of Stalinism on the other, was the strong Social Democratic flavour of much of the unrest. Many of the strikers explicitly demanded the re-foundation of the SPD in East Germany.[104] In many of the factories which did not strike, there were numerous reports of workers making pro-Social Democratic comments. On the building sites in Glösa in the *Bezirk* of Karl-Marx-Stadt, for example, the workers demanded free elections in which the SPD would emerge victorious, which in turn would lead to higher wages.[105] In the aftermath of the Uprising, twenty-five SED members at the Teeverarbeitungswerk in Leipzig refused to pay their subs, saying that they wanted to re-found the SPD in East Germany.[106] Amongst former Social Democrats, there was also a great deal of bitterness against their erstwhile leader Otto Grotewohl, who, they believed, had 'betrayed the SPD',[107] and who should now 'have his neck wrung'.[108]

There was also a strong correlation on 17 June between the intensity of protest and the existence of strong Social Democratic traditions. Leipzig, which had a long tradition of Socialist resistance both to Nazism and Communism, seems to have been a centre of SPD activity.[109] In the *Bezirk* of Karl-Marx-Stadt, one of the centres of unrest was the Kreis of Werdau, where there were short strikes at the Trikotage-Werken and the Wärmer-gerätewerk in Crimmitschau and the Wälzlagerwerk in Frauereuth. It was no accident that, during the Weimar period, Werdau had been a bastion of moderate Social Democracy. In 1933, the SPD in the area had six times more members than the KPD. In 1946, the towns of Crimmitschau and Frauereuth had both been centres of opposition to the merger of the Social Democrats and the Communists, and, ever since 1946, the SED authorities had complained about the continued existence of a strong Social Democratic tendency in the area.[110] It was thus entirely in keeping with the tradition of the district that it was once again in the forefront of unrest on 17 June, and that this unrest had a strong Social Democratic flavour.

A similar example is furnished by the giant Textima plant in Altenburg, also a long-standing stronghold of Social Democracy. On 18 and 19 June, some fifty-four SED members resigned from the party in protest at government policy and the shooting of workers in Berlin, Halle and Leipzig. Of these, no fewer than twenty-three were former Social Democrats, whose act of protest had been incited by a veteran Social Democrat who had refused to enter the SED on its foundation in April 1946.[111] The Textima plant, as will be seen presently, continued to be a centre of unrest for many months to come.

However, perhaps the most convincing evidence that 17 June represented a parting of the ways between the working class and the party comes, not from 17 June itself, but from what happened in the aftermath of the Uprising. Throughout the *Bezirke* of Leipzig and Karl-Marx-Stadt, hundreds of SED members, many of whom had spent decades in the labour movement, left the party in disgust at what had happened. In Leipzig, some 306 had handed in their party cards by 10 August. Of these, 69 per cent were working class, even though workers only accounted for 42.5 per cent of the SED membership in Leipzig.[112] Of the eighty-four SED members who left the party in Karl-Marx-Stadt, and whose details are known, thirteen were organised in the labour movement before 1933, and thirty-four had joined the KPD or SPD between 1945 and 1946.[113] At the Textima plant in Altenburg, no fewer than 450 SED members had left the party by 7 July, the vast majority of them workers, many of whom had long years' experience in the labour movement.[114]

Often such individuals were subsequently challenged by the SED authorities to justify their decision to leave the party. Veterans of the working-class movement, many of whom had participated in the anti-Nazi resistance, were not at all reticent about expressing their disgust at the regime, in general, and the shooting of workers on 17 June, in particular: 'I can't go along with it when workers shoot on workers'; 'the *Volkspolizei* have shot at workers and caused workers' blood to flow'; 'before there were bigwigs [*Bonzen*] and now there are bigwigs'; 'my proletarian conscience can no longer be reconciled to membership of the party and its policies'.[115] In Zschopau, an SED report noted that: 'In this area, it has been above all a large portion of the older comrades (VVN – organised before 1933) who have stood up energetically, and who have expressed the opinion that there is no longer any trust in the authorities.'[116] Such instances and reports were very widespread, providing us with clear evidence that, for many workers, their rejection of the SED regime was based not on a love of West Germany and capitalist democracy, but on a principled, Socialist rejection of Stalinism.

Another clear sign of this rupture between the party and the class it was supposed to represent was the widespread refusal of workers to pay their trade union subscriptions. Between April and August 1953, the payment of subscriptions fell by 15 percent in Altenburg, 18.5 percent in Leipzig, 22 per cent in Delitzsch and 26 percent in Döbeln. At the Thalysia plant in Leipzig, the payment of subscriptions fell by 78 per cent between April and August, whilst at the Hartpapier factory in Groitzsch they fell by 90 per cent during the same period. At the railway stations in Delitzsch and Colditz the workers stopped paying their trade union subscriptions altogether. There were numerous incidents in the aftermath of the Uprising of workers collectively refusing to pay their subscriptions until wages had been increased, until conditions improved or until former colleagues arrested during the Uprising had been released.[117] Under normal circumstances, workers look to their trade unions to defend and further their interests. In Stalinist East Germany, by contrast, the unions and the employers had become so closely associated that the workers sought to influence the latter by collectively refusing to pay their subscriptions to the former. Nothing could illustrate more clearly that, in the eyes of many workers, the organisations which had once represented their interests to the employers now performed exactly the opposite function.

The theory that 17 June constituted a 'workers' uprising' can take us a long way, but not, unfortunately, all the way to a satisfactory under-standing of the Uprising. Even though the workers did play a central role on 17 June, they were by no means the only group which participated in the unrest. It is unlikely that the many small farmers who in some way contributed to disturbances in the rural districts were in any way interested in the Socialist traditions of the German labour movement. Nor can the Nazi-influenced elements who made their presence felt during the Uprising be seen as part of a proletarian backlash against Stalinism. Even amongst the workers, not all of those who struck or protested on 17 June were as class conscious as the left-wing proponents of the 'workers' uprising' thesis would like to believe. As has been noted already, many strikers formulated the demand that their factories and workplaces be taken out of public ownership and returned to the original employers – hardly a traditional demand of the German labour movement!

Even more importantly, it is necessary to make a clear distinction between older and younger workers. In the strike committees that were elected on 17 June, it was usually the older workers who played a key role. On the demonstrations, by contrast, it was the younger workers who took the lead, particularly when it came to violent assaults on state property or on personnel of the security forces. The evidence clearly suggests that the majority of these young workers were not in the least bit interested in the Socialist traditions of their more elderly colleagues. Whereas the older workers had come to Socialism as a result of their own experiences of oppression during the Weimar and Nazi periods, for the younger workers – who had no memory of those times and whose formative years had been spent in the Hitler Youth – 'Socialism' was no more than a word used by party bigwigs and the Free German Youth (FDJ) to justify oppression. The majority of the hot-heads on the demonstrations were simply alienated young people who were more interested in western radio, western fashion and dancing than in politics. Their rejection of the East German state was based not on principled Socialist convictions but on a less politicised discontent with the stuffy and oppressive atmosphere of East Germany in the early 1950s.[118]

The single most important reason why 17 June can not simply be filed away under the heading 'workers' uprising' pertains to the stratum of workers who constituted the hard core of the East German labour movement. These were the workers who had been organised before 1933, who had often been active in the anti-Nazi resistance and who, at Zero Hour in 1945, had been the backbone of the workers' councils and the *antifa* movement. During the early months of Soviet occupation, these were the workers who had flooded into the ranks of the SPD and KPD, and who had set about rebuilding their parties at the grass roots. Throughout the first couple of years of the post-war period, before the process of Stalinisation had started in earnest, many of these workers had participated actively and enthusiastically in the task of political and economic reconstruction, believing that they were thereby laying the foundations of a new and better world. Many of these workers had, since 1945, become functionaries of the SED or of the FDGB, and had to some extent enjoyed the privileges which accompanied their posts. Even amongst those older veterans of the labour movement who had not become functionaries, one often finds that their criticisms of the Ulbricht regime were tempered by a pride in the achievements of the early post-war years, and a belief that, for all its numerous faults, the GDR was following a more progressive, more consistently antifascist course than was West Germany.

These veterans, many of whom were SED or FDGB functionaries, were surely the true bearers of the traditions and collective memories of the German labour movement. If 17 June was really about a confrontation between the German and the Russian traditions of Socialism, then one would have expected the hard core of the German labour movement to have taken the side of the demonstrators and strikers. In places this did indeed happen. As Klaus Ewers and Thornton Quest have pointed out, veteran trade unionists, Communists and Socialists played a considerable role in many of the strikes.[119] At the SAG Schumann in Leipzig, for example, a strike was sparked off by an SED veteran functionary who, on his own authority, convened a mass meeting of workers in the works canteen.[120] In the aftermath of the Uprising, as we have seen, many of these veterans resigned from the SED in disgust. Many more were expelled from the party on account of their behaviour on 17 June. In Magdeburg, 52 percent of those purged were former members of the KPD, in Leipzig 59 percent, and in East Berlin 68 percent. In the whole of the GDR, no less than one third of those expelled were veteran Communists who had been members of the KPD before 1933.[121]

In general, however, it was far more common for representatives of this stratum of the working class to vacillate, taking no firm position on either side. On 17 June, veterans of the labour movement found themselves having to choose between siding with the party and the state, which they had done so much to build up, or the working class, from whose ranks they had come. As one SED member in Leipzig put it on 17 June: 'Now I must decide either for the party or for the masses.'[122] Confronted by this stark dilemma, the majority of veterans were unable to make a clear decision. In the words of one report, describing the events of 17 June at a large Leipzig factory, 'they stood to one side, they vacillated to and fro'.[123] In the *Kreis* of Marienberg, old Social Democrats, whilst not directly participating in any of the disturbances, nonetheless 'lost their heads', arguing that it had always been their opinion that the SED had been pursuing too severe a line.[124]

Other veterans, when the crunch came on 17 June, chose the party over the class and acted vigorously to contain the unrest. In one incident in Stalinstadt, for example, a demonstration was confronted by a veteran of the SPD, who, even though he had been forced out of the local leadership, threatened to unleash his dogs unless the demonstrators desisted from tearing down party posters.[125] At the VEB Kombinat 'Otto Grotewohl' in Böhlen, the local party veterans, on their own initiative, seized control of the factory's telephones and PA systems, and formed a guard of reliable SED members to prevent any strikers from attempting to incite the workforce to strike action. As a result, there were no disturbances on 17 June at the factory.[126] At the RAW Engelsdorf in the suburbs of Leipzig, it was above all old trade unionists who, by arguing with the workers, persuaded them not to go out onto the streets to demonstrate.[127]

In short, if the Uprising really was above all a 'workers' uprising', a last violent outburst on the part of the native traditions of the labour movement against Stalinism, then why did the foremost bearers of that tradition behave in so ambivalent a fashion?

What was 17 June 1953?

It is thus far too simple and convenient to attach any single title to the June Uprising. As Mary Fulbrook has argued: 'Any attempt to label the Uprising under a single heading will inevitably fail to capture the multiple dissatisfactions, and the ways in which these interrelated, overlapped, and snowballed as events proceeded.'[128] The Uprising was in part a recrudescence of Nazism or Nazi-influenced German nationalism; however, it was also in part a struggle for western-style democracy and economic prosperity. In part, the Uprising really did represent the last violent spasm of the East German labour movement before it succumbed once and for all to Stalinism; however, it was also, in part, an expression of anger on the part of East German farmers, who had been ruthlessly oppressed in the preceding months. It was also, to a large degree, an outburst of violence on the part of disaffected but relatively apolitical East German youth. All these groups shared certain grievances in common. They all hated Ulbricht, and they all wanted to see an end to the fanatical, hard-line approach of the SED government. However, in many ways their motives and aspirations were quite different, even conflicting. Some wanted capitalism; some wanted democratic Socialism; some wanted a return to the authoritarian and imperialistic traditions of the past. Many simply wanted an easier life in material terms and an end to the government's hard-line economic policies. Additionally, amongst the young people who participated in the demonstrations, the majority simply wanted to be left alone by the state so that they could do all the things that young people usually want to do.

The starting point for any sophisticated analysis of the Uprising should therefore be a recognition that East German society in general, and the East German working class in particular, was not an undifferentiated whole, but in many ways had been deeply fragmented by the processes outlined in this book. The Nazi period, the war and eight years of Communist rule had left deep and often bitter divisions. There was, for example, the division between town and country. During the years of hunger after 1945 the majority of townsfolk, in order to survive, had been compelled to travel out into the country to buy food from farmers at exorbitant prices, or to exchange their most valued possessions for a dozen eggs, a few slices of meat or a handful of vegetables. This left such a deep legacy of bitterness that the SED leader-ship began to worry about the 'insuperable class hatred between farmers and industrial workers'.[129] There was little love lost between the town and the country in East Germany, and little sympathy amongst industrial workers for the troubles and tribulations of their rural counterparts.[130]

Another important cleft in East German society divided the working class from the group which the regime referred to as the 'technical intelligentsia' (technicians, engineers, specialists, managers, etc.). Whereas the workers had been ruthlessly squeezed as part of the 'planned construction of Socialism', the technical intelligentsia had in many ways been pampered with higher wages, better conditions, access to special shops and so forth. This division too became obvious on 17 June. The 'technical intelligentsia', for their part, largely abstained from the protests and demonstrations. Amongst many workers, by contrast, one of their chief demands was often the withdrawal of what they saw as the unfair privileges of the 'technical intelligentsia'.[131] Clearly, given the hostility felt by most workers towards both farmers and the technical intelligentsia, it is difficult to see how these social groups could ever have coalesced into a single, coherent political movement.

Even within the working class, there was a clear division between the older workers – who were usually more disciplined, more political conscious and more inclined to criticise the regime from a Socialist perspective – and the younger workers – for whom Socialism was an empty phrase and who were far more interested in all the good things and exciting experiences which the West appeared to offer. This division had an enormous impact on the character of the Uprising. Where the older workers took a leading role, above all in the strike committees, the protests were generally disciplined, organised and displayed a high political content. Where the younger workers took the lead, above all in the rioting of the afternoon and evening of 17 June, the protests were unorganised, spontaneous and violent.[132] It should also be noted that, by 1953, there were large numbers of former bourgeois, Nazis and professional soldiers working in East German workplaces. These elements often played a leading role in the disturbances, but had nothing in common with the traditions of the German labour movement.[133]

Important, too, was the fact that there were deep-rooted divisions within the ranks of the party itself. From the politburo down to the humble rank-and-file, the entire SED apparatus was riven by the political chasm between reformers and hard-liners. Though large sections of the SED wanted the party to adopt more moderate, less authoritarian policies, there were also considerable numbers of die-hard Stalinists who had been enthused by Ulbricht's announcement of the 'planned construction of Socialism' in 1952 and who were appalled by the New Course of June 1953. In Rochlitz, for example, a hard-line member of the local *Kreisleitung* denounced the recent political concessions, arguing that: 'If Comrade Stalin were still alive, there would be no New Course in the party.'[134] In Stollberg, a senior SED functionary refused to act as a speaker because 'he could not change his opinions so quickly', whilst a political lecturer denounced the New Course on the grounds that it was a deviation from the principles of Marxism–Leninism, and he could not teach it to others because hitherto he had been propounding a completely different set of policies.[135] In Leipzig, a member of the *Bezirksleitung* dropped out of political activity because 'as a result of the new government decisions, he has lost half his faith in the Central Committee and the government'.[136]

The cleft between hard-liners and reformers was further complicated by the many differences of political culture and tradition which sundered veteran SED members and functionaries from their younger colleagues. As was noted in the last chapter, an increasingly important role within the party was being played by a younger breed of apparatchiks and bureaucrats. Normally such elements had joined the labour movement only after 1946, often out of careerist motives rather than out of political conviction. The new breed of functionaries had been trained at the party schools unquestioningly to obey orders handed down from above, and to shrink from taking any independent initiative. As a consequence, it was often noted 'that those comrades who were organised before 1933 often approach questions more critically than those who have only come to the labour movement after 1945'.[137] From the point of view of the authorities, the political docility of younger apparatchiks was one of their greatest advantages. However, the problem with turning one's servants into puppets is that, when nobody is there to pull the strings, the puppets are incapable of independent action.

On 17 June, with the SED leadership in Berlin paralysed by factional struggles and indecision, functionaries on the ground were left to face a difficult situation with nobody to tell them what to do. Where older functionaries, like the ones at the Kombinat 'Otto Grotewohl' in Böhlen, kept a cool head and acted decisively and on their own initiative, the younger apparatchiks often failed completely to deal with the situation that confronted them. Many simply ran away and 'abandoned the field of battle to the provocateurs'.[138] Others lamely surrendered to the demands of the protesters, such as the functionaries in Leipzig city district (*Stadtbezirk* 10) who meekly complied with demands to take down party posters.[139] At the Betrieb Mifeu, the workers passed a resolution demanding that all SED functionaries leave the works immediately, whereupon the frightened young apparatchiks obediently went home and only felt able to return with a police escort.[140] Throughout the GDR, there were thousands of instances of SED functionaries falling prey to mysterious and sudden illnesses, or failing to return from holiday, or surreptitiously taking off their party badges, claiming that they had forgotten or broken them.[141]

The significance of all this for the character of the Uprising was profound. Where functionaries proved capable of vigorous independent action, as in

Karl-Marx-Stadt, the unrest was usually snuffed out before it had properly started. Where functionaries actually sided with the demonstrators, they lent the protest a more organised, disciplined and political character. Where they panicked or vacillated, as in Leipzig, the confusion on the ground was at its greatest, and so was the violence.

East Germany in 1953 was thus a deeply divided and fractured society. It was the unique achievement of Walter Ulbricht to alienate all the various groups that made up East German society simultaneously. The policies he launched at the 2nd party conference in July 1952 were so blinkered, counter-productive and destructive that they angered and alienated the workers, the middle classes, the farmers, the young people, former Nazis and former anti-Nazis; everybody. However, his policies impacted on these groups in different ways and with different results. When the explosion came on 17 June, the only characteristic that these groups had in common was their hatred of Ulbricht and his policies. Any lasting political movement presupposes at least some political common ground, and in East Germany this simply did not exist. The result of all this was that 17 June 1953 produced a furious cacophony of voices which drowned each other out and prevented any clear message from emerging. The Uprising, in short, was a tale full of sound and fury, but what it signified was unclear even to those who made it.

Notes

1   W. Loth, *Stalins ungeliebtes Kind*, Berlin, 1994, pp. 132–34.
2   N. Naimark, *The Russians in Germany*, Cambridge, MA, 1995, pp. 55–56.
3   Ibid., pp. 165–66.
4   SStA Leipzig, KV Leipzig, 379, 'Protokoll über die Kommunal-Konferenz', 29.4.47.
5   Ibid., Bl. 2.
6   See, e.g., ThHStA Weimar, MdI, 142, Bl. 1–2.
7   Bundesministerium für gesamtdeutsche Fragen, *SBZ [Sowjetische Besatzungszone] von A bis Z*, Bonn, 1966, pp. 198–200.
8   *Neues Deutschland*, 11.11.48, p. 4.
9   ThHStA Weimar, BPA Erfurt, IV/L/2/1-010 'Protokoll der Landesvorstandssitzung', 8-9.9.49.
10 ThHStA Weimar, MdI, 143, Bl. 4.
11 ThHStA Weimar, BPA Erfurt, AUV/2/3-95, Bl. 166.
12 Naimark (n. 2 above), pp. 43–44.
13 SStA Chemnitz, BPA Karl-Marx-Stadt, IV/2/4/46, Bl. 226. For further examples, see G. Pritchard, *German Workers under Soviet Occupation* (doctoral thesis, University of Wales, 1997), p. 327, n. 25.
14 See, e.g., SStA Leipzig, BPA Leipzig, IV/2/3/144, 'Protokoll der Sitzung der Bezirksleitung, Leipzig', 4.6.53, Bl. 59.
15 See, e.g., SStA Leipzig, BPA Leipzig, IV/2/3/40, Bl. 59 & IV/2/3/145, Bl. 29.

16 SAPMO-BArch, DY/30 IV 2/6.02, Nr. 96, Bl. 8.

17 SStA Leipzig, BPA Leipzig, IV/2/1/25, Bl. 69–71.

18 ThHStA Weimar, BPA Erfurt, IV/L/2/1-009, Bl. 33.

19 See, e.g.: SStA Leipzig, BPA Leipzig, IV/2/3/145, Bl. 20; SStA Chemnitz, BPA Karl-Marx-Stadt, IV/2/4/10, Bl. 270–71 & IV/2/4/14, Bl. 176.

20 SStA Leipzig, BPA Leipzig, IV/2/1/24, 'Bezirksleitungssitzung Leipzig', 15.12.52, Bl. 126–27.

21 SStA Leipzig, KV Leipzig, Bl. 3.

22 StA Chemnitz, Bezirksparteiarchiv Karl-Marx-Stadt, IV/2/4/46, Bl. 121.

23 See, e.g.: ThHStA Weimar, MdI, 141, Bl.91; SStA Chemnitz, BPA Karl-Marx-Stadt, IV/2/4/70, Bl. 3 & IV/2/4/4 (Bd. 1), anonymous letter to the workplace council and management of the Fabrik Baumwoll-Spinnerei Mittweida, 14.6.48.

24 S. Suckut, *Die Betriebsrätebewegung in der sowjetisch besetzten Zone Deutschlands* (doctoral thesis, University of Hanover, 1978), pp. 492–502. For the text of Befehl Nr. 234 see E. Deuerlein (ed.), *DDR 1945–1970*, Deutscher Taschenbuch Verlag, Munich, 1971, pp. 67–68.

25 See, e.g., K. Helbig, *Hennecke-Aktivisten schaffen das bessere Leben*, [East] Berlin, 1949.

26 SAPMO-BArch, DY/30 IV 2/6.02, Nr. 38, Bl. 61–66.

27 SStA Leipzig, BPA Leipzig, IV/2/3/40, Bl. 200–19.

28 SStA Chemnitz, BPA Karl-Marx-Stadt, IV/2/4/71, Bl. 94.

29 Ibid., Bl. 76.

30 SStA Chemnitz, BPA Karl-Marx-Stadt, IV/2/4/62, 'Ergänzungsbericht zum Informbericht über die Lage der Planer'.

31 See, e.g., SStA Chemnitz, BPA Karl-Marx-Stadt, IV/2/4/71, Bl. 118 & SStA Leipzig, BPA Leipzig, IV/2/1/25, Bl. 20.

32 See, e.g., SStA Chemnitz, BPA Karl-Marx-Stadt, IV/2/4/71, Bl. 46–49 & SStA Leipzig, BPA Leipzig, IV/2/3/144, Bl. 19–20.

33 See, e.g., SStA Leipzig, BPA Leipzig, IV/2/1/24, Bl. 126.

34 SStA Leipzig, BPA Leipzig, IV/2/1/25, Bl. 126.

35 SStA Chemnitz, BPA Karl-Marx-Stadt, IV/2/4/62, Bl. 57–98.

36 ThHStA Weimar, MdI, 141, Bl. 6.

37 Ibid., Bl. 18.

38 Ibid., Bl. 8.

39 ThHStA Weimar, BPA Erfurt, AIV/2/3-95, Bl. 166.

40 SStA Chemnitz, VVN, 43, 'Sonderbericht Hauptaufklärer Barthel', Bl. 1.

41 K.W. Fricke, *Selbstbehauptung und Widerstand in der sowjetischen Besatzungszone Deutschlands*, Bonn & [West] Berlin, 1964, p. 103.

42 SStA Chemnitz, BPA Karl-Marx-Stadt, IV/2/4/14, Bl. 179.

43 ThHStA Weimar, BPA Erfurt, IV/L/2-011, Bl. 28–32.

44 See, e.g., SStA Chemnitz, BPA Karl-Marx-Stadt, IV/2/4/61, Bl. 244.

45 See, e.g., SStA Leipzig, BPA Leipzig, IV/2/3/144, Bl. 58–59.

46 SStA Chemnitz, BPA Karl-Marx-Stadt, IV/2/4/4 (Bd. 1), Bl. 575–76.

47 Fricke (n. 41 above), p. 105.

48 See, e.g., SStA Chemnitz, BPA Karl-Marx-Stadt, IV/2/4/46, Bl. 292.

49 SStA Leipzig, BPA Leipzig, IV/2/1/27, Bl. 74.

50 SStA Leipzig, BPA Leipzig, IV/2/3/144, Bl. 20.

51 Ibid., Bl. 19–20.
52 B. Sarel, *Arbeiter gegen den 'Kommunismus'*, Munich, 1975, pp. 34–35.
53 SAPMO-BArch, DY/30 IV 2/6.02, Nr. 38, Bl. 54–57.
54 SStA Leipzig, KV Leipzig, 382, Bl. 4.
55 Suckut (n. 24 above), pp. 493–96.
56 Ibid., pp. 515–16.
57 Ibid., p. 517.
58 Sarel (n. 52 above), p. 39.
59 SStA Leipzig, BPA Leipzig, I/3/03, 'Die KPD, der Aktiv-Kader der Gewerkschaftseinheit'.
60 B. Bouvier & H. Schulz, '*...die SPD aber aufgehört hat zu existieren*', Bonn, 1991, p. 18.
61 ThHStA Weimar, BPA Erfurt, AIV/2/3-94, Bl. 24–29.
62 Suckut (n. 24 above), pp. 524–25.
63 ThHStA Weimar, BPA Erfurt, IV/L/2/1-009, Bl. 67–68.
64 'Only-trade-unionism' was a word coined by the authorities to describe trade union functionaries who persisted in believing that it was the function of a trade union to represent the direct, material interests of the workers in particular plants or industries, even if that conflicted with what the SED said was in the interests of the working class as a whole.
65 ThHStA Weimar, BPA Erfurt, IV/2/4/104, letter from Erfurt, 1.8.50.
66 ThHStA Weimar, BPA Erfurt, IV/2/4/139, letter from the LPKK to the SED Kreisvorstand Arnstadt, 18.7.50.
67 SStA Chemnitz, BPA Karl-Marx-Stadt, IV/2/4/61, Bl. 165.
68 SStA Leipzig, BPA Leipzig, IV/2/1/24, Bl. 114.
69 SStA Chemnitz, BPA Karl-Marx-Stadt, IV/2/4/62, Bl. 288–93.
70 SStA Chemnitz, BPA Karl-Marx-Stadt, IV/2/4/61, Bl. 255–56.
71 See: ThHStA Weimar, BPA Erfurt, AIV/2/3-96, letter from the SED Kreisleitung Suhl to the SED Landesleitung, 21.3.52; SStA Chemnitz, BPA Karl-Marx-Stadt, IV/2/4/61, Bl. 163 & 256.
72 Ibid., Bl. 165.
73 Ibid., Bl. 257.
74 SStA Chemnitz, BPA Karl-Marx-Stadt, IV/2/4/71, Bl. 137.
75 ThHStA Weimar, MdI, 142, Bl. 1.
76 SStA Leipzig, BPA Leipzig, IV/2/3/147, Bl. 21.
77 See, e.g.: A. Baring, *Uprising in East Germany*, New York, 1972; T. Diedrich, *Der 17. Juni 1953 in der DDR*, Berlin, 1991; A. Mitter & S. Wolle, *Untergang auf Raten*, Munich, 1993; U. Spittmann & K.H. Fricke, *17. Juni 1953: Arbeiteraufstand in der DDR*, Cologne, 1982.
78 See, e.g.: R. Badstübner et al., *DDR: Wachsen und Werden*, [East] Berlin, 1974, pp. 231–42; J. Heise & J. Hofmann, *Fragen an die Geschichte der DDR*, [East Berlin], 1988, pp. 111–18; E. Diehl et al., *Geschichte der SED*, [East] Berlin, 1978, pp. 288–98; Institut für Marxismus-Leninismus beim Zentralkomitee der SED, *Geschichte der deutschen Arbeiterbewegung*, Band 7, pp. 227–36.
79 Mitter & Wolle (n. 77 above), p. 105.
80 SStA Leipzig, BPA Leipzig, IV/2/1/28.
81 See, e.g., SStA Leipzig, BPA Leipzig, IV/2/1/29 & 30.

82   A. Merritt & R. Merritt, *Public Opinion in Occupied Germany*, Urbana, 1970, pp. 30–50.
83   See, e.g.: SStA Chemnitz, BPA Karl-Marx-Stadt, IV/2/4/62, Bl. 130–31, 139, 161–63 & 166; Mitter & Wolle (n. 77 above), p. 87; Institut für Marxismus-Leninismus beim Zentralkomitee der SED (n. 78 above), p. 233.
84   K. Ewers & T. Quest, 'Die Kämpfe der Arbeiterschaft in den volkseigenen Betrieben während und nach dem 17. Juni', in Spittmann & Fricke (n. 77 above), p. 27.
85   Diedrich (n. 77 above), p. 126.
86   See, e.g.: U. Rühmland, *Mitteldeutschland*, Stuttgart, 1959, p. 44; Bundesministerium für gesamtdeutsche Fragen, *SBZ [Sowjetische Besatzungzone] von A bis Z*, Bonn, 1966, pp. 229–30; W. Venohr, *Die roten Preußen*, Frankfurt/M & Berlin, 1992, pp. 85–105.
87   T. Prittie, *Germany Divided*, London, 1961, p. 143.
88   The policy, introduced by the West German government in the early 1970s, of seeking closer relations with the Soviet bloc and the GDR.
89   Mitter & Wolle (n. 77 above), p. 160.
90   See, e.g., ibid., pp. 158–61 & SStA Chemnitz, BPA Karl-Marx-Stadt, IV/2/4/ 62.
91   BPA Karl-Marx-Stadt, IV/2/4/62, Bl. 128–30.
92   Diedrich (n. 77 above), pp. 116–18 & 278–79.
93   D. Geary, 'Social Protest in Western Germany after 1945', *Contemporary German Studies, Occasional Papers No. 1*, University of Strathclyde, 1985.
94   SStA Chemnitz, BPA Karl-Marx-Stadt, IV/2/4/62, Bl. 126–27.
95   Ibid., Bl. 135.
96   SStA Chemnitz, BPA Karl-Marx-Stadt, IV/2/4/46, Bl. 203.
97   Ibid., Bl. 221.
98   SStA Leipzig, BPA Leipzig, IV/2/1/28, Bl. 34.
99   C. Kleßmann, *Die doppelte Staatsgründung*, Göttingen, 1991, p. 279.
100 L. Niethammer, 'Where were you on 17 June?', in *International Yearbook of Oral History and Life Stories, Vol. 1: Memory and Totalitarianism*, Oxford, 1992, p. 61.
101 Diedrich (n. 77 above), pp. 152–53.
102 SStA Leipzig, BPA Leipzig, IV/2/1/29, Bl. 216.
103 Diedrich (n. 77 above), p. 300.
104 SStA Leipzig, BPA Leipzig, IV/2/1/29, Bl. 21.
105 SStA Chemnitz, BPA Karl-Marx-Stadt, IV/2/4/62, Bl. 160–61.
106 SStA Leipzig, BPA Leipzig, IV/2/3/146, Bl. 9.
107 SStA Chemnitz, BPA Karl-Marx-Stadt, IV/2/4/62, Bl. 140.
108 Ibid., Bl. 143.
109 See: SStA Leipzig, BPA Leipzig, IV/2/1/29, Bl. 19–20, 126 & IV/2/3/148, Bl. 150; M. Fulbrook, *Anatomy of a Dictatorship*, Oxford, 1995, p. 186.
110 SStA Chemnitz, BPA Karl-Marx-Stadt, IV/2/4/46, Bl. 220.
111 SStA Leipzig, BPA Leipzig, IV/2/3/146, Bl. 2–10.
112 SStA Leipzig, BPA Leipzig, IV/2/1/29, Bl. 24–25.
113 SStA Chemnitz, BPA Karl-Marx-Stadt, IV/2/4/62, Bl. 145.
114 SStA Leipzig, BPA Leipzig, IV/2/1/28, Bl. 86.

115 SStA Chemnitz, BPA Karl-Marx-Stadt, IV/2/4/62, Bl. 145–59.
116 Ibid., Bl. 143–44.
117 SStA Leipzig, BPA Leipzig, IV/2/1/30, Bl. 103–05.
118 Diedrich (n. 77 above), 24–24, 83, 148–49.
119 Ewers & Quest (n. 84 above), p. 27.
120 SStA Leipzig, BPA Leipzig, IV/2/3/144, Bl. 229.
121 C. Harman, *Class Struggles in Eastern Europe*, London, 1988, p. 75.
122 SStA Leipzig, BPA Leipzig, IV/2/1/30, Bl. 71.
123 SStA Leipzig, BPA Leipzig, IV/2/1/28, Bl. 71.
124 SStA Chemnitz, BPA Karl-Marx-Stadt, IV/2/4/62, Bl. 154.
125 Niethammer (n. 100 above), p. 58.
126 SStA Leipzig, BPA Leipzig, IV/2/1/28, Bl. 39–44.
127 Ibid., Bl. 27–30.
128 Fulbrook (n. 109 above), p. 178.
129 SAPMO-BArch, DY/30 IV/2/6.02, Nr. 4, Bl. 66
130 See, e.g.: SStA Chemnitz, BPA Karl-Marx-Stadt, IV/2/4/46, Bl. 263; IV/2/4/ 10, Bl. 55, 78, 133, 155.
131 See, e.g.: SStA Chemnitz, BPA Karl-Marx-Stadt, IV/2/4/62, Bl. 136–37, 143– 44, 160–61; SStA Leipzig, BPA Leipzig, IV/2/3/40, Bl. 54–57 & 188; SStA Leipzig, BPA Leipzig, IV/2/3/144, Bl. 58–59.
132 Diedrich (n. 77 above), pp. 72–83, 127 & 155.
133 Baring (n. 77 above), pp. 69–72.
134 SStA Chemnitz, BPA Karl-Marx-Stadt, IV/2/4/62, Bl. 264.
135 Ibid., Bl. 154–55.
136 SStA Leipzig, BPA Leipzig, IV/2/3/145, Bl. 188.
137 SAPMO-BArch, NY4076/157, Bl. 2.
138 SStA Leipzig, BPA Leipzig, IV/2/3/28, Bl. 17.
139 Ibid., Bl. 15.
140 Ibid., Bl. 85.
141 See, e.g.: SStA Chemnitz, BPA Karl-Marx-Stadt, IV/2/4/62, Bl. 132, 146, 150–53 & SStA Leipzig, BPA Leipzig, IV/2/1/28, Bl. 15 & 85.

Conclusion:
from antifascism to Stalinism

The purpose of this study was to examine the interaction between working-class politics and Soviet occupation policy in East Germany in order to address three distinct questions. First, how did ordinary activists and functionaries in the labour movement respond to the Stalinist policies which were being initiated by the authorities, but which they themselves were having to implement on the ground? Second, to what extent did the existence in Germany of a native tradition of Marxism influence the process of Stalinisation? Third, what can the answers to the first two questions contribute to a broader understanding of Stalinism and the course of post-war German history? Having followed the story of the East German labour movement in the period 1945 to 1953, it should now be possible to provide some answers.

The answer to the first question is that, as one might have expected, the responses of individuals varied enormously, depending on their political background and personal experiences. Many hard-bitten Communists, particularly amongst those who had spent the Nazi period in exile in the Soviet Union, never wavered in their eagerness to put the will of Stalin or Ulbricht into practice. Many Social Democrats, by contrast, whose hostility towards Communism and the USSR had in no way been diminished by the years of Nazi dictatorship, were from the outset consistent opponents of the policies being introduced by the KPD and the Soviet military authorities. Only rarely, however, did their opposition translate into organised resistance.

The great majority of activists and functionaries in the East German labour movement were neither unquestioning servants nor outright opponents of Stalinism. The most prominent characteristic of the political views and behaviour of individuals falling into this category was the *ambiguity* of their response to the transformation of East Germany and of the East German labour movement. During the first weeks and months of occupation, they were reluctant to abandon the *antifas* and rank-and-file

225

unity parties which they had established, and were unhappy about the taming of the workplace council movement. Nonetheless, they allowed themselves to be corralled into the newly founded political parties and official trade unions, and they worked loyally and conscientiously within these organisations. During the period of the 'antifascist democratic transformation', they participated actively in the processes of land reform, denazification and reconstruction, even though they often had reservations about the manner in which these policies were being implemented. They also harboured ambiguous feelings towards the Soviet occupiers, for, on the one hand, they recognised that unlike the western occupying powers the Soviets had allotted the activists of the labour movement a considerable role in the refashioning of German society. On the other hand, they were only too well aware of the harshness and stupidity of many Soviet policies, and were appalled by the barbaric behaviour of many Soviet soldiers.

The ambiguous response of the East German labour movement to the process of Stalinisation was also a salient feature of the campaign to unify the KPD and SPD. Many Communists, and the majority of Social Democrats, had grave reservations about the foundation of the unity party. However, so great was their desire to avoid a repetition of the 'fraternal struggle' of the 1920s and early 1930s, which, in their view, had made it possible for the Nazis to seize and hold power, that they allowed themselves to be browbeaten and cajoled into giving up their separate organisations. The union of the SPD and KPD in 1946 was thus neither a 'forced merger' nor a voluntary union, but something in between the two.

During the later 1940s and early 1950s, many of these 'activists of the first hour' came under mounting pressure from a regime that was becoming more and more intolerant and authoritarian. Furthermore, as a new generation of Stalinist apparatchiks emerged from the party schools, the veterans of the labour movement found themselves being supplanted in the apparatus of the party and state. Many were thrown out of the party and cast into the political wilderness. Even now, however, the majority did not move into outright opposition, but either submitted to party discipline or retreated into disillusioned passivity.

With regard to the second question, it seems clear that the existence in East Germany of a native tradition of Socialism had a considerable influence on the process of Stalinisation. At Zero Hour, the unexpected activism of the 'active minority' of the population had confronted the Soviets with a dilemma. On the one hand, the Soviets were suspicious of the rank-and-file activism and indiscipline of the anti-Nazi activists. On the other hand, the Soviets' lack of personnel and experience, and the appalling material circumstances, dictated that they find some way of harnessing the energy and enthusiasm of the reviving labour movement. The solution the Soviets found to the problems was to suppress or neuter the initiatives which had emerged spontaneously at Zero Hour, and to create in their stead a range of alternative organisations which could be more easily controlled from above.

This, in turn, had a number of important consequences for the subsequent political development of the Soviet zone. In the short term, the readjustment of Soviet occupation policy led, in the summer of 1945, to the re-founding of the SPD and KPD, the creation of the FDGB and the taming of the workplace council movement. In the longer term, the Soviet response to the labour movement established East Germany on a political trajectory which for two reasons would culminate in the emergence of the SED dictatorship and a separate East German state.

First, in order to try and bring the 'active minority' and 'passive majority' of the population into the same anti-Nazi united front, the Soviets and KPD leadership promoted a moderate but reformist political approach which, it was hoped, would be sufficiently radical for the activists without being so radical that it would scare off the majority of the East German people. The attempt, however, was to fail miserably, for the political gulf dividing the two groups was too great ever to be bridged. This, however, was to have fateful consequences, for once the attempt of the authorities to control the population through political methods had miscarried, they had no alternative but to secure their rule through violence and intimidation.

Second, by seeking to channel the energy of the anti-Nazi minority of the population the Soviets effectively confirmed the dominant position which the activists had assumed at Zero Hour, albeit in a different form. In the course of time, however, the activists of Zero Hour were transformed by their powers and privileges into a new ruling elite. Most importantly, the Soviets, through their constant insistence on discipline and ideological conformity, managed to break the bonds between this layer of activists and functionaries and the bulk of the working class, for the more disciplined and obedient the functionaries became, the more estranged they grew from the workers from whose ranks they had originally sprung. The organisations of the labour movement were thus deprived of their roots in the working class, and, as an inevitable result of this, they withered and died.

This process, however, was not completed without a struggle on the part of those activists and functionaries who were still steeped in the German tradition of Socialism, and who, either deliberately or involuntarily, impeded the introduction of Stalinism. After 1948, the regime attempted to overcome all such opposition by identifying and obliterating the anti-Soviet, Social Democratic, 'reconciliationist' or 'sectarian' tendencies of many SED members. The more the authorities searched for such oppositional views, the more they found. To this extent, the fact that the rank-and-file party members were still strongly under the influence of their old, German traditions was a spur to the Stalinisation process, for it induced the regime to become yet more suspicious and dogmatic.

Ironically, however, the survival of traces of the German tradition inside the SED, at the same time as being a stimulus to the Stalinisation process, also acted as a brake upon it. Even the organisations most responsible for changing the SED from a German political party into a Soviet-style party – such as the police, the legal system and the PKKs – were influenced by the 'reconciliationist' tendencies which they were supposed to be destroying. Fortunately for East Germany, Stalin died before this 'resistance' of the SED party apparatus to the purge could be broken, thereby sparing the country from the same level of terror which had been experienced by the Hungarians, Poles and Czechoslovaks.

What, then, can all this tell us about the broader issues of Stalinism and the course of post-war German history? To begin with, it seems that the division of Germany into two separate states was not determined solely by the clash between the Soviet Union and the western powers. On the contrary, the roots of the division were already there in 1945, in the political chasm which divided the anti-Nazi 'active minority' of the population from the pro-Nazi or Nazi-influenced 'passive majority'. The divergent occupation policies of the Soviets and the western powers acted upon and mutated these divisions. In the Soviet zone, the military authorities fostered the 'active minority' at the same time as disciplining it and subordinating it to control from above. In the western zones, by contrast, the military governments held back the 'active minority', thereby allowing conservative political forces to regroup and, with the electoral support of the 'passive majority', to go on to rule in West Germany for the next twenty years. In short, the various military governments effectively *displaced* the divisions which were there at Zero Hour. By 1949, the gulf between the 'active minority' and 'passive majority' of the population had been transformed into the geo-political divide between West Germany and the GDR.

All of this was to have an enormous impact on the subsequent course of German history.[1] In East Germany, the regime which emerged from the interaction between the German and Soviet traditions of Socialism never had any democratic legitimacy, but it did have a degree of anti-Nazi legitimacy, at least in the eyes of its supporters at home and its sympathisers abroad. Even after the collapse of the GDR in 1989, this has continued to be an important factor in East German politics, for it is within this radical anti-Nazi tradition that the PDS locates itself. According to Gregor Gysi, the most prominent PDS leader:

> I believe that the positive element was the attempt to follow a non-capitalist path. Positive, as well, was an antifascist state which developed something which I still today maintain as important: one thinks of the minimal social differences, of the fact that the line between rich and poor was very small compared to that which occurs in all capitalist states.[2]

In West Germany, by contrast, the radical anti-Nazi section of the population never quite forgave the 'passive majority' for having supported Hitler in the 1930s, and for having turned their backs on radical anti-Nazism and Socialism in the immediate post-war period. Ever since, a very prominent feature of West German politics has been the ongoing controversy between those on the Left who feel that the German nation has never properly confronted its past, and those at the centre or on the right of the political spectrum who see no reason why Germany should for ever remain 'in Hitler's shadow'.[3] This conflict has been part and parcel of almost all political debate in the Federal Republic since 1949, and can still be discerned in the controversy surrounding issues such as how to deal with refugees and 'guest workers' (*Gastarbeiter*), and the role which Germany should play in the new Europe. At times, the conflict has even been the cause of bloodshed. Particularly in the late 1960s and early 1970s, a number of anti-Nazi radicals became so frustrated at what they perceived as the obdurate refusal of the West German population to confront the past that they resorted to violence. In the new united Germany of the 1990s, the desire of extreme right-wing fanatics to nail what they call the 'Auschwitz lie' has been an inextricable part of their violent and racist political project.

Finally, with regard to the question of Stalinism, one of the most salient points which emerges from a study such as this is how effective Stalinism proved at manipulating, exploiting and eventually neutralising the idealism and enthusiasm of the German Left. To some extent, the relative ease with which Stalinism overcame the native German traditions of Socialism can be explained by the physical, psychological and above all political wounds which the previous three decades had inflicted upon many German Socialists, Communists and trade unionists. Equally important, however, was the skill and the patience displayed by the Stalinists in terms of choosing the right moment to pick off their opponents. The Soviets and the KPD/SED leadership took great care to avoid provoking all their real or potential opponents at the same time, but instead, using what the Hungarian Communist leader Matyas Rakosi called 'salami tactics', non- or anti-Stalinist political tendencies were sliced off the body politic one by one.

Thus, during the first months of occupation, the fire of the authorities was concentrated almost exclusively on former Nazis and reactionaries. Once the old order in East Germany had been thoroughly smashed, the authorities turned their attention to subduing the two 'bourgeois' parties and the SPD. In the later 1940s and early 1950s, it was the turn of members of the former splinter parties to be humiliated, broken or expelled. Eventually, in the early 1950s, and particularly in the aftermath of the workers' uprising of 17 June 1953, the veteran 'old believers' of the KPD were either forced to capitulate or were cast into the political wilderness.

However, perhaps the most important single reason for the success of Stalinism in manipulating the German labour movement was its trick of seizing on the real aspirations of German workers and holding these out as a greater and higher goal in the name of which all present policies were justified and explained. As a result, discontented functionaries and activists held back from making a stand on any particular issue because they were afraid that, by so doing, they might jeopardise the attainment of the higher goals towards which they believed they were working. Social Democrats, for example, swallowed their doubts about the creation of the SED because they were told, and believed, that the unity of the German working class was of overriding importance. In the later 1940s and early 1950s, many of those who experienced considerable 'political qualms' (*politische Bauchschmerzen*) nonetheless remained true to the regime, for they believed that, despite all the mistakes, problems and abuses they could see around them, East Germany was still on the road to Socialism. Herbert Prauss, for example, justified to himself his continued loyalty to the East German regime in the following manner:

> Everything that happened in the East was also for me basically good, at best there existed only temporary growing pains and childhood illnesses. What happened in the West, by contrast, was basically bad. If anything good happened there, it only appeared as good, in its essence however it definitely had to be bad.[4]

If, however, Stalinism in East Germany in the period 1945 to 1953 proved to be adept at exploiting and manipulating people's idealism and enthusiasm, it also demonstrated that it was extraordinarily bad at sustaining these qualities. To this extent, Stalinism showed itself to be an essentially parasitic force, destroying the life of the labour movement at the same time as feeding upon its energy. The end result of this process was that, whilst the SED and FDGB retained the outward form of genuine workers' organisations, they had been corroded from within to such an extent that they had become empty and brittle husks.

Nothing demonstrates this point more clearly than the events of 17 June 1953. With the leading echelons of the SED embroiled in internecine turmoil, no clear instructions were passed down the party apparatus to the masses of middle- and low-ranking functionaries. Confronted by a dangerous and violent situation, and with nobody around to tell them what to do, the Stalinist apparatchiks and careerists who now made up the bulk of the party apparatus were paralysed by fear and indecision. In many cases, SED functionaries removed their party badges and scuttled off home, abandoning their factories and party offices to the strikers and demonstrators. It was only the timely intervention of the Red Army that saved the SED regime from complete disintegration. It is here, perhaps, that we can see most clearly the impact of eight years of Soviet occupation upon the East German labour movement. In 1945, the activists in the antifascist committees, workplace councils and rank-and-file party cells were often veterans of the anti-Nazi resistance, many of whom had suffered for the faith in the concentration camps and torture chambers of the Third Reich. Amidst the rubble of Germany's towns and cities, they had displayed the utmost ingenuity and initiative, and, against all the odds, had been able to restore some degree of order out of the chaos. Over the next eight years, however, these 'activists of the first hour' were either disciplined and broken by the regime, or cast out of the party to be replaced by careerists and yes-men who were incapable of either self-sacrifice or independent initiative, and who fell to pieces at the first serious challenge to the regime's authority. Whereas the veterans of the anti-Nazi resistance had withstood the might of the Third Reich, their Stalinist successors did not even hold their nerve in the face of a strike wave and a few violent demonstrations.

Notes

1 See G. Pritchard, 'National Identity in a United and Divided Germany', in R. Pethybridge & R. Taylor (eds.), *European Integration and Disintegration*, London & New York, 1996, pp. 154–71.
2 S. Vastano, 'Germany United and Divided', in H. James & M. Stone (eds.), *When the Wall Came Down*, London & New York, 1992, p. 149.
3 See R. Evans, *In Hitler's Shadow*, London, 1989.
4 H. Prauss, *Doch es war nicht die Wahrheit*, [West] Berlin, 1960, p. 84.

Index

Note: 'n' after a page number indicates the number of a note on that page. Where antifascist committees or industrial enterprises are listed, their location is indicated in brackets. Between 1945 and 1952 the territory of the Soviet Zone (excluding East Berlin) was divided into five *Länder* (Mecklenburg, Brandenburg, Saxony-Anhalt, Saxony and Thuringia), and where villages, towns or cities are listed, the *Länder* in which they were located are given in brackets. The villages, towns and cities listed in this index are also divided into eight categories according to their approximate population in the early 1950s. These eight categories are: S1 under 1,000 inhabitants; S2 1,000 to 2,000 inhabitants; S3 2,000 to 5,000 inhabitants; S4 5,000 to 10,000 inhabitants; S5 10,000 to 20,000 inhabitants; S6 20,000 to 50,000 inhabitants; S7 50,000 to 100,000 inhabitants; S8 100,000 or more inhabitants.